THE STATE IN Q

THE STATE IN QUESTION

*Transformations of
the Australian State*

Edited by Paul James

Allen & Unwin

Copyright © Paul James, 1996

All rights reserved. No part of this book may be reproduced or transmitted in any form or by any means, electronic or mechanical, including photocopying, recording or by any information storage and retrieval system, without prior permission in writing from the publisher.

First published in 1996 by
Allen & Unwin Pty Ltd
9 Atchison Street, St Leonards, NSW 2065 Australia
Phone: (61 2) 9901 4088
Fax: (61 2) 9906 2218
E-mail: 100252.103@compuserve.com

National Library of Australia
Cataloguing-in-Publication entry:

The state in question: transformations of the Australian state.

Includes index.
ISBN 1 86373 673 5.

1. State, The. 2. Australia—Politics and government—
1990– . I. James, Paul (Paul Warren), 1958– .

320.994

Cover painting copyright © John and Helen Brack

Typeset by Pauline Dwyer
Printed by Australian Print Group, Maryborough, Victoria

To Hugh

Contents

Acknowledgements viii
Notes on contributors ix

1 Introduction
  Paul James 1

2 Debating the state: the real reasons for bringing the state back in
  Hugh V. Emy and Paul James 8

3 Laborism and the state: confronting modernity
  Rob Watts 38

4 Greening the modern state: managing the environment
  Robyn Eckersley 74

5 The poverty of the welfare state: managing an underclass
  Rob White 109

6 Australian feminism and the state: practice and theory
  Ann Curthoys 138

7 Beyond foreign policy: state theory and the changing global order
  Christian Reus-Smit 161

8 The state of postmodernity: beyond cultural nostalgia or pessimism
  John Hinkson 196

9 As nation and state: a postmodern republic takes shape
  Paul James 224

Index 252

Acknowledgements

The original conception of the study was very much a collaborative effort with Hugh Emy, professor in the Department of Politics at Monash University. We jointly commissioned the chapters and asked each of the authors to present their work in the critical forum of the Department's staff seminars. Unfortunately, Hugh was unable stay with the project to its end, but the final product still very much bears the imprint of his abiding concern with the problem of rethinking the state.

I need to also thank those members of the Department of Politics who took an active part in those seminars, in particular Michael Janover, Peter Lawler, Andy Butfoy and Ray Nichols. Pauline Dwyer carried the brunt of the enormous task of typing the manuscript and its various editorial revisions. Mark Tredinnick waited patiently while we slowly worked over the chapters, and John Iremonger, Julia Hancock and Margaret Jones took the manuscript quickly through the final stages. All the while, Stephanie Trigg gave me intellectual support and much more.

Notes on contributors

Ann Curthoys is in History at the Australian National University. She is author of *For and against feminism: a personal journey into feminist theory and history* (1988), co-editor of six books on Australian history, and author of many articles and chapters on feminist theory and Australian women's, Aboriginal, immigration, political, media, and cultural history. She has recently completed a study of the role of women in the anti-Vietnam-war movement, and is currently engaged in three projects: a history of the 'Freedom Ride' protesting against discrimination against Aboriginal people in rural New South Wales in 1965; with Paula Hamilton and Julianne Schultz, a history of journalism in twentieth century Australia; and, with John Docker, a book entitled *The orientalising of desire: western women in popular romance*.

Robyn Eckersley is in Politics at Monash University where she is Programme Director for 'Environment and Development' with the Institute of Ethics and Public Policy in the Graduate School of Government. Her teaching and research focuses on environmental politics and green political theory and her recent books include *Environmentalism and political theory: toward an ecocentric approach* (1992) and *Markets, the state and the environment: towards integration* (1995).

Hugh Emy is in Politics at Monash University where he teaches Australian politics and democratic theory. His recent books include *Australian politics: realities in conflict* (with Owen Hughes, 2nd edn, 1991), *New Political horizons: essays with an Australian focus* (edited with Andrew Linklater, 1991) and *Remaking Australia: the state, the market and Australia's future* (1993).

NOTES ON CONTRIBUTORS

John Hinkson is in Education at La Trobe University where he teaches cultural theory. He is convening editor of *Arena Journal*. and has published widely on cultural politics and the culture of economics, including *Postmodernity: state and education* (1991).

Paul James is in Politics at Monash University and is an editor with *Arena*. His publications include *Technocratic dreaming* (1990), *Critical politics* (1994), and *Nation formations* (1996).

Chris Reus-Smit teaches international relations in the Department of Politics at Monash University. He has been awarded fellowships by the MacArthur and Mellon Foundation, and held visiting positions at Princeton University and the University of Melbourne. His current research integrates international relations theory, international history, institutional analysis and social theory. His book *The moral purpose of the state* is forthcoming with Princeton University Press.

Rob Watts teaches social policy and social theory at RMIT, Melbourne, and is currently writing two books: one on group work and the other on state violence in the twentieth century.

Rob White is in Criminology at the University of Melbourne. He has written widely in the areas of youth studies, juvenile justice and social policy, and has been active in a variety of anti-poverty and anti-racist campaigns over the years. His recent publications include *No place of their own: young people and social control in Australia* (1990), *The police and young people in Australia* (with C. Alder, 1994), *Youth subcultures: theory, history and the Australian experience*, and *Juvenile justice: an Australian perspective* (with C. Cunneen, 1995).

1

Introduction

Paul James

Everybody seems to have some response to the state. It is an abiding institution of contemporary politics and social life. In its different guises the state elicits a panoply of emotions, from irritation, resentment and boredom, sometimes horror, to enthusiasm and fascination, loyalty and self-sacrifice. These responses may be in tension with each other, but most us manage to swing comfortably between them without feeling the burden of contradiction. It is an indication not of our stupidity, but of the complexity of the roles and structures of the state in contemporary society. Despite the pronouncements of some ideologues, it is hard to have a simply consistent position when the outcomes of state practices are so contingent and structurally contradictory.[1] For example, one of the outcomes of the welfare state, as through this century it developed important structures for supporting the needy, was an ever-increasing degree of intrusion into people's lives: the gentle welfare state and the hard-edged surveillance state developed hand-in-hand. Or again, one of the accompaniments to state regulation of the economy was the development of increasingly powerful economic interests which,

---

1   This is not to suggest that it is impossible to develop a consistent set of principles and theoretical proposition about the roles and structures of the state. It is to imply that they will need to be a bit more sophisticated than those raised by the current debates between the protagonists who suggest that the state should withdraw from all possible macro-regulatory functions and those who look back to the Keynesian interventionist state with nostalgia. It should also be noted that in using the word 'contingent' I am not backtracking from a structuralist recognition of trajectories and patterns of practice, only from the view that treats structures as things which fix the future.

in an exponentially globalizing world, came to seek ways of bypassing old-style state regulation.

Hence, we have arrived at the situation when responses to the state are in flux. As one writer notes:

> One of the oddities of our times is that radicals who theoretically abhor the state, almost invariably vote for the political parties that endorse *more* state action, while capitalists, who supposedly have the state in their back pocket, almost invariably vote for parties that preach a minimalist state.[2]

In Australia this confusion is compounded by the peculiarity that it is the party which ostensibly endorses more state action, the Labor party, that has been at the forefront of both withdrawing the state from certain kinds of regulatory practices and rationalizing the provision of social security.

In the 1990s the size of the state and its penetration into everyday life are becoming contentious public issues. For the most part, however, we have tended to treat the form of the state as a background consideration. While in Australia we argue, and are constantly kept informed by the media, about the comings and goings of party politics, about the personality and fitness for office of particular politicians, and about the various policy pronouncements and broken promises of governments, it has been rare to see extended public debates over more general questions such as what shape the state should be, what should be the relationship between the state and civil society, what grounding principles best allow us to determine the state's role in protecting the environment (Robyn Eckersley's chapter) or providing support for the poor or the less powerful (Rob White's chapter).

As such the dominant sense of the state has been invested with a dual character, at once taken for granted as legitimately operating across the core of our economic and social lives—whether framing, governing, protecting, intruding or coercively controlling—and yet treated in the main as an institution which should, in all its complexity, be left to theorists, jurists and political analysts. Two apparent counter-examples

---

2 John McGowan, *Postmodernism and its critics*, Cornell University Press, Ithaca, 1991, p. 226.

INTRODUCTION

stand out, but they remain ambiguous: firstly, the Australia Card debates during 1985–88 raised fundamental questions about the nature of the surveillance state, but within months of the card proposal being abandoned, a tax-file-number system, very similar in structural effect but less public in manifestation, passed into law with little public consternation; secondly, the right-wing, anti-state demonstrations of the early 1990s were notable for their vocalizing of intense dissatisfaction, but when asked what they wanted the demonstration organizers replied only in negative and vague terms saying that it was up to the politicians to get their house in order. In short, neither episode generated sufficient momentum to translate into discussions of what alternative form the state might take.

There are many reasons for this leaving of the big questions concerning the state to 'experts'. Social developments such as the confirmation of politics as largely a spectator sport mediated by television and the press, and intellectual developments such as the increasing difficulty, self-referentiality and arcane intricacy of the theoretical debates, redoubled by the ideological surety of the protagonists, have contributed to a wariness about explicit political change. In Australia there has been a reluctance to endorse constitutional change,[3] a circumspection, even paranoia about other political systems, and a naturalization of the kind of state we have. While this may be changing, the form of the state has long been seen as written into the stone of our past and relevant in perpetuity into the future. Through the post-war years and into the 1980s there was a dominant settled sense that however much we might complain about the liberal democratic state it continued to work well enough to muddle on. Spates of marginal change were largely accepted and routinized as the outcome of the different parties putting their stamp upon government.

Taken together all these minor changes *were* adding up to a dramatic pattern of transformation. Nevertheless, for a long time it did not translate into public debate.[4] There was apparently no need to discuss

---

3   In 1988, Australians recorded the highest ever 'no vote' in a referendum. See Shaun Carney, 'Following the leader', *Age*, 8 April 1995.
4   This has been taken to exemplify a refutation of 'legitimation and steering crisis' arguments as presented by theorists such as Habermas, Offe and O'Connor, but as Michael Muetzelfeldt and Richard Bates suggest in their excellent chapter ('Conflict, contradiction and crisis',

the big issues too long and hard. All may not be right with the world, but at least we thought we knew where we stood. The Whitlam government may have got a bit carried away at one stage, but at least the subsequent governments of the 1970s and 1980s did not seem to try anything too radical. (In hindsight, people look back to the set of policy decisions of 1983 as a turning point—in particular, the deregulation of the exchange rate, of banking capital and of the national financial system—but at the time there was a relatively comfortable response to the moves.) The floating of the Australian dollar led more to an unprecedented fascination with its fluctuations in value, than it did to any discussion about the role of the state in the global exchange system: for the first time on Australian television the value of the dollar became the subject of a new segment at the end of the daily news.

All the while, despite this faith in continuity, both the state and our society were fundamentally changing. It was the Australian Labor Party (ALP), while presenting itself as continuous with the old tradition of social democracy, that for good or ill began the more serious renovation of the state, particularly in the area of economic policy. Some theorists had been talking for some time about the changing form of society—depending upon one's political position described variously in terms of post-industrialism, globalizing capitalism, and late-modernity or postmodernity. However, it is only quite recently that the policy changes in the areas of deregulation, privatization, corporatization, micro-economic reform, changing criteria for welfare provisions, and constitutional and legislative reform over Aboriginal land rights, equal opportunity, racial vilification and the national sovereignty question that commentators have begun to treat the changes as part of a larger picture.[5] The implications of these changes have crept up upon all

---

in *Society, State and Politics,* ed. Muetzelfeldt, Leichhardt, Pluto Press, 1992) the subjective response to the crises of the state can be offset by changing political and economic strategies while ongoing and emerging structural contradictions continue to place the modern state under immense pressure.

5   The literature on post-industrialism goes back to the right-wing theorists of the 1970s and 1980s; the first Australian book which drew a connection between the changing state, the globalizing of capitalism and emergence of a setting of postmodernity was written from a left perspective by John Hinkson (*Postmodernity: state and education,* Deakin University Press, Geelong, 1991). His chapter in the present volume extends beyond that book to focus upon the relationship between the state and the postmodern market.

of us, including upon many mainstream political analysts. Thus in the late twentieth century, as the scale and depth of the changes have finally started to hit, debates about the state have begun to cross the public and academic realms. In particular, the debate over the coming republic (discussed in the final chapter, 'A postmodern republic takes shape') is, as Hugh Mackay reports, 'closely related to the underlying sense that Australia is overdue for some kind of examination of its political institutions ...'[6] Whether or not this examination or the possible changes wrought will have any depth to them is still an issue to be fought over.

All of this provides the context for book. In the 1990s the state is very much coming into question, but apart from those marketeers who confidently argue that 'getting the state off our backs' is the only answer, the rest of us are still formulating the questions and grounds for debate rather than assuming the answers. *The state in question* attempts to combine a concern for the big picture—drawing upon theoretical analyses about the changing kind of world in which we live—with more specific forays into the ways that modern state practices in Australia are being affected by and contributing to these general changes. (Chris Reus-Smit's chapter is especially exercised by the way in which the state is itself part of the process of transformation rather than simply determined by larger social changes.) In other words, the book attempts to draw connections between the raging debates in contemporary social theory and what is happening on the ground in Australia today.

The chapters vary in how they go about fulfilling our intention of bringing together theory with empirical description and political argument, but all of the contributors to this volume have four starting points in common: (i) Australia, as society and polity, faces significant challenges and choices, with pressures both from within and without bringing about changes of an unprecedented kind; (ii) the modern, liberal, Keynesian welfare state is part of the process and it too is changing; (iii) changes in the state and the socio-economic setting are bound up with each other; (iv) however dramatic the changes might be, transformation and continuity remain caught up in a contradictory bundle

---

[6] Hugh Mackay, *Reinventing Australia: the mind and mood of Australia in the 90s*, Angus and Robertson, Sydney, 1993, p. 182.

of outcomes and possibilities;[7] and (v) the state will, and should (within constantly assessed and debated limits), have a role to play as one level of political practice in the administration of the common good.

Within this shared ground, the most significant areas of contention between the writers are over the nature and extent of change, and secondly, over how to locate and explain its significance. The contributors express a range of positions about the relationship between change and continuity, modernity and postmodernity: from Rob Watts who emphasizes the continuities which have traversed the vagrant journey into late-modernity (his chapter explores the relationship between the labor movement and the state); through Robyn Eckersley who contends that despite the way in which politicians and bureaucrats are digging their heels into the mire of environmental pragmatism the modern state is being dragged uncomfortably into a new era of evolving ecological globalism; to John Hinkson who focuses upon what he argues are utterly fundamental transformations, discontinuities which lead him to talk about the development of a postmodern society and a postmodern state.

The contributors also express a range of political and philosophical conclusions about the state of debate and the possibilities for political practice. Ann Curthoys in her chapter on the relationship between feminism and the state concludes that theory and debate are 'at a crossroads, looking for a way to combine a postmodern awareness of difference, ambivalence and fragmentation with a coherent political philosophy capable of sustaining the important political struggles still to come'. Other contributors, including Hugh Emy, John Hinkson, Rob White and myself remain much more suspicious about the 'postmodern turn' to the extent that it tends to gloss over new and old inequities, increasing social divisions and changing structures of direct and indirect power.

---

[7] For example, if the Hilmer report recommendations to create a 'national competition regime' come into effect, they will confirm a paradoxical development with precedents in the Keating government's *One Nation* policy document: namely, that the pressures of globalization are leading to an increasing nationalization of the economy. Victorian premier Jeff Kennett described the development as based on the necessity to 'think of ourselves as a borderless country' (*Age*, 12 April 1995).

INTRODUCTION

As we get closer to the end of the century the state is coming back as a focus of debate. *The state in question* is intended as political contribution to that discussion. In the next chapter (Hugh Emy and Paul James,) we begin a political assessment of the dominant theoretical approaches to the state as they have developed over the last few decades and up to the present. The authors attempt to make explicit a core concern of the whole anthology—namely that if we dismiss the state as an unnecessary burden rather than debating the form it should take, then other people and other pressures will determine the future for us.

2

Debating the state: the real reasons for bringing the state back in

Hugh V. Emy and Paul James

One of the major areas of debate today is what we are to make of the state. It is possible that we are watching the gradual transformation of the modern state into something else, the contours of which are by no means clear. This observation relies a good deal on changes occurring in and to the theory and practice of sovereignty.[1] Sovereignty, meaning the effective right of one government to exercise exclusive control by varying combinations of law and force, consent and coercion over all the people and resources within a bounded territorial area, has been the central defining characteristic of the modern state. Two powerful forces appear to be undermining it: firstly, globalization—in particular the growth of a new kind of global economy, coupled with an information revolution and the rapid diffusion world-wide of a number of new technologies, especially in computers and electronics. This first set of changes make it easier for capital in various forms to bypass state boundaries and controls.[2] Secondly, the modern state is being challenged by an increasing internationalization of law and the development of a supra-state framework of norms, rights and institutions. Both forces restrict the operational autonomy of governments and make sovereignty a less

---

1   E.g. Joseph A. Camilleri and Jim Falk, *The end of sovereignty? The politics of a shrinking and fragmenting world,* Edward Elgar, Aldershot, 1992.
2   See e.g. Hugh V. Emy, *Remaking Australia: the state, the market and Australia's future,* Allen & Unwin, Sydney, 1993, ch. 7; Walter B. Wriston, *The twilight of sovereignty,* Charles Scribner's Sons, New York, 1992.

absolute concept than it once was.

However, it is not so clear whether we are looking at an epochal and qualitative change in the meaning and powers of the sovereign state, changes which have been gathering momentum since at least the beginning of this century, or at the overlaying of competing, sometimes contradictory practices and discourses of sovereignty, new upon old. Querying the meaning and relevance of sovereignty is not new.[3] Its meaning *has* changed, but has it changed so much that we must revise our standard understanding of the state, for example that contained in Weber's classic definition?[4] This chapter will suggest that our improved understanding of the logic of state-building, of how states develop, how they maintain their viability in the face of uncertainty or insecurity, and how they are structurally constrained, should make us chary of de-emphasizing the political efficacy of the modern state too soon. Even if we are entering a new world increasingly framed by what writers from various theoretical traditions are calling 'postmodernization', it does not mean that all the practices associated with the modern state will simply disappear. Just as the transformation from the traditional state to the modern state in Europe during the sixteenth centuries was replete with continuities, the contemporary state will carry much of its past with it into the future.

There is, too, the political question of whether we should not resist the forces undermining sovereignty. These forces also undermine the capacity, and to some degree the accountability, of elected governments to make and deliver policy. Some conservatives and social democrats share reservations over just how far governments should be willing to surrender their autonomy and responsibilities to impersonal market and technological forces. It is

---

3   E.g. Heinz Eulau, 'The depersonalization of the concept of sovereignty', *Journal of politics*, vol. 4, no. 1, February 1942; W.J. Stankiewicz, ed. *In defense of sovereignty*, Oxford University Press, New York, 1969.

4   Max Weber, *Economy and society*, eds G. Roth and C. Wittich, University of California Press, Berkeley, 1978, vol. 1, p. 54: 'A compulsory political organization with continuous operations ... will be called a "state" insofar as its administrative staff successfully upholds the claim to the *monopoly* of the *legitimate* use of physical force in the enforcement of its order' (original italics). See pp. 54-6 and ch. 9 in vol. 2 for extended discussion of the nature of political communities.

not impossible that, in countries most vulnerable to the competitive pressures unleashed by globalization, governments will be forced to act to protect sources of employment and social cohesion. Acting in defence of territorial integrity may still have another lease of life. For different reasons, countries like Britain, Japan, some of the smaller social corporatist democracies in Europe, and France perhaps, are worried by the continuing erosion of state sovereignty, economic and cultural autonomy. Loss of sovereignty brings perceived costs as well as possible benefits.

We should also bear in mind that at least some of the impetus to winding down the concept of sovereignty comes from liberals whose long-term project has been to advance the cause of free trade and international markets. The existence of sovereign states has always been a serious obstacle to achieving their goals. Liberals have always believed that commerce and free trade were self-evident goods, forces for peace. On that, they have been in error before, notably before 1914, in part because they have never really understood the nature of states or the kind of dynamics present in the state-building process. The current critique of sovereignty is not just a response to observable, empirically grounded events, although it is informed by these. For some commentators, there is also a hidden normative agenda: to replace states with markets wherever possible. There is a suggestive similarity between this critique and the critique of the state advanced by American political science, which this essay will discuss.

Today the state is simultaneously at the height of its powers and very much in question. The modern state has grown to become the universal model of political association, in the process destroying all competing models. Notwithstanding the ever-increasing centrality of transnational corporations in global economic relations, states have parcelled up the world and all its resources between them. For both individuals and ethnic groups, having a state of one's own is a prerequisite for cultural and/or economic survival. In July 1993, Andorra in the Pyrenees, a country with a population of 47,000, became the 184th member of the United Nations. Perhaps it is time to query this extraordinary reliance on the state as the sole vehicle of political association. Other facets of globalization, notably awareness of global environmental problems (see Robyn Eckersley's chapter) and the growing numbers of migrants moving from state to state in search of work, conflict with our established view of the state as, in effect, a legitimate territorial monopolist and decisive arbiter of the rights of all people living within its borders.

It has been suggested that we are watching a pulling apart of the concepts of state and nation: that it might be possible to imagine stateless nations, built around internationally recognized unions of peoples as distinct from territorially-based states.[5] Conceivably, the classic or modern idea of the nation-state as well as of the sovereign state is beginning to change. This may not be a wholly positive development either. The disintegration of the Soviet Union, events in Eastern Europe, recurrent tribal and ethnic conflicts in Africa, show what can occur when state prohibitions on long-standing ethnic, religious or national rivalries are removed. Paradoxically, the wars in the old Yugoslavia and in Rwanda are being fought in the name of both the modern nation-state *and* traditional attachments to tribe or religion, but they can not be explained in terms of either. Overall, the situation is extremely confusing. On the one hand, the state does not seem to be the best tool for dealing with the problems created through globalization. Rising consciousness of one planet, one species, implies that we should try to build supra-state institutions—and a new world order. On the other hand, as we are made aware of both the artificiality and ambiguous relevance of many nation-states, we have to recognize that nationalism and tribalism are by no means dead: the alternative to the centralizing state in some parts of the world is fragmentation and violence. While for many peoples, such as the Palestinians, the Kurds and the *Quebecois*, statehood is still a valued means to preserve national identity.

The state has been questioned in another sphere too: in liberal democracies especially, but in all industrial societies to some degree, there has been recently a great effort to re-structure the state vis-à-vis the market economy. In several cases, including

---

5   Gideon Gottlieb, 'Nations without states', *Foreign affairs*, vol. 73, no. 3, 1994; also, Anthony D. Smith, *National identity*, Penguin Books, Harmondsworth, 1991, ch. 7.

Australia, this has led to prolonged attempts to reduce substantially the size and responsibilities of government and the public sector. At one level, this was caused by dissatisfaction with the rising cost of big government and evidence of government failure. At another, it was caused by an ideologically-driven desire on the part of many contemporary liberals to dismantle the legacy of welfare-liberalism, shift the balance from positive to negative liberty, expand the scope of markets and revive the classical liberal model of the minimum state. There is reason to suspect that the tidal wave of free-market liberalism has slowed down.[6] What remains, however, is a sense of uncertainty. Neither statism nor a dogmatic faith in the virtues of free markets now seems sufficient by itself. The challenge is to know how to re-design the province and responsibilities of government in the light of all that has happened to both capitalist and communist societies over the last ten years. At a theoretical level, there are no obvious or clear-cut answers to the question 'what should governments do?'

However, this is not just a question about government. The issues are wider because they involve re-thinking the balance between state and society, or between the more altruistic and cooperative moral values which help to legitimate the democratic state, and the stress on competition, self-interest and profit-seeking behaviour integral to the market economy. (This is part of the focus of John Hinkson's chapter.) The follow-up question has to do with working out whether, and if so how and how far, the state should be invested with explicit responsibility to oversee and steer the long-term development of the productive system, and to ensure the integrity of society as a whole. Should its role be seen simply as one of clearing away obstacles in the path of the market, creating the kind of environment now required by business to succeed in the global economy?

---

6   Note the growing number of substantial critiques: Peter Self, *Government by the market? the politics of public choice*, Macmillan, London, 1993; John Gray, *Beyond the new right: markets, government and the common environment*, Routledge, London, 1993; Hugh Stretton and Lionel Orchard, *Public goods, public enterprise, public choice: theoretical foundations of the contemporary attack on government*, Macmillan, London, 1994.

The real issue that confronts us in liberal democracies especially is not just the proper size or cost of government. It is whether the market as an organizing idea and practice is to subsume the state. Is the political organization of society to be determined by the functional requirements of the market? Part of the reason why, in recent years, there has been so much emphasis on cutting government down to size and deregulating the market, has to do with the eclipse of the state as a valued organizing concept for discussing the nature and purposes of social life. It is difficult to discuss the role and functions of government without having some idea or preconception of the kind of society one wishes to create. Currently, the dominant ideas about how to re-organize society are derived from economic models of society which take market-related behaviour as the norm. Stretton and Orchard, Gray and Self have argued strongly that this involves a dangerous over-simplification of our understanding of human association, and of the nature and functions of government. It cuts us off from, arguably, older and richer notions of community.[7] For those unhappy with the current dominance of these economic models, the challenge is to find a satisfactory alternative way of conceptualizing the issues. Conceivably, one strategy is to take the concept of the state more seriously, to reassess and qualify the negative image of the state which has developed in the social sciences in the latter half of this century (and which derives from an odd combination of liberal, Marxist and, more recently, post-structuralist theorizing). If the nineteenth century was, in certain respects, inclined to idealize or exaggerate the state's potential, the twentieth century is now in danger—for understandable historical reasons admittedly—of erring in the opposite direction. The time has come for a balanced but critical reassessment.

To voice such a thought at once runs counter to the prevailing cast of contemporary thinking about the state. In fact, two currents

---

[7] The task of re-thinking the balance between state and market really centres on this issue: whether one thinks that the same kind of rationality, broadly functional rationality, applies to all the institutions and major decision-centres in society, or whether 'the state' provides us with intellectual and institutional resources to override the claims of functional rationality in the name of other values.

of liberal scepticism come together here to reinforce each other's antipathy towards the state. First, there is the more immediate mind-set of today's liberals, especially neo-classical economists, for whom any hint that the state should oversee the development of the market raises the spectre of intervention and, even worse, planning. In Australia especially, the received dogma is that any attempt to qualify the autonomy of market processes, to subject the market to political guidance, is to place it in jeopardy. Markets everywhere work best when left alone, as far as possible.

But one important reason why this neo-classical mind-set has emerged triumphant in recent years is that political science—specifically American, liberal, empirical political science—helped to prepare the way for it. The second current of scepticism is the hostility towards the concept of the state expressed by American political science for much of this century, but especially between 1945 and the late 1970s. American pluralists and behaviouralists denied the utility of the term for directing empirical research. They preferred to disaggregate 'state' into its component bits and pieces to facilitate the behavioural study of government, power and the policy process. One might say that American scholars pursued a strategy of 'deconstructing' the state some decades before that term became fashionable. The effect was to remove the state as a suitable object for study by the mainstream profession. It was even in effect to deny the state's existence. Pluralists and empirical realists were also sceptical of attempts to invest the state with normative qualities, or higher responsibilities to safeguard the public interest, or articulate and uphold a framework of moral rules, or a distinctive sphere of justice. Such language, let alone any suggestion that the state, as the political arm of the community was the (potential) site for reasoned deliberation of a kind qualitatively distinct from the kind of rational choice strategies which became increasingly popular in the 1980s, was regarded with amusement—or derision: it was pre-scientific or, worse, verged on the metaphysical.

The scepticism towards the state maintained by a majority of political scientists[8] for thirty years or more had two consequences:

---

8 Given that, in the 1980s, at least three-quarters of political scientists worked in

(i) it limited the contribution which political scientists felt able to make to debates about the role of government, or the relationship between state and society in the 1980s. It meant that the initiative passed to those who preferred to work with analytic models of political life, usually drawn from economics, which paid little attention either to history or to the normative discourse which had influenced the development of particular states. (ii) The dismissal of the state as a generic term, a device for ordering our ideas about the nature and purpose of public life, for making and upholding important normative distinctions between the public realm and private life, created the opportunity to replace it with another generic term—'the market'. In effect, the eclipse of the state created a large intellectual and political space into which marched the 'market men' in the 1980s. These included some empirically oriented political scientists as well as economists: the two formed an alliance grounded in their common liberalism which was reinforced by the spread of rational actor-public choice models in both disciplines.

The upshot is that although we may think today that the state is very much in question—that is, that we should ask questions about whether the modern state (or some reconstituted form of state) should be an important institutional level in the organization of political life; whether states should seek greater control over impersonal market forces in the interests of the community—it is unsatisfactory to do so within the conventional terms of political science. This is because, for a mixture of methodological and ideological reasons, 'the state' remains a suspect concept. It is more respectable to talk about government, or the actions of specific public-sector agencies. It is more respectable to conceptualize the area of government itself as non-market institutions and to treat each part or agency of government as if it were a business like any other. The combination of disaggregating the state into its component parts and privileging the market as the key generic

---

America. Erkki Berndtson, 'The rise and fall of American political science: personalities, quotations, speculations', *International political science review*, vol. 8, no. 1, 1987, p. 85.

term for conceptualizing social order, has produced significant political effects: as scholars and citizens, it is more difficult to make sense of the whole in which we live. It is harder to deny or resist the supremacy of 'market forces', whether domestically or globally. We are indeed left afloat on 'a boundless and bottomless sea ... [in which] there is neither harbour for shelter nor floor for anchorage ...' and where 'the enterprise is to keep afloat on an even keel'.[9] And this is a situation recommended, in effect, by those who look to the market as the real source of order as well as by those critics of both the state and the market (for example, by those advocating a politics of postmodernism) who see all institutional structures as oppressive.

Between them, behavioural political science and neo-classical economics have marginalized normative discussion of the state, its links with justice and community, and replaced it with the 'natural' order of the market. And strangely, the further entry into the debate by postmodern*ist* writers has exacerbated this trend. In treating the state as an institution to be actively deconstructed, and viewing the market passively as a fluid process of open choice always in the process of deconstructing itself, the state always seems to come off second best. For those of us concerned at the implications of this death of the state, there is a case for reclaiming the state as a major organizing concept which can help us to conceptualize and assess society as a social whole, and provide the resources, both intellectual and institutional, for treating the market as one contributory element of that whole; that is, recovering the concept of the state can help to resist claims that the market is synonymous with society, and that society and government must be subordinated in practice to the functional requirements of the market.

To say this, however, is to challenge what is still a powerful position within political science, not to mention contemporary liberalism: namely, that talk about the state, especially talk that is overtly normative or philosophical, belongs to the pre-scientific

---

9   Michael Oakeshott, *Rationalism in politics and other essays*, Methuen, London, 1962, p. 127.

stage of the discipline. To bring the state back in, some writers argue, would be to return to the kind of conceptual morass which existed before the behavioural revolution replaced it with the concept of political system. In 1981, for example, David Easton wrote that 'the state, a concept that many of us thought had been polished off a quarter of a century ago, has now risen from the grave to haunt us once again.'[10] He regarded the re-emergence of the concept as a retrograde step, a view with which another member of the old guard, Gabriel Almond, heartily concurred in 1988.[11]

To understand how we have arrived at the present it is worth briefly recalling the recent history of the debates.

The first retreat from the state

It is no secret that the social sciences lost interest in the state after 1945. In political studies, where the state had been a key concept for centuries, it was a major casualty of the behavioural revolution and the drive to create a more rigorous, empirical science of politics. However, the retreat from the state began between 1900 and 1920 when English pluralists challenged prevailing notions of sovereignty. During the same period, American political scientists also began to criticize the concept of the state for reasons of their own. The first wave of English pluralists contributed towards the mood of intellectual scepticism towards the state emerging in America, and this was taken much further by American pluralists after 1945.[12]

There is a lot to be said for their criticisms of received (traditional) state-theory, even if their alternative generated its own problems. In England, the pluralists criticized the received idea of

---

10 David Easton, 'The political system besieged by the state', *Political theory*, vol. 9, no. 3, 1981, p. 304.
11 Gabriel Almond, 'The return to the state' reprinted in his *A discipline divided: schools and sects in political science*, Sage, Newbury Park, California, 1990.
12 See generally David Nicholls, *The pluralist state*, Macmillan, London, 1975 and *Three varieties of pluralism*, Macmillan, London, 1974. Also Henry Kariel, 'Pluralism', *International encyclopaedia of social science*, Macmillan, New York, 1968.

the state as an all-powerful organization which existed above society and controlled it by laws which expressed the state's sovereign will. They did this for two reasons. First, they found this idea empirically inaccurate because it ignored the presence of other significant organizations whose resources, together with the loyalties of their members, counterbalanced the formal powers said to reside in the sovereign state. Pluralists on the right, such as J.N. Figgis, stressed the autonomous rights of the Church and professional associations like the law. On the Left, pluralists sympathetic to notions of guild socialism argued in favour of the autonomy of trade unions from the state. Second, many pluralists considered the belief in a sovereign state to be politically undesirable because it kept alive values which really belonged to the pre-modern era, and notably to the age of absolutism.

First in England and later in America, the emergence of a distinct modern tradition of liberal-pluralism not only strengthened the classical anti-state position within liberalism in favour of a strong emphasis upon the individual, group autonomy, and on limiting and decentralizing state power. On the positive side it also opposed any attempt to deify the state, to invest it with superior rationality, spiritual or metaphysical properties. Liberal-pluralists adopted a self-consciously sceptical and realist stance towards philosophic (or ethical) defences of the state. Later pluralists were also avowed methodological individualists hostile to any suggestion that the state was more than the sum of its parts. Such an argument they thought had the potential to reify the state, to endow the concept with a degree of concreteness which it did not have in fact, and with powers which it should not possess either.

Such a perspective contained familiar implications for conceptualizing government and state, implications which are readily apparent in latter-day economic rationalism. Social order is largely natural, or it is implicit within society. Therefore, it does not have to be created by government, still less a state. It is also self-sufficient, running on potentially limitless supplies of energies supplied by individuals (and the market). The task of government is to do only what is necessary to maintain this state of affairs, to promote individual freedom, protect natural rights and remove any troublesome friction between the parts. The point is two-fold: American liberalism, very much a type of neo-classical liberalism, viewed government as an adjunct to society and saw the coercive powers of the state as a continual threat to individual liberties. Furthermore, because social order and individual liberty were 'natural', Americans never had any real need for some kind of unified, sovereign public power to create these, either out of chaos or out of a medieval past.[13] America was not only born modern, it was ideologically believed to have been born as a unique type of stateless society.

We have to look back to 1926 to read what was virtually the last major study of the state by an American political scientist.[14] Then, Robert MacIver saw the modern state in pluralist terms as one association among many with the special characteristic that a government could back up its lawful commands throughout its defined territory by means of force. In 1933, the eminent theorist George Sabine, having surveyed the range of political units to which the term 'state' could apply, noted: 'the word commonly denotes no class of objects that can be identified exactly'. It did not stand for any common list of attributes and had to 'be defined more or less arbitrarily'. Sometimes it was identified with a legal order or with a system of legal norms. Sometimes sovereignty was invested in the state and sometimes in the people. It was difficult to distinguish between state and government, and between state and society. The notion of a sovereign state was clearly on the wane and 'it seems not improbable that some new type is in process of formation'. Just what, was not clear. What was clear was the highly problematic status of the concept itself. The outstanding question was what to put in its place.[15] The answer, according to Easton, was 'political system'.

Structural-functionalism in the shape of Parsonian systems theory emerged as the major post-war theoretical expression of

---

13   See especially Samuel P. Huntington 'Political modernization: America vs. Europe', *World Politics*, vol. xviii, 3, 1996; J.P. Nettl, 'The state as a conceptual variable', *World Politics*, vol. xx, 4, 1968.
14   R.M. MacIver, *The modern state*, Oxford University Press, London, 1926.
15   George Sabine, 'State', *Encyclopaedia of social sciences*, Macmillan, New York, 1933.

societal liberalism,[16] a theory which provided Easton in 1953 with the final justification he needed to strike out the state from the vocabulary of political science: the concept of system became one of the keywords of politics. Easton had three major objections to using the term 'state': (i) it was too difficult to define. He suggested there were at least 145 ways of describing the state.[17] Since political science now required precise orienting concepts to direct empirical research, a term like state, which lacked an operationally precise definition and fomented conceptual confusion should be jettisoned. (ii) It was too political. It carried too much ideological baggage. Especially, it was over-imbued with the symbolism of order: 'it was an instrument to achieve national cohesion', a crucial myth in the struggle for national unity and sovereignty.[18] It was not a tool for promoting thoughtful analysis. (iii) It limited the scope of political research. It appeared to prevent political science from studying political processes in acephalous or non-state societies. It was also used too simplistically in complex societies to give 'the appearance of a single, easily identified entity which makes and implements policies'. As such, it gave a false guide to real world practice.

His opposition to the state also followed from his support for the behavioural agenda, especially the goal of making politics a science by developing a new body of empirical or causal theory, to be built from the ground up. Normative theorizing about the nature of the state did not belong in that agenda. In sum the

---

16 Cf. Göran Therborn, 'Two thinkers on different sides of the barricades' (a comparative obituary notice of Herbert Marcuse and Talcott Parsons), *Times higher education supplement*, 18 January, 1980. See also William Buxton, *Talcott Parsons and the capitalist nation-state: political sociology as a strategic vocation*, University of Toronto Press, Toronto, 1985, on the way in which structural functionalists nevertheless treated the political subsystem (the state) as an instrument in the maintenance of consensual order and social integration.

17 David Easton, *The political system: an inquiry into the state of political science*, Alfred Knopf, New York, 1953, p. 108. The authority for this claim was a curious article by Charles Titus which did not discuss the state or give any details about the definitions. It also recorded a similar multiplicity of meanings for law, government, administration and political ('A nomenclature in political science', *American political science review*, vol. 25, no. 1, 1931, p. 45).

18 Easton, *Political system*, pp. 112-13.

methodological reasons advanced by American political scientists for rejecting the state are the tip of a larger iceberg. Their methodology, especially their methodological individualism,[19] is one expression of a dominant ideology, a kind of monolithic liberalism which can also function as a closed system of ideas.[20] Their opposition to the state is based in the political self-understanding of a particular kind of 'stateless' society, one which views its own order as rational and natural, and further progress as inevitable; which has no room for any separate theorization of the state and which views any attempt to provide one as a retrograde step because it will awaken a demon its social theory has conveniently buried.

Arguably, American political science over-reacted against the state.[21] When it rejected the German state tradition because of its excessive formalism and abstraction, it also lost interest in the concept of justice and in theories of political right. When it discarded juridical-ethical approaches, it cut itself off from western traditions of inquiry into the nature and purpose of political association.[22] Philosophic concern with such issues was seen as belonging to the pre-scientific stage of the discipline and normative political theorists were often dismissed as philosophic dreamers.[23] Once again, this reflected American experience: the terms and conditions of political association, the relationship between government and society, was regarded as settled.[24] State formation and the concept of public order posed fewer problems for Americans. The completeness of this reaction left two problems. First, as a discipline, American political science has largely dismissed the rel-

---

19 Cf. Steven Lukes, *Individualism*, Blackwell, Oxford, 1973.
20 The point behind Robert P. Wolff et al., *A critique of pure tolerance*, Beacon Press, Boston, 1969, and recognised by Louis Hartz' classic *The Liberal tradition in America*, Harcourt, Brace and World, New York, 1955.
21 Cf. Harry Eckstein, 'On the "science" of the state', *Daedalus*, vol. 108, no. 4, 1979: over-fascination with the German state-tradition perhaps provoked an equivalent reaction.
22 Bernard Crick, *The American science of politics: its origins and conditions*, University of California Press, Berkeley, 1959, pp. 97, 213, 234.
23 ibid. p. 100.
24 See generally Huntington, 'Political modernization'.

evance of other, approaches to and understandings of, politics in which the state has remained a central focus. Political science in Australia has been very much an American product: its field of inquiry, methods of inquiry, almost the whole language of politics, reflects a distinctively American understanding of politics. The whole agenda, including especially opposition to the state, reflects the hegemonic influence of American ideas.

Second, in finding little of interest in the normative concept of the state,[25] American political science lost touch with the problem of normative order, i.e. with the tradition of normative inquiries, centred on the state, which sought to explore the double problem of how to identify, and how to ground, the first principles on which political association could or should be based, and how to make these effective in practice. In other words, American political science lost sight of the link between public power and public order, of the potential role of the state as the agency most responsible for securing a just public order. Political science in America grew up with a weak sense of the need to examine, in order to renew, the superordinate set of values on which the whole political association was based.[26] It has lacked a critical theory of its own polity. Its working assumption has been that social forces were more important than constitutional arrangements:[27] a just public order would emerge spontaneously out of society because the latter's growth was benign and rational. The problem for America is what happens when evidence accumulates to disprove this assumption, when it appears that American liberalism may not be,

---

25 Frederick M. Watkins, 'State: the concept', *International encyclopaedia of social sciences*, Macmillan, New York, 1968, pp. 152-4, explains the reasons for the 'marked devaluation of the normative concept of the state'.

26 L.J. Sharpe, 'American democracy reconsidered', *British journal of political science*, vol. 3, parts 1 and 2, 1973. Not everyone of course: the criticism applies to the discipline collectively. Political theorists especially (e.g. Wolin, Jacobson) and some political scientists (notably Lowi and the later Lindblom) have criticized the presumptions of American political science. So too did the critics of behaviouralism. There has always been tension between the proponents of science and those of democracy, and this re-surfaced in the 1980s, in books by David Ricci and James Ceaser.

27 M.C.J. Vile, *Constitutionalism and the separation of powers*, Clarendon Press, Oxford, 1967, pp. 303-14.

after all, self-sufficient? To whom or what does it turn? For other societies, such as Australia, there are risks in accepting at face value the American agenda for political studies.

American political scientists especially are fond of pointing out that the state is a value-laden term: its meaning is obscured by ideological baggage. That is undoubtedly true. What is also true is that their own hostility towards the state is grounded in a very particular set of cultural and intellectual factors, notably in the case of mainstream writers the uniqueness of American liberalism, the highly decentralized bargaining style of American politics and, overall, a fierce attachment to the political arrangements of a certain kind of 'stateless society'. As Bernard Crick argued provocatively some time ago, one should understand the programme of, and the ambitions for, the American *science* of politics as very much the product of America's own indigenous political and philosophic traditions—notably, realism, pragmatism, a certain theory of progress and distinctive ideas about democracy. It was also informed in this century by a conscious reaction against the theory and practice of the state in Europe. Europeans, by and large, have theories of the state but mainstream American social scientists have been much more interested in devising a systems theory of society, one which totally subsumes the state as a separate or subordinate structure. The latter have also been supremely confident in the potential universal applicability of their own theories—of development, of the social system, of personality, of pluralist democracy—offering them enthusiastically as models for other cultures and societies to emulate.

The point is that we need to be aware of just how much the negative view of the state which has grown up over the last fifty years is a product of America's own distinctive society and traditions, reinforced by the scepticism towards the state found in the classical liberal tradition. We might remember that in Europe the view of the state, both in theory and practice, has always remained much more positive, despite the appalling record of certain European states this century. In Europe, notably in Germany and France, the normative dimensions of the state remained alive and the state has been regarded as an important intellectual resource for both nation-building and post-war reconstruction. In Australia there has developed a profound ambivalence with regard to the state as we have, despite notable exceptions,[28] tended towards the American tradition.

Given the influence that American political (and social) science exerts by sheer weight of numbers and scholarly output, we in Australia might do well to be more sceptical towards the hegemonic impact of American ideas on our understanding of our own political traditions. In particular, we should be cautious about transplanting ideas emanating from a very particular kind of 'stateless society', into this society where the state has played a much more active and positive role in nation-building. It may be that the state represents for us, as in Europe, a more important resource to be utilised than it ever has in America. To dismiss the state too readily may be to cut ourselves off from ideas about how best to organise our collective existence which might be of real value at the present time. There is also something ironic, to put it mildly, about American scepticism towards the state as the final custodian of justice and public order when such scepticism forms part of a syndrome which has helped to bring about 'the decline of the United States into a sort of chronic, low-intensity ethnic civil war, a proto-Lebanon held together only by a dwindling capital of legalism ...'[29]

Bringing the state back in

The rejection of the state was never as widespread as Easton clearly assumed in 1981. At the time (1968) when Watkins was writing a qualified obituary notice for the state in the IESS, the term was already coming back into vogue on the other side of the Atlantic. Kenneth Dyson's book, among others, re-established the

---

28 For example, Boris Frankel, *Beyond the state? dominant theories and socialist strategies*, Macmillan, London, 1983; however, while we agree with much of his critique of common tendencies to reify or homogenize the state as a thing or actor, we part company with him when he says that it is unhelpful to use generalized concepts such as 'the capitalist state' or 'the modern state'. We contend that they are of use in making broad comparisons.

29 Gray, *Beyond the New Right*, p. ix.

significance of the state as a central ordering concept within the discourse of European politics.[30] In Britain, although the state fell out of fashion in the 1950s and 1960s, it was not completely jettisoned in the way it was in America. The concept lived on in the teachings of political theorists, especially within the three main traditions of ethical liberalism, reformist socialism and conservatism. It was also present in teaching the *misterie* of the British Constitution: responsible government was a *de facto* philosophy of the state.

By the later 1970s, a steady stream of publications on the state, from different quarters of political science, signalled that the term was well on the way to reinstatement.[31] *Daedalus* devoted a special issue to the state in 1979 (volume 108, number 4) while the American Political Science Association took as its theme for the 1981 Conference 'Restoring the State to Political Science'. Liberal social scientists as well as Marxists were increasingly willing to modify their respective 'society-centred' paradigms, and to acknowledge that state officials, under certain circumstances, enjoyed significant autonomy to articulate and impose their own policy preferences even in the face of dissent from other powerful social interests.[32] Interest in the state and state theory was further stimulated by two emerging realms of debate: first, over the nature of the capitalist state. This became a central focus of neo-Marxist theory—key writers included Nicos Poulantzas, Jürgen Habermas, Claus Offe and Bob Jessop. Second, historical sociologists debated the causes of state formation and the reasons why some states and state systems grew and prospered—particularly the European —while others collapsed. Leading writers here included Charles Tilly, Theda Skocpol, Michael Mann and Anthony Giddens. Their work both drew on and overlapped with very extensive research

---

30 Kenneth Dyson, *The state tradition in Western Europe: A study of an idea and an institution*, Oxford University Press, Oxford, 1979.
31 E.g. Stephen D. Krasner, 'Approaches to the state: review article', *Comparative politics*, 16: 2, 1984.
32 Much of this literature is summarised in Peter Evans, Dietrich Reuschemeyer and Theda Skocpol eds, *Bringing the state back in*, Cambridge University Press, Cambridge UK, 1985.

carried out by political anthropologists and, in particular, by American cultural anthropologists, into the origins of states, classes and the beginnings of socially differentiated, complex societies. Their collective output highlighted the nexus between state and war, identified several distinctive trajectories of state formation, and showed that it was possible to use the term 'state' to draw attention to a different set of structural regularities within the processes of social and political evolution, complementary to those for which empirical-behavioural scholars had previously understood themselves to be searching.

Reviewing this literature falls outside the province of this chapter. Much of it is of very high quality and reading it, especially that dealing with the way in which states establish themselves and grow, a process which is by no means self-evident and which was described by one cultural anthropologist as 'an evolutionary paradox',[33] should be sufficient to counter the kind of doubts and criticisms Easton expressed towards the 'operational utility' of the state in 1953. The volume and quality of this research is the main reason for a recent student text on the state beginning thus: 'the period in which social science "lost interest" in the state ... is now over'.[34] However, the flood of research upon the state creates new drawbacks. There is so much of it, a synthesis is lacking, and because much of it is historical and anthropological, it seems to have passed by the Politics mainstream. Consequently, it is still open for members of the Old Guard, such as Almond, to query whether bringing the state back in really will add to rather than diminish the explanatory resources of the discipline at large. That argument still has to be made. For another thing, some of this material may be criticised as overly-abstract. This is a particular fault of neo-Marxist theorizing. With some notable exceptions such as Stuart Hall, neo-Marxists have become more theoretical as socialism has declined in status as a practical political program. The historical sociologists, too, are

---

33 David Webster, 'Warfare and the evolution of the state: a reconsideration', *American antiquity*, 40: 4, 1975.
34 John A. Hall and G. John Ikenberry, *The state*, Open University Press, Milton Keynes, 1989.

open to criticism over the range of their generalizations. It is also possible for neo-Marxists to argue that although historical sociologists like Skocpol have brought the state back in, they have done so at a certain price: the concept has been sanitized, the link between the state and force, the Marxist insight into the role the state necessarily plays in a stratified (i.e. unstable) society, has been pushed to the intellectual margin.[35]

Still, these are matters for another essay. Here, the real drawback of recent work on the state is that, by concentrating on the state-in-history and the transformation from the traditional to the modern state rather than on more contemporary developments, those theorists who wanted to 'bring the state back in' inadvertently left the way open for a new theoretical challenge to sneak in the front door. It quickly took over the front rooms in the house of state-theory.

A second retreat from the state?

During the 1980s and 1990s we have seen the development of a new and much more theoretically sophisticated retreat away from directly addressing the state as a general institution and structure of power. It was not that the orthodox core of the Australian discipline of politics needed to find new reasons for not studying the state-as-such. A glance at even the most recent university political science text books confirms that the state continues to be prominent in its absence. Under the heading of 'Government', the state continues to be the implicit subject of political studies, but it is hardly ever directly mentioned. The texts do not even broach questions about the historical form of the state or its changing institutional practices. As a Derridean deconstructionist might express this peculiar absence-presence, the writers of politics text books in effect treat the state as a hidden signifier, a master concept that could be said to connect all of their analysis but is always under erasure. The texts cover almost every aspect of the

---

35 Paul Cammack, 'Review article: bringing the state back in?', *British journal of political science*, vol. 19, part 2, 1989.

state from the conduct of government enacted via the party system, the public face of politics fought out in the houses of parliament, through to the role of bureaucracy and other agents of the state involved in the implementation of policy directives, but they consistently and comfortably avoid ever talking about broad structural continuities and transformations in the state as a whole.[36]

When Rob Watts begins his chapter with the sentence 'The *modern* state is everywhere the object of widespread analysis and concern' (emphasis added) he is rightly pointing to the contemporary currency of surface debates over the role of state apparatuses in the regulation or deregulation of the economy and civil society. However, the question remains, how long will such debates—full of sound and fury as they are—continue to have any substance at all? Just as discussions over 'what form of economy is a good economy?' have largely been overtaken by debates over 'what kind of micro-economic reforms are necessary for increased global "efficiency"', discussions over 'what is a good state?'[37] have been reduced to debates over 'how big or small should the state be'; 'how might we proceed with micro-reforms to various state apparatuses'; 'how might we write some minimal changes into the constitution which would nevertheless confer on Australia the status of republic?'

In the disciplines of sociology, criminology and social welfare, studies of the state in the guise of the welfare-surveillance state had been given a new lease of life during the 1980s. (Rob White draws upon some of this material on the theme of social control in his chapter.) However, in the 1990s these disciplines too are beginning to come under the influence of a 'second retreat' influenced by trends outside them all. It is a retreat with many apparent similarities to the first. The central difference, which might be described in terms of a shift from an emphasis on 'Government' to

---

[36] The one notable exception is *Society, state and politics in Australia*, ed. Michael Muetzelfeldt, Pluto Press, Leichhardt, 1992. See particularly Aynsley Kellow's appropriately titled chapter 'The curious case of the vanishing state'.

[37] See Peter Lawler, 'Constituting the "good state" ' in *Critical politics: from the personal to the global*, ed. Paul James, Arena Publications, Melbourne, 1994.

a concern with 'governance', is based on a methodological aversion to considering the state as anything other than a contingent collection of contingent processes. This moves the debate an epistemological step beyond the pre-1980s' propositions that all state decision-making processes are messy, no more than a matter of muddling through. If some neo-Marxists had responded to the first retreat by re-emphasizing, and sometimes over-emphasizing, the state as structured whole,[38] by contrast, the new trend goes further along old pluralist lines: it involves understanding the state as always dissolved into multiple and changing sites of micro-power. The theoretical rationale for this move comes from the emerging field of post-structuralism, particularly influenced by Michel Foucault. Its political orientation ranges from left-liberal to postmodernist.

The contemporary theoretical retreat from the state is taking three main forms: (i) to treat the concept of the state as a useless or over-generalized abstraction; (ii) to implicitly treat the state as everywhere and nowhere, the metaphoric naming of one of the discursive closures in the flow of ubiquitous power; and (iii) to treat the postmodernization process as a comprehensive process acting to fragment, decentre and deterritorialize the modern state. As you can see these trends contradict each other.

The first trend is part of the backlash against structural theories of the state, both Marxist and Weberian. As one of the postmodern turns there has emerged a tendency to treat the state as either a useless abstraction, an abstraction in the sense that it is not real, or as a discursive abstraction, only real to the extent that it discursively names a set of 'shifting and temporary connections'. For example, Judith Allen gives voice to this turn when she writes:

---

38   Most of the well-known neo-Marxists bent over backwards not to over-generalize their claims and not reify the state, not to treat the state structures as things. For example, going back to Nicos Poulantzas, he writes: 'it is precisely one of the merits of Marxism that ... it thrust aside the grand metaphysical flights of so-called political philosophy—the vague and nebulous theorizings of an extreme generality and abstractness that claim to lay bare the great secrets of History, the Political, the State, and Power' (*State, Power, Socialism*, Verso, London, 1980, p. 20). However, as later Marxists pointed out, Poulantzas somehow thought he could do this in the abstract, hardly referring to actually existing states to illustrate his general arguments.

'The state' is a category of abstraction that is too aggressive, too unitary and too unspecific to be of much use in addressing the disaggregated, diverse and specific (or local) sites that must be of most pressing concern to feminists. 'The state' is too blunt an instrument to be of much assistance (beyond generalizations) in explanations, analyses or the design of workable strategies.[39]

Writers of these kinds of statements are reacting to an earlier tendency to treat the state as a monolithic whole, as an institution which was given unproblematic anthropomorphic agency: that is, a state was said to be able to act as if it had a life beyond the people who made it up; sometimes it was even invested with a personality, usually masculine. There are deep problems with classic and modern theory insofar as it treats the state in this way (see both Rob Watts' and Ann Curthoys' chapters). However, by refusing to make generalities about the state-in-history the alternative (postmodern) approach simply turns the problem on its head, and in the process the state has had to disappear (or rather, as we would argue, has come to exist as a concept under erasure).

The power of this move has begun to inveigle its way into both the Marxist and liberal tradition alike. In his latest book, the Marxist Bob Jessop finds it necessary to include a section entitled 'Does the state exist?' He concludes that as a social relation it does exist (phew), but along the way he presents as one of his major theses the dubious proposition that 'as an institutional ensemble the state does not (and cannot) exercise power: it is not a real subject'.[40] Similarly, commenting on the liberal tradition, Clyde Barrow writes:

---

39 Judith Allen, 'Does feminism need a theory of "the state"?', in *Playing the state*, ed. Sophie Watson, Verso, London, 1990, p. 22; see also the critical discussion by Jane Kenway, 'Feminist theories of the state: to be or not to be?' in *Society, state and politics in Australia*, ed. Muetzelfeldt.
40 Bob Jessop, *State theory*, Polity Press, Cambridge, 1990, p. 366. It is possible to sympathize with him in attempting to bypass the theoretical problems that post-structuralists have rightly criticized; however, it can be done without throwing the baby out with the bathwater.

the ambiguity in the boundaries of the state concept is compounded by the analytic requirement that, for political authority to achieve stateness, there must be a relative unity to the apparatuses exercising that authority within the boundaries of what we call the state. However, as a result of its internal development and expansion during the twentieth century, Poggi argues that it is now 'totally unrealistic ... to conceive the state as making up *an* organization,' as suggested in the definitions proffered by Skocpol, Skowronek, and others. In fact, their emphasis on the unevenness of state development suggests a research agenda in which it is possible to talk about organizations that wield state powers, but in which one cannot any longer talk realistically about *the* state or *a* state.[41]

In both of these cases we find the assumption that an entity can wield no power if it is more than the sum of its parts.

There is a simple way out of this problem, simple at least in its saying. States do exist and they are much more than transitory discursive formations. However, the way in which they are described depends upon what level of generality *and* what level of theoretical abstraction we want to begin the description (see Appendix 1 to Chapter 9). At the most abstract generalizing level, while they may be contingent and changing, historically they have tended to be relatively stable structures of governance. They operate as a more or less co-ordinated ensemble of agents who draw on sets of juridical procedures to administer (by consent and coercion) a given territory and people. The state, as for example it exists in Australia, may be an abstraction, but it is a material abstraction, a lived structure of unevenly integrated and patterned practices and ideologies.

At a more concrete theoretical level, the state in Australia *is* much more messy. The closer one gets to the ground the more the state does disappear into a disorganized ensemble of individuals battling it out over micro-issues in their micro-settings. Such analyses do help us to avoid the problem of treating the state as an homogenous, undifferentiated whole. However, it makes no sense

---

41 Clyde Barrow, *Critical theories of the state*, University of Wisconsin Press, Wisconsin, 1993, pp. 144-5.

to valorize less generalized and less abstract descriptions if by doing so we can no longer talk about the state as such: to modify a common aphorism, a detailed description of every leaf in the forest is not sufficient to come to an understanding of the forest itself. Both of these levels of description are useful in combination. As the contributors to this volume attest, ranging across different levels of theoretical abstraction, and qualifying each level of analysis by other levels, enables a much more nuanced understanding than does heading off in the direction of either empiricism or theoreticism. (See in particular the chapters by James and Hinkson on the use of different levels of theoretical abstraction and how they can be used to understand the lived abstraction we call the state.)

The second postmodern trend which has made it hard to 'bring the state back in' is a tendency to treat the state as a nodal point in the ubiquitous circulation of power. In this move the state is at once treated as having enormous power and reduced to nothing but a symptom of the circulation of power in general. This is a bit confusing, but bear with us. The following quote from the poststructuralists Gilles Deleuze and Félix Guattari will need translating into more common English but with careful reading it does give a direct rendition of this double move:

> the modern nation-States ... take decoding even further [than traditional and early modern states] and are models of realization for an axiomatic or general conjunction of flows (these States combine social subjection and the new machinic enslavement, and their very diversity is a function of isomorphy, of the eventual heteromorphy or polymorphy of the models in relation to the axiomatic).[42]

In this description the modern state is said to offer a place for the temporary slowing down of abstract capital: their phrase, the 'axiomatic ... of flows', is Deleuze and Guattari's metaphor for describing global capitalism. When they describe the state as 'models of realization for an axiomatic' they are trying to under-

---

42 Gilles Deleuze and Felix Guattari, *A thousand plateaus: capitalism and schizophrenia*, University of Minnesota Press, Minneapolis, 1991, p. 459.

stand why, despite the fact that capitalism can do without states, states are given new strength by the deterritorializing flow of capitalism. In other words, they see states as contradictorily an expression of the global flow of power even though they inhibit it. States become megamachines of enslavement just as globalism contributes to a generalized regime of 'voluntary' subjection. The effect of all of this is to overstate the role of the state as a comprehensive machine of internal control, and at the same to over-reduce it to a residual effect of grander external processes.

Michel Foucault makes something of a parallel move when on the one hand he says that we live in the era of 'governmentality', but then on the other hand he reduces the form of state we experience today to an effect of the whole discursive formation—'a society controlled by apparatuses of security'.[43] Accordingly, he writes:

> the state is no more than a composite reality and a mythicized abstraction, whose importance is a lot more limited than many of us think. Maybe what is really important for our modernity—that is for our present—is not so much the *étatisation* of society, as the 'governmentalization' of the state.[44]

Foucault wants to take the state out of the centre of discussions of contemporary power and replace it by governmentality, but ironically his own analyses centre upon state apparatuses—such as the prison and the clinic, and upon state practices such as policing and welfare provision—all seen as key institutions in the globalization of bio-power. It is no wonder that some commentators have accused Foucault of underestimating the state, and others have said that he makes the state everything.[45]

As with the first problem, we think there is a relatively simple

---

[43] Michel Foucault, *The Foucault effect: studies in governmentality*, eds Graham Burchell, Colin Gordon, and Peter Miller, University of Chicago Press, Chicago, 1991, p. 104.
[44] ibid., p. 103.
[45] Jean Cohen and Andrew Arato, *Civil society and political theory*, MIT Press, Massachusetts, 1992, pp. 280-6.

way out. It is possible to say that the state is a central institutional ensemble with enormous actual and potential power at its disposal without either demonizing it as the source of that power, or reducing the state to the kinds of power it uses. We have choices about the ways in which the state will act. What Foucault calls modern governmentality is part of what we would prefer to call the legal-rational mode of organization, that is, the means, techniques, procedures and cultural assumptions practiced in administering the activities of people and the movement of objects such as commodities. The legal-rational is the dominant mode of organization across the late-modern/postmodern world including Australia. Economic rationalism is an extreme form of this kind of rationality. However, the state and the dominant mode of organization are not the same thing. The state, just like the multinational corporation, is an institutional structure through which its agents draw upon various modes of organization; it is not reducible to a 'model of realization' of something beyond itself.

The third postmodern retreat from the state arises out of flawed attempts to understand the transformations of the modern state into what John Hinkson (Chapter 8) calls the postmodern state. Hinkson in his chapter argues that 'A dualism between modern 'totalizing' forms ... and a postmodern specificity and decentredness leaves little conceptual space for a post-modern state'. In a new book called *Postmodernization*, three Australian authors attempt to look into this space, but in doing so they lose sight of the state in the glare of their own theoretical apparatus. They conclude that the state is devolving into a postmodern 'disorganization complex':

> the general direction of change can be charted with modest accuracy. It involves a general shift away from corporatist centralism and towards a more decentralized and fragmented minimal state. More specifically, the vector of change involves shifts from centralized to decentralized state apparatuses and from authoritative to manipulative forms of control. This may prove to be the best *temporary* survival strategy for the state ... The current process of devolution seems to follow logic of ironic reversals ... differentiation and centralization [under modernity] give way to fragmentation of domains, each with

fuzzy boundaries and unspecific functions.[46]

Any force the argument might have is undermined by its radical overstatement. Crook, Pakulski and Waters set up a totalizing view of the nature of the transformation, misunderstanding very real emergent trends including privatization, corporatization, deregulation, and globalization as harbingers of the end of the state as we know it. It all becomes so fuzzy that they have to employ unhelpful oxymorons to label the disappearing state, renaming the postmodern state as a 'disorganization complex'. By contrast, while the authors of the present volume take a variety of views upon whether or not, and to what extent, we are witnessing a transformation of modernity and/or the development of postmodern structures and sensibilities, none of them sets up a dichotomous schema for understanding historical change. From a range of perspectives they all attempt to analyse the dialectic of continuity and discontinuity, and the overlaying of various modes of practice.

Conclusion

In 1988 a pro-state theorist, Stephen Krasner, observed: '*Sovereignty* is a term that makes the eyes of most American political scientists glaze over. It has lost meaning and analytic relevance.'[47] Despite the appearance of a book such as *Bringing the state back in*, the debate about the state within political science is far from over. It is not only the old guard but their many followers, as well as a whole new generation of commentators influenced by post-structuralism, who need to be convinced that reviving the state will add to rather than diminish the explanatory resources of the discipline of politics as a whole. It has been argued that the state has only been reinstated partially—that the way in which it has been brought back in is limited by the preconceptions and agenda of liberal social science which prefers not to dwell on the

---

46 Stephen Crook, Jan Pakulski and Malcolm Waters, *Postmodernization: change in advanced society*, Sage, London, 1992, pp. 103-4
47 Stephen D. Krasner, 'Sovereignty: an institutional perspective', *Comparative Political Studies*, vol. 21, no. 1, 1988, p. 86.

links between state and class, or state and power.[48] This is thoroughly in evidence in the huge review-volume put out recently by the American Political Science Association called *Political science: the state of the discipline*.[49] Unlike the first volume a decade ago, there is a section devoted to the state, but, in keeping with our argument, any general concern with questions about 'what kind of state?' disappears into dreary chapters such 'Legislatures: individual purpose and institutional performance'. It is indicative that the book *Bringing the state back in* does not get a mention in this section, but Blanche d'Alpuget's biography of Robert J. Hawke does.

There are stronger reasons for bringing the state back in than political science as a discipline has acknowledged. These are to be found in the literature on state formation. This book will suggest in due course that re-examining the state can add to our conceptual resources by focussing attention on the way in which the interlocking processes which occur in state formation help to both fashion political identity (see Paul James' chapter) and construct the political reality which political scientists engaged in 'normal science' tend to take for granted (see in particular Chris Reus-Smit's chapter). It *is* possible to use the term 'state' to draw attention to a different set of structural regularities in political life. In this way generalized studies of the state can complement the micro-political analyses favoured by liberal pluralists and postmodernists alike.

Meanwhile it must be argued that we do have reasons in the shape of hard political issues to make the state a focus for study: that the state represents an important conceptual resource to be recovered and developed, subject to a proper regard for certain of the criticisms levied. The core of the opposition to taking the state more seriously stems from a strong normative preference for treating markets and free trade, individuals and sites of micro-power, as more important objects of study than the state, entities

---

48 Paul Cammack, 'Review article: bringing the state back in?', *British journal of political science*, vol. 19, part 2, 1989.
49 Ed. Ada Finifter, APSA, Washington, 1993.

which are intrinsically more valuable in themselves. Unless we take the state seriously and address it in its generality (as well as its particularity), old-fashioned questions such as 'how might we reform the relationship between state and society?' will be reduced either to slanging matches over micro-economic 'reform' versus welfare provision, or to postmodern debates over whether or not the state exists.

3

Laborism and the state: confronting modernity

Rob Watts

The modern state is everywhere the object of widespread analysis and concern. The 'crisis of the welfare state', the limits to governance and the prospects for dissolving the state in the conditions of postmodernity are variously the object of enthusiastic promotion by the Right, anxious sentimentality on the part of the Left, or nihilistic malice on the part of some postmodernists.[1]

Since the 1980s, parallel anxieties and criticisms have swirled around the Australian Labor Party. Critics have argued that the Hawke-Keating governments have terminated the history of the ALP by allegedly breaking with labor tradition and radically revising the traditional ALP view of the State.[2] Maddox suggests that under Hawke, the ALP has been 'courting Labor's traditional adversaries in the business and financial communities ... adopting many of its opponents' favoured policies ... and abandoning many

---

1   The literature on these themes is immense. For representative treatments see   A. Kroker and D. Cook, *The postmodern scene: excremental culture and hyper-aesthetics*, St Martin's Press, New York, 1986; C. Offe, *The contradictions of the welfare state*, Blackwell, Oxford, 1984; Evatt Foundation, *State of siege*, Evatt and Pluto Press, Sydney, 1988, and   P.G. Cerny, 'State capitalism in France and Britain and the international economic order', in *Socialism, the state and public policy in France*, eds P.G. Cerny and M. Schain, Methuen, London, 1985.
2   C. Johnson, *The Labor legacy: Curtin, Chifley, Whitlam, Hawke*,   Allen & Unwin, Sydney, 1989;   D. Jaensch, *The Hawke-Keating hijack: the ALP in transition*, Allen and Unwin, Sydney, 1989; G. Maddox, *The Hawke government and labor tradition*, Penguin, Ringwood, 1989, and T. Battin, 'A break from the past, *Australian journal of political science*, vol. 28, 1993, pp. 221-41.

of its own'.[3] These commentators interpret the Hawke and Keating governments' preference for market forces, a minimalist state, deregulation, privatization, and the rhetoric of economic rationalism, as marking a fundamental break with 'labor's mission' and 'tradition'.[4] Battin, commenting on the alleged 'abandonment of traditional Labor ideology' since 1983, claims that 'no other Labor government has felt the need to pour [such] scorn on previous labor thought'.[5] This chapter begins its foray into the relation between laborism, the state and modernity, by expressing a radical scepticism about the value and validity of these arguments. Whilst it does not systematically essay the arguments here, this chapter also rejects the proposition that something called a postmodern society or economy has emerged, rendering everything before it obsolete.[6]

Much of the criticism of the modern ALP is a form of sociocritique that begins with the politically charged premise that the ALP *ought* to reflect its working-class origins.[7] For some the 'betrayal' of the Labor tradition by Labor governments since 1983 is tied to larger structural matters like the decline—or demise—of the working class in postmodern society accompanying the rise of new social movements.[8] Others see betrayal following the middle-class lawyers, teachers and social workers joining the ALP in the 1970s.[9] Crisp argued in 1983 that the ALP has lost its 'true' blue-collar working-class base, and that the *embourgeoisement* of the ALP explains both the betrayal and the breach with its original

---

3   Maddox, *The Hawke government and labor tradition*, p. 12.
4   G. Maddox, 'Language, tradition and Labor's business orientation', *Business and government under Labor*, eds B. Galligan and G. Singleton, Melbourne, 1991.
5   Battin, 'A break from the past', p. 233.
6   See R. Watts, 'The pseudo-history of postmodernism: restoring social theory', mimeo, RMIT, 1994, for a summary of arguments against the postmodernist thesis.
7   On 'socio-critique' see N. Rose, *Governing the soul*, Routledge, London, 1988, pp. 3-5.
8   Karl-Werner Brandt, 'New social movements as a metapolitical challenge', *Thesis Eleven*, no. 15, 1986, pp. 60-7, and J. Cohen, 'Strategy or identity', *Social research*, no. 52, 1985, pp. 663-716.
9   See A. Scott, 'Root and branch', *Australian left review*, October 1990, pp. 32-3.

class links.[10] Scott argues that in Victoria the ALP lost the support of its 'traditional blue-collar manual working-class' base and that 'there have been new sources of support for Labor from workmen and young people, inspired in part by the social movements from feminism, peace and the environment'.[11] Others, taking a longer view, see more than mere coincidence in the demise of the traditional ALP, the rise of new social movements, and the radical transformations in economy and society that began in the 1960s.[12] The rise of a new ALP under Hawke and Keating is in this way connected to the rise of new social movements, like feminism and eco-politics, which it is claimed has both eroded the old base of the Labor party and its tradition *and* diverted the Left with bewitching new items for political action.

There can be little doubt that much of this recent literature reflects real changes within the labour movement and its context. Some of these changes are occurring as a result both of new forms of integration and re-differentiation of capitalism at the global level, and of the 'restructuring' of the Australian state, the economy and the labour market.[13] Certainly the social conditions which sustained Australian laborism at its birth, and defined its role in shaping the Australian welfare state in the 1940s, in most cases no longer exist. Yet grasping the significance of *these* changes may well be larger or more complex than current simplifications about the betrayal of Labor's mission suggest. Equally I am not persuaded, whatever its many grievous, even objectionable,

---

10 L. F. Crisp, 'The Labor party then and now', in *Labor essays 1982*, eds G. Evans and J. Reeves, Drummond Press, Carlton, 1983.
11 A. Scott, 'Root and branch', pp. 32-3.
12 B. Frankel, in his *From the prophets deserts come*, Arena Publications, Melbourne, 1992, suggests the loss of 'true' working-class consciousness. On social movements see K. McDonald, 'The unmaking of the labour movement', *Social alternatives*, vol. 6, no. 4, 1987, pp. 12-16; B. Frankel, 'Whither the social movements?', *Arena magazine*, no. 2, 1992, pp. 17-22; and V. Burgmann, *Power and protest*, Allen & Unwin, Sydney, 1993, pp. 262-77.
13 Organizationally the proportional membership of blue-collar workers within the ALP decreased from 63 percent in 1901 to only 12 percent in 1981. See Jaensch, *The Hawke-Keating hijack*, p. 51 and A. Scott, *Fading loyalties*, Pluto Press, Sydney, 1991, pp. 43-8.

LABORISM AND THE STATE

political and moral failings, that laborism has yet become the irrelevant or obsolete social movement that so many critics claim for it. Like Mark Twain's celebrated premature death-notice, reports of laborism's death are somewhat exaggerated.

In raising the question of how best to characterize the past achievements and the present prospects of the ALP, I focus here on the concept of laborism and the practices to which it refers and its relationship with the state.[14] After a brief historiographical survey of the idea of laborism, I offer some suggestions about the character of the ALP under Hawke and Keating, before pursuing the question of the future of laborism, modernity and the state.

Some arguments

Against those who identify a radical break between an Australian Labor Party tradition, and the Hawke-Keating ALP, I suggest that there are discernible threads of continuity, however thin or tatty, running between the 1890s and the 1990s. That century-old thread is 'laborism'. Laborism has held out the promise that through parliamentary control of the state by a Labor party and a special relationship between the party and the organized labour movement, protection, however scant, might be afforded to the most vulnerable members of 'the working class'. It is this thread which, however often stretched, frayed, even snapped, and endlessly repaired, provides a clue to the tenuous continuity and famous survival ability of the labour movement, the oldest and most successful of the great modern social movements in Australia.

---

14. I acknowledge here the assistance of T. Irving's 'Do we still need the concept of labourism?', (unpublished paper). Two further points. The spelling of 'labor' and 'labour' has often been both a lexical and a substantive issue. In this chapter I use 'labour' to refer to the labour movement, 'Labor' to refer to the ALP, 'labourism' to refer to the first and more general category that has been at issue in the historiography, and 'laborism' to refer to the political continuities I argue for here. Secondly I concentrate on the federal Labor party. An interesting but impossibly diverse set of stories can be told about each of the state Labor parties. See D.J. Murphy, ed. *Labor in politics: the state Labor parties in Australia 1880-1920*, University of Queensland Press, St Lucia, 1975.

Secondly, rather than identifying the current crisis of laborism or crisis of the state, it seems plain that both laborism and the state in the 1990s continue to be what they have always been, historically contingent. Those who would argue for an essential labor tradition face real problems in defining the line which separates tradition from the new heresies. This is so especially because laborism as a body of ideas, policies and doctrines has always been to a considerable extent field-dependent. That is, the ALP has embraced major ideological and discursive fashions, often fashioned outside the labour movement, producing major shifts by the ALP. It has lurched from the experiment of 'new liberalism' in the 'Lib-Lab' alliances of the pre-1914 period, to the more serious embrace of Keynesian social-liberalism in the early 1940s, to the current enthusiasm of key strategists and leaders for the economic liberal nostrums that Michael Pusey has so memorably described as 'economic rationalism'.[15] In the periods of its greatest electoral success or policy influence, the ALP leadership has selected, in something like magpie fashion from available intellectual and discursive fashions, packages of ideas and policies which sit best with their sense of what laborism is all about. If the ideas have changed, the underlying strategic threads of laborism have not.

Unlike more recent social movements, leading laborists have accepted the discipline and the contradictions of the electoral project. For good or bad, key figures within the ALP recognized early that they would need to expand their electoral appeal beyond the boundaries of their class-base if the party were to win office or to maintain government. For a good part of its history this recognition has sat uneasily with members of its social-movement base, especially those with a more teleological view of history committed to a view of the working class as the agent of historical progress. They expected purity of commitment rather than the grubby compromises electoralism seemed to constantly demand of its parliamentary wing.

---

15 M. Pusey, *Economic rationalism in Canberra*, Cambridge University Press, Melbourne, 1991.

LABORISM AND THE STATE

Contemporary debates about the past

If we are to make sense of the ALP's prospects for the 1990s, there is little point in doing this by looking for some essential ALP identity to act as a benchmark against which critics can accuse it of betraying its mission or losing touch with history. Making sense of the ALP's enthusiastic flirtations with ideas and political programmes over the last century is no easy matter. Equally, catching the character of the ALP has never been simply an academic exercise. Defining the identity of the ALP has itself been central to its political life, providing a focus for political struggles both within the ALP and between it and its adversaries.

Sometimes it has seemed that the ALP was more to be characterized by the things it was not. In a process of typification by subtraction, especially for those who began with the premise that the ALP *ought* to be a worker's party and were then puzzled when it did not always conform to a European-style socialist party, Metin's 1904 claim that the ALP practised a 'socialisme sans doctrine' could serve doubly as an analysis and as a standing reproach.[16] In 1921 Gordon Childe chastised the ALP for not being a *proper* workers' party, in large measure because of the absence of a suitably explicit intellectual and socialist element within it.[17]

Among academics, for whom typologies matter, the conclusion was reached that if the ALP was neither Fabian, Bolshevik nor social-democratic, then these absences must mean that the ALP was essentially pragmatic or even anti-intellectual, a party where ideas have not mattered. Burchall suggests, typically, 'Laborism, the traditional ethos of the labour movement, was in effect anti-theoretical; it held that the prime goal of the labour movement was to strengthen the power of the labour movement'.[18]

More recently, some have uneasily acknowledged that it is a

---

16 A. Metin, *Socialism without doctrine*, Longman, Melbourne, 1987. See also R. Catley and B. MacFarlane, *From Tweedledum to Tweedledee*, ANZ Books, Sydney, 1974.
17 V.G. Childe, *How Labour governs* (reprint), Melbourne University Press, Melbourne, 1967.
18 D. Burchall, 'After social democracy', *Australian left review*, September 1992, p. 25.

'confused party, both organizationally and ideologically'.[19] Yet even a perfunctory, let alone sensitive, reading of the ALP's history suggests that ideas and theoretical frameworks have always mattered, even if they were not always articulated in the self-consciously intellectual style favoured by European social-democratic parties.[20] By the 1960s the previous 'intellectual desert' model had been abandoned and the ALP was rediscovered as a doctrinal land of plenty, as utopianism, populism, 'labour developmentalism', 'democratic socialism' and 'social democracy' were all rediscovered.[21] Attempts to persuade us that the ALP is a social-democratic party or a democratic-socialist party continued to have a good run, and the idea of labourism was introduced.[22]

Irving suggests the concept of labourism itself has only recently achieved currency, even though the characteristics that labourism was designed to catch have been around a long time. He also notes that the concept is neither innocent nor neutral. Deployed critically by the New Left in the 1960s, it has since been adopted in a more self-congratulatory way by the New labour Right, thereby rendering its contemporary use suspect—at least in the

---

19 J. Wheeldon, 'The problem of the ALP', *Quadrant*, March 1983, p. 42.
20 Failure to deal with ideas in the ALP is one of several weaknesses in both L.F. Crisp, *The Australian federal Labor party, 1901-1951*, Heinemann, London, 1955 and R. McMullin, *The light on the hill*, Oxford University Press, Melbourne, 1991.
21 On utopianism and populism see R. Gollan, 'American populism and Australian utopianism', *Labour history*, no. 9, 1965, pp. 15-21; P. Love, *Labour and the money power*, Melbourne University Press, Melbourne, 1984; and R. Markey, *The making of the Labor party in New South Wales, 1880-1900*, UNSW Press, Sydney, 1988. On developmentalism see G. Maddox, 'The Australian Labor party', in *Political Parties in Australia*, eds G. Starr et al., Richmond, 1978, pp. 220-44, and on social democracy see S. Macintyre, 'The short history of social democracy in Australia', in *Blast, budge or by-pass: towards a social democratic Australia*, ed. D. Rawson, ANU Press, Canberra, 1984.
22 S. Macintyre, 'The making of the Australian working class: an historiographical survey', *Historical studies*, vol. 18, no. 71, October 1978, pp. 233-53; J. Camilleri, 'After social democracy', *Arena*, no. 77, 1986, pp. 48-73, and R. W. Connell, 'ALP: A basis of the Left', *Arena*, no. 78, 1987, pp. 31-42. A recent study of the Cain-Kirner governments in Victoria identifies Victorian Labor as Keynesian *and* social democratic: *Trials in power: Cain, Kirner and Victoria 1982-1992*, eds B. Costar and M. Considine, Melbourne University Press, Melbourne, 1992, pp. 284-5 whilst P. Beilharz, *Labor's utopias*, Routledge, London, 1992, would seem to leave the ALP out on a limb.

eyes of some.

An early development of the labourist idea by the American labour historian Commons identifies some of the key connotations of its more contemporary definitions-in-use, suggesting why the politics of the idea of labourism might become controversial. Commons, writing in 1918, noted how:

> a more 'pragmatic' or 'opportunistic' philosophy, based on the illogical variety of actual conditions and immediate necessities has taken form in the American Federation of labour, the railway brotherhoods and industrial unionism, which is neither anarchism nor socialism, but a species of protectionism combining both, and is analogous to the 'solidarisme' of recent movements in France, and the 'labourism' of England and Australasia.[23]

Here was a set of typifications that stressed pragmatism, the avoidance of socialist commitment, and as Macintyre notes, it was grounded in 'the immediate concerns of the worker'.[24]

By the late 1960s the revisionists were in full flight under the impact of the British New Left and their highly combative use of the idea of labourism.[25] Deploying Gramsci's notion of hegemony, labourism was identified in Britain as the expression of ruling-class hegemony within the Labour Party which was preventing the British Labour Party from fulfilling its role as a socialist workers' party. 'Labourism', variously identified as anti-intellectualism, parliamentarianism, rampant empiricism, trade-unionist consciousness, pragmatism, or simply as out and out pro-bourgeois sentiment, plainly had a lot to answer for. In Australia, a group of local New Left intellectuals (including Catley, Wheelwright, Rowley, McQueen and Connell and Irving), cheerfully repeated the analysis and found the ALP as wanting as its British cousin.[26]

---

23 Cited in Irving, 'Do we still need the concept of labourism?', p. 3.
24 S. Macintyre, *The labour experiment*, History Department, University of Melbourne, Melbourne, 1989, p. 35
25 Irving, 'Do we still need the concept of labourism?', pp. 9-11.
26 H. McQueen, 'Laborism and socialism', in *The Australian new left*, ed. R. Gordon, Heinemann, Melbourne, 1970; McQueen, *A new Britannia*, Penguin, Ringwood, 1970; J. Playford, 'The aristocracy of labour', *Arena*, no. 29, 1972, pp. 29-42; and Catley

Either historically or in its most recent manifestations under the leadership of Whitlam, the ALP too had fallen prey to bourgeois hegemony and slunk down the parliamentary road. Worse, it expressed the viewpoint and needs of a working class that ought to have known better. That working class had ended up either embracing political passivity in return for the 'living wage' and a modicum of welfare, or worse, had even embraced bourgeois values and aspirations![27] Anxious to preserve the appearances, Connell and Irving argued that the workers *qua* working class were essentially anti-capitalist; only the Australian state of the 1890s was pro-capitalist. Regrettably, as the union movement and the newly formed Labor parties enjoyed the warm embrace of the state, the evolution of state-sponsored arbitration meant that the unionist impulse was strengthened. Whatever oppositional or revolutionary potential the working class and its labour movement should have had was inexorably drained away.[28]

If some disapproved, others like Hagan stressed the essentially commonsense nature of the ALP; 'their faith was not in socialism, but in labourism'. This meant a belief in the neutrality of the state and a faith in the capacity of the labour movement, using parliaments, to win justice for workers without having to overthrow capitalism. In a way that was subsequently mirrored by Markey, Kelly and others, Hagan saw in labourism a cluster of policy intentions and achievements spanning much of the twentieth century, all designed to achieve a high average standard of wages and thereby of standards of living.[29] Markey too stressed its character as a practical/intellectual manifestation of something called 'the working class'. Yet like parallel accounts Markey's account is ultimately unhelpful since it relies on an essentialist, that is an undifferentiated, gender-blind and racist construction of

---

and McFarlane, *From Tweedledum to Tweedledee*.
27 See, for example, W. Higgins, 'Reconstructing Australian communism', in *Socialist Register 1974*, eds R. Miliband and J. Saville, Pluto Press, London, 1974.
28 R.W. Connell and T.H. Irving, *Class structure in Australian history*, Longman, Melbourne, 1980.
29 J. Hagan, *The history of the ACTU*, Cheshire, Melbourne, 1981, pp. xi-ii, and pp. 3-49. Much of this reappears as Kelly's version of the 'Australian settlement', in P. Kelly, *The end of certainty*, Allen and Unwin, Sydney, 1992.

the working class.[30] Markey's formulation, unlike Castles', ignored the profoundly masculinist preferences involved in using the state to secure the wages and working conditions of predominantly male unionists and male breadwinners. And as Calhoun reminds us:

> the nineteenth and early twentieth century working-class movement (if it even can be described more than tendentiously as a single movement) was multi-dimensional, only provisionally and partially unified, and not univocal.[31]

Others like Castles and Beilharz have extended the critical purchase of labourism. Castles' 1985 account has rightly proven influential as he examined the effect of the early political interventions which took as their privileged and undisclosed subject the male white wage-earner.[32] At the least Castles' comparative perspective revealed what was obvious yet had escaped too many Australian writers; that the particular form that Australian state interventions had taken presupposed not a citizen with rights, but a male wage-worker exercising political muscle to extract entitlements within the hurly-burly of political deals.[33] Castles' formulation of a 'wage-worker's welfare state' is at least a better start to grasping some of the peculiarities of the evolution of Australian state interventions, such as the limited scope for arguments to rights to be treated seriously.

Yet too much theory untempered by an historical eye for difference can also lead one astray. Beilharz, for example, relies on a theoretical typology of reformist parties that ends up characterizing labour parties like the ALP, as he rightly insists, by

---

30 M. Lake, 'The independence of women and the brotherhood of man', *Labour history*, no. 63, November 1992, pp. 1-24.
31 C. Calhoun, 'Postmodernism as pseudohistory', in *Agency and structure: reorienting social theory,* ed. P. Sztompka, Gordon and Breach, Reading, 1994, p. 181.
32 See Francis G. Castles, *The working class and welfare*, Allen & Unwin, Sydney, 1985.
33 Irving argues for the ALP as a bearer of the citizenship idea, but not convincingly; see T. Irving, 'Introduction', in *Challenges to labour history*, UNSW Press, Sydney, 1994, p. 10.

a convergence of many traditions that do not include socialism. His resulting account of laborism is accurate, however, I believe only for the period *since* the 1970s, when he claims that laborism's goals included:

> national equity achieved through the market, organized via the formal mechanisms of democracy, [which] could only result in the reproduction of capitalist relations, privileging the interests of employers over those of employees and those of both, over those outside the labour market.[34]

This will not do as an *historical* reading of the political twistings and the organizational turnings in the orientations and the policy approaches of the ALP over the past century because it ignores too much. In part and in spite of the many virtues of Beilharz's reading, it attempts an essentialist reading that seeks to leap out of time.

This leads me to suggest that the Australian Labor Party has historically been for most of the twentieth century a laborist party.[35] By *laborism* might be meant many things, and it usually has. Here I propose only that we use 'laborism' as an analytic device to catch the ambiguities, contingency and change in the content of the ALP's political and policy interventions, whilst seeing in it a tenuous continuity as both a political strategy, and as a way of orienting the ALP to the often heterogenous and contradictory agencies and policies of Australian state and social formations.

At its birth the ALP was a workers' party reflecting the experiences, aspirations and fears of some of Australia's unionized workers. Formed first in New South Wales in 1891–92, the aim

---

34 See P. Beilharz, 'The labourist tradition and the reforming imagination', in *Australian Welfare: Historical Sociology,* ed. R. Kennedy, Macmillan, Melbourne, 1987, pp. 132-53 and P. Beilharz, 'The Australian left: beyond labourism?', in *Socialist Register 1985-86,* eds R. Miliband and J. Saville, Pluto Press, London, 1986, pp. 210-32. See also his 'Australian laborism, social democracy and social justice', *Social justice*, vol. 16 no. 3, 1989, pp. 15-29.
35 D. W. Rawson, 'Labour, socialism and the working class', *Australian journal of politics and history,* vol. 7, no. 1, 1961, pp. 51-63.

of the ALP was to ensure that the working class would be represented by working-class people in the parliament with the hope that one day there would be a Labor government. The invention of the ALP bears testimony to the legacy of the radical intelligentsia and organized labour movements in the second half of the nineteenth century in producing class-based 'constitutive abstractions'—or categories grounded in the discourse of class. Where once there had been representations of the diverse social conditions of the 'labouring and perishing classes' this gave way to the rise of a solidaristic working-class.[36]

Laborism was limited both by the differences and by the modesty of the competencies, intentions and aspirations of the early Labor men. They brought with them the rituals of working-class life-worlds centred around the pubs, the Mechanics' Institutes, the chapel or the mass, the union office, numerous 'improving' associations (that embraced everything from phrenology through socialism and progressivism to rationalism), and the male-breadwinner-dominated respectable household. They were divided profoundly by male 'tribal associations' in which cloth cap or collar and tie mattered as much as did belonging to the Masons or taking mass. Social solidarity was expressed in habitual modes of address, 'mate' and 'comrade', deployed in the conviviality of the pub, as well as in such 'eccentric' devices as caucusing, pledges of solidarity, and the election by the whole caucus of leaders and ministers. These behaviours and institutions embodied the distinctive perspective of a subordinate class looking up at a vast and hierarchical network of class relations and institutions.[37]

Since then the ALP has proved to be a mansion with many rooms, filled with the clamour of contested ideas. Its members have embraced racism, populism, Fabianism, socialism, republicanism, democratic egalitarianism, internationalism, Bolshevism,

---

36 See H. Perkins, *The making of modern English society*, Routledge, London, 1976. And on recent theoretical work on the conditions of modernity and the work of the intellectually-trained see especially G. Sharp and D. White, 'Features of the intellectually trained', *Arena*, no. 15, 1968 pp. 30-3; and G. Sharp, 'Constitutive abstraction and social practice', *Arena*, no. 70, 1985 pp. 48-83.
37 W.M. Hughes, *The case for labour*, Cassell, Sydney, 1970, pp. 65-84.

eugenics, vegetarianism, pacifism and many other 'isms', but laborist it has always been. I do not think that laborism has ever been 'essentially' anything in particular except an orientation to action shaped by very diverse intellectual fashions. That diversity certainly had its origins in the very different histories of six labor parties where:

> each state Labor party developed a character and structure that were dependent on the geography, type of migrant and economics of the colony concerned and on the aims and capabilities of those who sat on its executives and in its Parliamentary Labor Parties.[38]

The highly gendered character of laborism has also been important. Much of the distinctive ritual, modes of address and policy preferences have been until the 1980s grounded in the figure of the male. In policy terms laborism produced discourses and policies about a male wage-earner rather than the potentially more generic and strategically more open discourse about citizenship which some parts of European social democracy have sustained.[39] Laborism's 'workers' are 'men' and 'mates' rather than 'citizens'.[40] Yet if the ALP could do so, historians can no longer ignore the fundamental character of the labour movement and its political expression of patriarchal practices and preferences in which the sexual division of labour was the fundamental structuring principle.[41]

In defence of the interests of workers and mates, laborism maintained until the early 1980s a relatively inflexible commitment to a number of settled policies and preferences. These included a white Australia, high tariffs and, after 1945, full employment.

---

[38] Murphy, ed., *Labor in politics*, p. 10.
[39] A. Yeatman, *Bureaucrats, technocrats, femocrats*, Allen & Unwin, Sydney, 1990, p. 164; C. Pateman, 'The patriarchal welfare state', in her *The disorder of women*, Cambridge University Press, Cambridge, 1989, pp. 180-5.
[40] On the citizen as male see C. Pateman, *The sexual contract*, Oxford University Press, Oxford, 1987.
[41] Lake, 'The Independence of Women'; pp. 4-23, S. Shaver, *Gender, social policy regimes and the welfare state*, SPRC Discussion Paper no. 26, SPRC, Kensington, 1990.

LABORISM AND THE STATE

Laborism until quite recently worked through the organized union movement, using the refracted and actual preferences of (white male) wage-earners organized in various union and party factions as its benchmarks for policy formulation. The consequences were serious for those outside the labour market and labour unions. The unemployed, those in receipt of welfare, women, blacks, recent immigrants, gays and young people were to all practical intents and purposes—and until quite recently—rendered invisible or irrelevant in the practices and discourses of laborism. This rendering can no longer be ignored either politically or theoretically.

Electoralism and social movements

Laborism until recently was successful in 'blank-maleing' those elements of the population who were neither white nor male out of its field of vision or interest. It has been far less successful in dealing with the political contradictions of electoralism that all social movements seem to confront sooner or later.

The ALP has struggled often to deal with the ambiguous and tension-filled relations with its social-movement base. On occasion these tensions ripped the heart out of the parliamentary party (in 1916–17, 1931–33 and 1954–57). The ALP was originally formed by the trade unions to represent working-class men and to win parliamentary office, two not necessarily compatible aims. From time to time it also formally endorsed its identity as socialist—whilst in practice eschewing socialist objectives. (The socialization plank of the ALP platform was only definitively buried in 1982 long after any support for it had died.) These chronic tensions within the ALP, and between it and the union movement, were based on its inability to identify a solution to the problem of reconciling its representation of working-class interests with the electorally driven logic of appealing to broader social interests or, on those occasions when it formed government, of dealing with the imperatives of governing in the 'national interest'.[42] In this respect the ALP was to learn, in the hardest way possible, the lesson all social movements treading the electoral path have to learn; electoralism and parliamentary politics are as much a problem as a solution.

The ALP's experience has proved exemplary for any mass party based on a social movement working in the modern electoral market. One condition of electoral success is that such a social movement must dilute and broaden its often sectarian narrow focus on issues and its utopian policy and discursive formulations so as to better appeal to the far broader and more diverse constituency. Reaching out to a more diverse constituency, however, also threatens to rupture the links to the original base of social-movement support.[43]

In the midst of the most successful period of ALP in government, this experience has been at the heart of the current claims about betrayal by the contemporary ALP of a traditional ALP vision. Yet in terms of political and policy content, no essential Labor vision or tradition has been there to betray. Rather laborism is, and has been, only a strategy of using the state to advance the interests of workers, deploying whatever political and discursive material is to hand. The more interesting problems that Labor and laborism confront have more to do with the contemporary social, cultural and politico-economic transformations involved in a cycle of heightened modernization since the early 1970s.

Modernity and the ALP

In 1949 Chifley defined Labor's mission in these terms, 'I try to regard the labour movement in the same light as the leaders of the great religious faiths regard their organization. *We are social evangelists* who are charged with a great responsibility.'[44] The ambiguity of this needs emphasizing. Chifley understood, in ways

---

42 R. Watts, 'Revising the revisionists: the ALP and liberalism 1941-1945', *Thesis eleven*, no. 7, 1983, pp. 37-49.
43 Jaensch, *The Hawke-Keating hijack*, pp. 16-19 and pp. 61-77.
44 J. B. Chifley in *Labor call*, 17 July 1949.

perhaps few of his colleagues did, that central to laborism's capacity to realise its ethical mission would be its capacity to deploy the state in an increasingly technically rational way.[45] This observation leads to a larger point: the Australian Labor Party and its movement base has always occupied an ambiguous position in relation to those practices and discourses characteristic of capitalist modernity.[46]

Modernity, under the conditions of capitalist accumulation and the structuring of work processes and social relationships in ways that facilitate capitalist accumulation, has entailed a ruthless assault on pre-modern life-worlds and social practices. In particular it has involved an incessant stripping away of those practices and conventions in time and space typical of pre-modernity and its small-scale and face-to-face interactions and knowledges. In this sense, modernity is characterized by the increasing abstractness and disembodied character of social relations in which metaphors of 'system' increasingly catch the quality of experience, as ideas of rationality are intended to signify the distance modernity has travelled away from tradition. Capitalist economic processes and styles of organization of work have seen a special role assigned to—or grabbed by—the intellectually-trained, and their management of technical rationality and 'expert systems' within both the capitalist market mechanisms and the state.[47] The evolution both of market economic processes and of state regulation over increasing areas of activity within civil society in the twentieth century has owed much to the distinctive work processes of the intellec-

---

45 This is exemplified in Chifley's enthusiastic patronage of the first generation of Keynesian econocrats. See L. F. Crisp, *Ben Chifley*, Angus and Robertson, Sydney, 1965.
46 I rely on A. Giddens, *The consequences of modernity*, Polity Press, Cambridge, 1988.
47 It is not I think a matter here of whether we are 'for' or 'against' modernity. M. Berman, 'Why modernism still matters', in *Modernity and identity*, eds S. Lash and J. Friedman, Polity Press, Cambridge, 1993, pp. 33-4; J. Hinkson, 'Post Lyotard: a critique of the information society', *Arena*, no. 80, 1987, pp. 123-55; A. Caddick, 'Feminist and the post-modern: Donna Haraway's cyborg', *Arena*, nos. 99/100, 1992, pp. 112-28 and G. Sharp, 'Extended forms of the social', *Arena journal, new series*, no. 1, 1993, pp. 221-37. See also P. James, 'National form and popular culture' in eds S. Alomes and D. den Hartog, *Post pop: popular culture, nationalism and post modernism*, Footprint, Melbourne, 1991.

tually-trained. This has opened up new and increasingly difficult tensions for an ALP which has traditionally identified its constituency as male productive workers. In the second half of this century it has been unable to defer its rendezvous with modernity and the increasing reach of new modes of work and social integration produced by the intellectually-trained.

The Labor party, perhaps most notoriously in the 1970s and again in the 1980s, portrayed itself as a zealous modernizer. Yet the Labor party and the labour movement has until recently preserved a large internal space for a pre-modern, communal and highly defensive ethos of near 'tribal' masculine sentiment and respect for tradition which stands out against the hard heads of rationality and their enthusiasms for the modernizing project. In one sense the very commitment to a project of collective defence of workers' interests, and the reliance placed on intense forms of social co-operation (exemplified in laborist institutions like the caucus or collective industrial action), were not only anti-capitalist, they were the residual of pre-modern forms of collective action by workers. (An oft-cited sign of a radical shift in Labor practice is the fact and the manner of Hawke's demise in late 1991. Yet this does not quite catch the pathos of Hawke's roles as an agent of a belated lurch into late-modernity in terms of his personal enthusiasms for globalizing imperatives, even as he clung to the mythos of mateship and conviviality, now reworked into a larger and more abstracted vision of a society committed to social harmony and co-operation.)

The ALP has long had an ambiguous relationship to modernity and to the state, possibly because the modern Australian state itself has been an ambiguous agent of modernity. At Federation the ALP could well believe that whilst the state had played and would play a vital role as a collective investor in infrastructure and as an employer of labour, it could also defend the interests of the working class. The rest of the century has suggested how the relationship of state to modernity itself is a dubious foundation on which to rest the overarching strategy of laborism.

From the start of the twentieth century, laborists focused on the state as a defensive agent able and willing to protect workers' interests. This view was encapsulated in the NSW Labour Council's view of its mission in 1870 as being to defend workers interest 'in case of oppression'.[48] This involved protection from exploitation, ameliorating the inconsistencies of the labour market and protecting workers from the harshest effects of employer lockouts. Labor's preference, only reluctantly accepted first in NSW in 1899, for state arbitration of industrial conflict, focused on passing state and national legislation to regulate wages and conditions, to outlaw 'sweating' and to provide arbitration tribunals to manage inter-class disputes.[49] By the end of the first decade of the twentieth century, laborism had embraced the policies of the New Liberalism within a 'Lib-Lab' alliance that produced the beginnings of a settled policy at the national level which stayed more or less intact until the 1980s. This included a centralized wage-fixing system (well in advance of most comparable countries in the early 1900s), and a new national Conciliation and Arbitration Court (established in 1904) designed to deliver 'a new province of law and order' in industrial relations.[50] A settlement between labour and industry ushered in the distinctive Australian pattern of very high and generalized tariffs to protect local manufactures. (Nationalist and racist sentiment combined with paranoia about the effects of cheap coloured labour to foreshadow the restrictions of the White Australia immigration policy legislated for in the Immigration Restriction Act of 1901.)

What began as a defensive coalition of interests was to be reworked in the crucible of Depression as a story about rationality. The crisis of the 1930s' Depression was read by contemporary laborists and by a significant fraction of intellectually trained liberals as the consequence of an absence of planning and rationality by either market or state. The crisis of total war after 1939 provided both laborists and the new technicians of modernity, the economist-administrators, with the opportunity to rectify these failures and omissions. Both Keynesian liberalism and the

---

48 See R. Markey, *In case of oppression: the NSW Labour Council*, Pluto Press, Sydney 1994.
49 M. Easson, ed. *The foundations of labor*, Pluto Press, Sydney, 1990.
50 See J. Rickard, *H.B.Higgins*, Allen & Unwin, Sydney, 1986.

ALP came to hold common responses to the Depression of the 1930s. Rationality would realize the shared vision of a harmonized society purged of class conflict by progressive refinements of the techniques of mass production and state planning. Rational state interventions would guarantee full employment and the steady supply of consumer goods and services for an Australian consumer-oriented lifestyle. Later analysts would call it the emergence of a Fordist society.

In May 1945 the Curtin Labor Government released its epochal *White paper on full employment*, signifying a major addition to the 'settled policy' of national government, and a major addition to laborism's statism.[51] The *White paper* signified the ALP's dramatic, if selective, embrace of Keynesian liberalism and its underpinning promise that the right economic theory would deliver rationality and order to the capitalist economy by harnessing a project of economic growth to the defence of workers' interests. In this way an antipodean version of the Keynesian welfare state evolved after 1945, with a subsidiary pattern of restrictive and means-tested social security benefits underpinning the priority of Keynesian demand-management techniques to maintain full (male) employment.

In effect the laborists of the 1940s proved to be the progenitors of a liberal welfare state, characterized as much by the minimalism of its level of public provision and of its level of capital investment, as by the relatively large scope retained for the 'free market' to determine the well-being of citizens.[52] In this way, Labor's mission of defending and enhancing welfare, through protecting access to employment and the wages and conditions for (male) wage labour without altering the fundamental constraints of

---

51 L. Black, 'Social democracy and full employment: the Australian white paper 1945', *Labour history*, no. 46, 1984, pp. 34-51.
52 Shaver notes; 'As a type, the liberal welfare state tends to be highly residual, maintaining selective arrangements for the poor, while other groups are supported through occupational and voluntary arrangements rooted in the market and class society'. S. Shaver, *Body rights, social rights and the liberal welfare state*, SPRC, Kensington, Discussion paper no. 38, 1992, p. 5.

a capitalist wage-labour market, was substantially confirmed and amplified after a decade in the wilderness up to 1941.

Modernization in the 1970s

Until 1975 successive Labor and non-Labor governments accepted the burden of responsibility imposed by the 1945 *White paper* to make full employment the first priority of national government.[53] Yet when Whitlam returned to office in 1972, a renewed cycle of modernization was already beginning. The ALP's conception of the relationship between state and economy increasingly privileged market-forces over state interventions through the 1970s. Yet by the 1970s there was evidence of a further cycle of modernization, in the cultural and social spheres as much as in the economy, that created new challenges for laborism.

The 1970s saw the start of far-reaching social and economic changes involving family formation, women's labour-market participation and the gendered relations between men and women. It also saw new forms of work, especially in human service work, which became a major sphere of work opportunities for women wage-workers. Between 1975 and 1994 the industry saw the highest rate of employment growth. New forms of service work, with their base either in information technology or in community-services work, were to sustain the long-term shift to a service-based economy that was to leave the old blue-collar working class, with its base in production and manufacturing work, increasingly vulnerable to permanent unemployment as the larger globalization of capital took hold.

Running in parallel, intellectual challenges shadowed these processes. The older social liberal and Keynesian welfare discourses were challenged from both the New Right and the New Left. The 'bourgeois counter-revolution' staged by a revived neo-classical economics and anti-modernists who self-identified as the New

---

53 See W.J. Waters, 'Australian labour's full employment objective, 1942-1945', in *Australian journal of politics and history*, vol. 16, no. 1, pp. 48-64. See also S.J. Butlin and C.B. Schedvin, *War economy 1942-1945*, Australian War Memorial, Canberra, 1983.

Right proved more influential. (This highly unstable alliance on the right only came unstuck in the 1990s; leading anti-modernists like Manne and Carroll now lead the attack on neo-classical economics.) Amongst the victims was the long-standing Australian version of social liberalism. The embrace between Keynesian Liberals and laborists in the 1940s was a Faustian pact. That initial embrace of Keynesian-as-economic-politics had left the ALP vulnerable to takeover by whatever economic paradigm proved discursively superior, should Keynesianism prove either deficient or obsolescent.

Contrary to widely held perceptions about Whitlam's government as a glorious, because reforming, Labor government, and of a subsequent betrayal of Labor's tradition by Hawke and Keating, the Whitlam government signified the start of the shift towards a greater role for market forces, a criticism made at the time.[54] As Robinson argues, under Whitlam, 'traditional [Labor] suspicions of market outcomes were abandoned and the ideal of competitive capitalism enthusiastically embraced'.[55] Whitlam forced his cabinet to adopt a national policy which would create 'a more efficient competitive Australian industry', one more open and sensitive to the global economy. As Frankel notes, the Whitlam government—like its predecessor Curtin-Chifley governments—was captivated by modernization:

> Labor's post-war reconstruction and the classic giganticism of modernist projects such as the Snowy Mountain scheme ... was renewed under Whitlam. Chifley, Evatt and Whitlam desired an independent Australia which was industrially, fiscally and socio-culturally based on a strong neo-Keynesian public sector and welfare state. During the Whitlam period the ALP advocated 'buying back the farm' in order to end old forms of colonial submission.[56]

---

54 See Catley and McFarlane, *From Tweedledum to Tweedledee*.
55 Robinson, 'Labor and market forces', p. 95. See also Fabian Papers, *The Whitlam phenomenon*, Drummond, Melbourne, 1986, pp. 135-49.
56 Frankel, *From the prophets deserts come*, p. 49.

LABORISM AND THE STATE

Contemporary anger about the Hawke and Keating assaults on tariffs forgets that Whitlam and his treasurer Cairns began the process of dismantling the long-established protectionist framework. Whitlam gave the Tariff Board under Rattigan its head, establishing the Industries Assistance Commission in 1973 and in July 1973 introducing a 25 per cent general cut in tariffs.[57] Whitlam's enthusiasm for tariff cuts, and 'freeing up' market forces and competition from institutional inhibitions, led him to curb restrictive trade practices, protect consumers, abolish the federal wealth tax and initiate an anti-inflationary policy. All of this signified Labor's acceptance that state interventions should promote increased economic competition, productivity and efficiency.

The heady if somewhat florid days of Whitlam's government of 1972-75 also marked the final apotheosis of a moderately social liberal conception of the state in its redistributive role. This was as much an electoral programme designed to win seats in the new suburbs of Australia's cities as anything else. Expenditure on urban planning, health, welfare services, infrastructure, education and the arts began to lift off after a long plateau during the Menzies years. This reformism was linked quite uneasily to a new modernizing project centred on an emphatically competitive market model.

Whitlam's aborted rendezvous with destiny has not largely been read as a consequence of enchantment by the spirit of modernity. Rather, Whitlam's experiment was interpreted in the years after the trauma of 1975 in a new context of crisis which, if it lacked the awesome drama of the 1930s' Depression, was to prove no less profound in its long-term consequences. The politics of the 1975 crisis have helped to obscure this underlying crisis.[58]

Firstly, the 'failure' of the Whitlam experiment suggested to key ALP power-brokers that a concern with a broad programme of citizenship issues and rights bypassed the traditional concerns of

---

57 A. Rattigan, *Industry assistance: the inside story*, Melbourne, 1986, pp. 146-212.
58 G. Whitlam, *The truth of the matter*, Penguin, Ringwood, 1979 and P. Kelly, *The unmaking of Gough*, Allen & Unwin, Sydney 1976; B. Head, ed. *The politics of national development*, Allen & Unwin, Sydney, 1986.

laborism and threatened its emotional and true electoral basis. The reaction against Whitlam's social liberalism is best grasped in the emotional vehemence of Hawke's reassertion of the traditions of Labor mateship and in the need to manage the Accord process on behalf of the union movement. (Politically, the animus against Whitlam was to do with the new leadership reasserting traditional Laborist sentiment and enlisting it in a radical and novel cause.)

Secondly, the significance of the Whitlam era lay in the judgment made belatedly—and from which numerous unwarranted conclusions were drawn by more traditional laborists like Hayden and Hawke—that Whitlam's framework of moderate regulatory interventions had not worked and that more not less space needed to be given to market forces to work their magic. Notwithstanding all the differences between the two governments, the Hawke government's deregulatory policies in fact built on Whitlam's privileging of market forces. It was but one small step to take to observe that if the state was also a constraint on market forces then those constraints had to be removed. From 1975 on, the 'new laborists' in the party machine and in the ACTU had to look no further than the economic departments of the nation's universities to find what they had been looking for—a new basis for yet another go at modernization.

They did not have to look too hard. Whitwell and Pusey have ably traced the rise of economic rationalism in the bureaucracy.[59] That triumph grew on the back of the intellectual effects of the critiques of Keynesianism surfacing both among economists and inside key agencies of government in the 1960s and early 1970s.[60] A full-blown neo-classical economic *revanche* against Keynesian interventionism coincided with the rise of the so-called economically literate laborists of the late 1970s and 1980s. The time was ripe for another discursive capture, this time by resurgent neo-classical economists who abhorred the contemporary scale and form of government interventions. Economic rationalism was as

---

[59] G. Whitwell, 'The triumph of economic rationalism: the treasury and the market economy', *Australian journal of public administration*, vol. 49, no. 2, 1990, pp. 17-31, and Pusey, *Economic rationalism in Canberra*, pp. 111-58.
[60] Groenwegen and McFarlane, *A history of Australian economic thought*, pp. 210-14.

much a discursive shift as a generational shift, as the products of the new university economics departments of the 1960s climbed into the seats vacated by the last of the post-war Keynesian mandarins and by the older generation of union and Labor leaders.

With the incalculable advantage of hindsight we now see that the *White paper on full employment* (1945) was for Labor a Faustian pact. Labor's embrace of Keynesianism in the 1940s initialled a pact between economic techniques and policies on the one hand, and the ALP as putative economic managers on the other. The advent of Keynesianism marked the triumph of a whole new conception of the state as economic manager, in which voters had now to discriminate between the economic management competencies of parties marketing themselves as would-be governments.

The Hawke-Keating years

From 1983 the Hawke government continued Whitlam's enthusiasm for free-market forces within a policy framework which bonded the union movement to the government with uncommon success. The first policy casualties included policies which had stood at the centre of laborism for decades. Labor's adoption of the Accord as the framework for a national policy signified a politics which parts of its social movement base frequently found difficult to swallow, yet it nonetheless provided a durable political structure of uncommon strength and flexibility.

In a spirit of zealous modernization beginning in 1979 after a visit by Willis to check out the social contract of Britain's Callaghan Labor government, the ALP leadership renovated its model of laborism. The laborism of the 1980s and 1990s relied on a highly ambiguous statism inscribed in the Accord.[61] The Accord (1983–1995) is best understood as another highly unstable but ever-so-typical laborist accommodation between the will to defend the interests of the (male) working class and to promote a

---

61 See G. Singleton, *The accord and the Australian labour movement,* Melbourne, 1990 (especially chapters 1-7); P. Ewer et al., Politics and the accord, Allen & Unwin, Sydney, 1991 and F. Stilwell, *The accord and beyond*, Pluto Press, Sydney, 1987.

new 'modernizing' project using the latest fashion out in the public sphere. From 1978 on, key architects of the Accord (including Hayden, Hawke, Crean, Dolan, Kelty, and Willis) held that simple Keynesian pump-priming interventions would no longer work, and that job creation without wage restraint and a reduction of production costs would be fatal to long-term recovery. The new laborists accepted that the imperative to win government took precedence over any other considerations.[62] Defence of the union movement, protection of jobs and securing an ALP government became the centre pieces of the revised laborist agenda of the late 1970s, and with it came acceptance of a politics which privileged market forces well beyond Whitlam's initial forays in this direction.

Hayden, Hawke, Kelty, Crean, Weaven, Dawkins, Keating and Willis dominated both the organized moderate trade unions and the leadership of the ALP. What was left of the Left (under the leadership of Uren, Howe et al.) either traded away their 'traditionalist' principles for access to decision-making, or else accepted the new model of modernization.

The Accord, through successive major modifications between 1983 and 1993, was a consequence of the unlikely union of Thatcherite economics legitimized by contradictory appeals to the need to modernize the economy and to protect the interests of the least well-off, and implemented within a modicum of Swedish corporatist and welfarist institutional arrangements.[63] Electorally this eclecticism has produced outstanding results for the ALP. It has assured itself of a stable relationship between it and its social-movement base. More substantively, these successes have not covered up the deep-seated structural contradictions attendant upon the contemporary cycle of social and economic transformation.

Contrary to recent discussion about a lapse from Labor tradition, the intent of the politics and policies pursued by the Hawke

---

[62] ALP Secretary Bob McMullan defined the 'predominant new development in the party in the early eighties ... [as] a commitment to winning elections', R. McMullan, 'Management and decision making within the Australian Labor Party', *Australian institute of public administration seminar*, Canberra, 1990, p. 3.

[63] P. Boreham, 'Corporatism', in *Hawke and Australian public policy,* eds C. Jennett and R. Stewart, Longman Cheshire, Melbourne, 1990, pp. 42-53.

and Keating labor governments since 1983 is generally consistent with the laborist impulse, and represents an evolving line initiated by Whitlam and Hayden. This is so even though Hawke's laborism, or Labor's vision of the state, and the substance of its policies were increasingly refracted through an economic rationalist discourse which seemed often to collide with older labor preferences.[64] Whatever the mutterings of the Left, the impulse to protect and to defend workers' interests was at the very heart of the ALP's Accord. It has, however, done this in ways which have significantly altered the traditional role of unions as agents of collective working-class interests, whilst also stripping away the mediatory role of the old arbitration system. In the partially deregulated labour markets of the 1990s, collectives of workers now confront collective employers in a modified 'market game' to negotiate enterprise agreements on an industry-by-industry basis. In a context of mounting unemployment, severe wage restraint and a major redistribution of national incomes, it is clear that only those remaining in work have been protected and then only minimally.

The Hawke-Keating model of modernization has privileged market forces in a radical way that marks out the 1980s from the preceding decades of this century. The older liberal-Keynesian model emphasized a minimally rational, bargaining framework supervised by a 'gentleman' nation-state, drawing on a normative framework of national policy oriented to full employment. The 1980s model construes the market place as the motor-force in modernization. The state plays a negative regulatory role by deconstructing older forms of state regulation and intervention, now defined as impediments to market rationality. Most importantly, it has marketized the provision of public policy, forcing the state sector to embrace increasingly the ethos, goals and practices—real or mythic—of the market sector. Muetzelfeldt has accurately summed up this central effect of the resurgent economic discourse: 'the trend towards the marketization and design of

---

[64] M. Costa and M. Duffy, *Labor prosperity and the nineties: beyond the bonsai economy*, Pluto Press, Sydney, 1991.

public policy ... positioned people less as citizens with rights to controlled benefits and more as participants in markets through which those benefits were privatized.'[65]

Modernization was now clearly defined through the lens of market rationality.[66] Laborism's modernization project in the 1980s and 1990s envisaged an Australia made strong and vital by a strengthened and revitalized business sector oriented to the global markets and with a strong export orientation, supported by a public sector oriented to efficiency, accountability and the pursuit of strategies including privatization, deregulation, corporatization and managerialism.

This outcome involved a reworking of the public sphere, embracing schools, universities and the public sector generally, via the adoption of an enterprise culture and managerialist procedures increasingly aping private sector behaviours, including greater reliance on the user-pays principle and a strengthening of management prerogatives in the name of 'clever solutions' and 'enhanced organizational rationality'.[67] The result in the universities has been predictable; on the one hand the drift on the part of some intellectuals to postmodernism and their metaphors of open-ended, non-hierarchical networks of communication, has had a lasting and pernicious effect.[68] On the other hand, a whole new generation of managerialist administrators has arisen, leading to a debauching of intellectual standards and an extraordinary growth in absurd and totally inefficient administrative cultures.

The rationale for this? Economic reconstruction would be the consequence of a thorough-going structural redesign of Australian institutions, including new discourses and practices designed to

---

[65] M. Muetzelfeldt, 'Economic rationalism and its social context', in *Society, state and politics in Australia*, ed. M. Muetzelfeldt, Deakin University Press, Geelong, 1992, p. 202.
[66] Pusey, *Economic rationalism in Canberra*, pp. 59-64.
[67] M. Considine, 'The corporate management framework as administrative science: a critique', *Australian journal of public administration*, vol. 47, no. 1, 1988, pp. 47-64.
[68] See for example J. Matthews, *Tools of change: new technology and the democratisation of work*, Pluto Press, Sydney, 1989.

subordinate the schooling and education systems to a globalized and information-based economy.[69]

Travails of laborism, the state and modernization

If the modern ALP is politically and electorally successful, this should not mean we stop asking questions about its capacity to manage the current cycle of modernization. The Australian political and state apparatus, in common with many Western governments, has through the 1980s had to come to terms with (i) major changes in the constraints operating with increasing rigour on the capacities of states to make effective policies at the national level, and (ii) recognize and address urgent changes in the social fabric which have rendered the post-war 'welfare state' less and less relevant. In effect, as in earlier stages in the project of modernity, the social and economic practices which sustained that project confronted obstacles derived in part from the past and in part from the modernizing process itself. Labor's modernizing agenda relied in particular on a belief in the continuing capacity of the nation-state to manage the processes of transition even as the very process of modernization it envisaged was undermining the capacities of the state to do the job. Worse, the consequences of modernization are calling out for far-reaching state action to limit the damage done by modernization, even as the shift in political culture makes this more and more difficult to realize, or to pay for.

Against this backdrop, Labor's Accord has been a triumph of optimism over realism. The architects of the Accord have always presupposed a continuing capacity to shape state policy in ways that were actually increasingly compromised by the very processes of internationalization that the ALP government was sponsoring. Stuart Holland had pointed out back in the early 1970s that the scale of internationalization of corporate manufacturing and finan-

---

[69] S. Marginson, 'Education as a branch of economics: the universal claims of economic rationalism', in *Rationalising education (Special issue of Melbourne studies in education)*, LaTrobe University Press, Bundoora, 1992, pp. 1-14.

cial capital was rendering more and more tenuous the capacity of nation-states to govern effectively. The paradox, in a context of failing national sovereignty, as the victory by the Federal ALP in March 1993 rammed home, is that into the mid-1990s, the labor party and its social movement base remains the most significant of the social movements, to which the others must still merely aspire.

By the 1970s and 1980s the conditions which had sustained the creation and growth of the Australian welfare state from the 1940s to the 1960s were either disintegrating or becoming obsolete as new waves of modernizing continued to revolutionize productive, cultural and social action. The keystone of the welfare state that emerged after 1942 in Australia was full employment, and not the emergent social security programme. Full employment presupposed constant growth in an economy steered by a technically proficient state, reliant on Keynesian-like technique and the operations of a heavily protected free-market economy. The real crisis of the welfare state is the unbridgeable gap between those foundational assumptions of its architects in the 1940s, and the remarkable transformations which have taken place in the social and economic fabric of Australia, especially since the 1980s.

Five key structural assumptions that imbricated state and civil society in the 1940s and 1950s have all come undone. Firstly, it was held that wage-work in combination with the social security safety net would be adequate to prevent poverty. Secondly, paid labour was held to be both desirable and to actually be available on a full-time basis (certainly for males). Thirdly, the sexual division of labour and the distinction between paid and unpaid labour which it sustained was assumed to be a normal, natural and inevitable feature of Australian social relations. Full employment and high rates of economic growth were assumed to be both feasible and desirable objectives of national economic policy. Finally, it was widely assumed that a reasonable degree of equitable income distribution would be achieved as a consequence of Australia's progressive income-tax system along with full employment and a social security system.[70]

---

70 See B. Gregory, 'Aspects of Australian labour force living standards: the disap-

In effect, the white heat of modernization has meant a meltdown of these assumptions by the 1980s. This has occurred as a product of deliberate policy interventions and/or the unforeseen effects of policy. It is a result of changes in social and cultural practices, and a consequence of the new globalization of trading and investment. It is imperative to an understanding what is happening that the economy is reconceptualized as a system of social action, interdependently interacting with other forms of social action.

Australia in common with other Western economies now confronts the nightmarish novelty of a regime of economic growth not linked to employment growth.[71] Accompanying these transformations have come alarmist discourses about the creation of an underclass of emiserated workless and 'feral' youth, and an X Generation of pessimistic middle-class young people.[72] The most tangible social, economic and cultural effects of the great transformation of the past two decades have included the near-destruction of the youth labour market, the de-industrialization of major industrial centres, the downsizing of primary industries with the attendant social and economic dislocation of rural Australia, the institutionalization of long-term unemployment, the extension of the dependence of adolescence into early adulthood, and a marked increase in income inequality. Consideration by policy-makers of the OECD's 'active society' model of welfare (to deal with the eventuality that full employment was no longer achiev-

---

pointing decades, 1970-90', Copland Oration, Conference of Economists, Melbourne 1992; B. Bradbury, *Unemployment and income support: challenges for the years ahead*, SPRC Discussion papers, May 1993, SPRC, University of New South Wales; P. Saunders, 'Income inequality in Australia: lessons from the Luxembourg income study', in *Income distribution seminar papers of economic and social policy group*, SPRC, Kensington 1993, and N. Warren, 'The effect of Australian taxes and social welfare on the distribution of income in 1975-6, 1984-5 and 1988-9', *Conference on economic and social inequality*, SPRC, 1991.

71 Employment Task Force, *Employment growth for Australia: a discussion paper*, AGPS, Canberra, December 1993.
72 See J. Bessant, 'Feral policy', *Arena magazine*, March 1994, and on the X Generation see the *Sun*, 10 January 1994.

able) was a sign that the real crisis was being acknowledged, however inadequately, in official circles.[73]

The disintegration of the foundations of Australia's liberal welfare state regime and the increasing likelihood that both high growth and a return to full employment are increasingly problematic have (i) rendered the existing architecture of state interventions increasingly obsolescent and yet (ii) increased the call for new kinds of state intervention, possibly more far-reaching than anything that the liberal welfare state regime could ever have envisaged.[74] As the new wave of modernization takes hold, it has lessened the capacity of nation-states to effectively manage the transition or even to hold the policy of transformation more or less steady. Since 1983, Australia's national economic policy reveals this problem clearly.[75] Keating and the Treasury after 1986 embraced the twin dogmas of deregulation of the banking and finance sectors and zero tariffs, as well as an insistence on continuity with the Whitlam and Fraser governments' policies of 'fighting inflation first' by restraining real wage increases. In common with most other OECD countries, Australia has seen full-employment goals abandoned to market forces, government deficits targeted for elimination so as to better control inflation and release resources for private investment, profitability defined as a major victim of 'big government', which crowded-out private initiative, and spending measures especially in capital investment severely restrained.[76]

Yet by 1991–92 the entire strategy was in tatters. Cuts to government outlays had led the Hawke government in 1990 to brag—prematurely—about its timetable to reduce public sector outlays (as a proportion of GDP) back to the level they were at in

---

[73] B. Cass, 'Fightback! The politics of work and welfare in the 1990s', in *Markets, Morals and Manifestos,* eds P. Vintila *et al.*, Curtin University Press, Perth, 1992, pp. 45-66.

[74] See R. Watts, 'A welfare state for the twenty-first century: renovating citizenship and basic income', *SPRC Social Policy Conference*, Kensington, July 1993.

[75] A. Glynn, 'The costs of stability: the advanced capitalist countries in the 1980s', *New left review,* November 1992, pp. 71-95.

[76] F. Gruen and M. Grattan, *Managing government*, Longman, Melbourne, 1993.

the late 1960s.[77] The recession of 1991–93 revealed one more time how little a highly vulnerable economy like Australia's, with its narrow base of primary and mining exports, could hold at bay a tidal wave of international recession, the effects of subsidized export production and trade wars, and its own catastrophic decline in its balance-of-trade deficit. At the same time 'spokesmen' for the all-important financial markets and credit rating agencies increasingly intervened in a detailed way into state macro-economic policy making.

Cerny has argued forcefully for the effects on state policy of the long-running recession of 1974–93:

> it has tended to undermine a range of policy measures ... earlier identified with the 'welfare state' ... the provision of welfare services, ... Keynesian macro-economic policy ... and the maintenance of basic or strategic industries (including natural monopolies and public goods (through regulation, subsidy and /or public control) ... But despite the increasing openness and interpenetration of the world economy, these measures are still essentially national, and their political legitimacy rests on their appeal to and impact upon the body politic of a particular nation-state. And at the same time transnational integration has made these policies more and more difficult to effectuate at national level.[78]

Since the 1980s, a combination of discursive strategies originating in the private sector, built primarily around notions of the optimal size of state debt and the need to remove micro-economic rigidities (such as 'excessive' inflexibility in wages and conditions), have combined with quite real market manipulation of the exchange and interest rates to force or cajole governments into adopting appropriate policies. At the same time as facing an economy with an historic problem about its balance of trade, Australian governments have ruefully been forced to admit that macro-economic policy can be counter-productive, especially when stimulatory policies can

---

[77] Commonwealth Government, *Budget statement 1990-91, no.1*, AGPS, Canberra, 1990.
[78] P.G. Cerny, *The changing architecture of politics*, Sage, London, 1990, pp. 220-1.

increase the level of imports to a level likely to invoke sanctions by the international finance community.

This is but one example of the way that the experience of the late 1980s and 1990s points to the fundamental problems that nation-states are having in dealing with the combined effects of modernization—conceived here in its most limited sense as a strategy of becoming more open to global/market pressures and opportunities—whilst maintaining an effective policy setting to manage the both the process and the consequences of that modernizing.

The actual shifts towards transnational economic organization, the recasting of global markets in new strategic ways and the revival of economic liberalism have all led to demands for smaller government. The pursuit of smaller government has led, however, not to smaller government but to chronic deficit-financing by governments. This is to maintain basic services or, as in the case of *One nation*-type stimulations, to lift economies out of periodic downturns. The actual effects of post-1986 policies on governance have been more contradictory. Firstly, the long-term trend since the 1940s to reduce the role of public-sector capital formation has been confirmed. There was a further dramatic decrease in capital investment by the state, achieved by draconian treatment of state government capital needs accompanying an increased interest bill on overseas debt.

Secondly, the Hawke-Keating governments have striven but with limited success to return government tax raising and expenditures as a proportion of GDP back to the levels they were at under Menzies in the 1960s. It would seem on this measure that the scale of state interventions peaked in the years up to 1986–87 and have since been somewhat reined in. Yet they have certainly not produced any significant decrease in the scale of the Australian state. Using public sector outlays, revenues and the public sector borrowing requirement as a ratio of GDP, all show a similar pattern of growth, partial decline in the late 1980s and growth in the 1990s.[79] The Hawke government used its considerable authority

---

79 Commonwealth Government, *Budget statement, paper no.1*, 1991-2, 6.5, Canberra, 1991.

to coerce the state governments into following its lead in a partially forcing restraint on the states. Yet its restraints have been hard to maintain against insistent pressures for continuing economic interventions, especially after Keating announced the *One nation* measures early in 1992. In this regard there is some evidence to suggest that whatever the commitment to deregulation, privatization and tariff abolition, all in the name of freeing market forces which Labor governments have promoted since the mid-1980s, its capacity to reduce state expenditures and revenues significantly has been limited by the imperatives of economic stabilization.

It was little wonder that the rhetorical stress on smaller government, and related aspects of the Hawke government's policy setting, persuaded many of its critics that the Hawke government had created a minimalist state and thereby betrayed its historical social base and mission.[80] Little wonder too that Keating as Prime Minister should grimly reach for the appearance of stimulatory policies in his *One nation* package, and that neither policy interventions fully recognized the extent to which the national government was less and less able to control the local effects of global transformation.

Conclusion

For most of the 1980s the many stings in the tail of ALP policy interventions, such as growth in underlying and long-term unemployment, the destruction of large sections of the manufacturing sector, rising economic inequality and irresponsible and reckless activity by the financial sector were camouflaged by the mobilization of an egalitarian rhetoric which self-consciously drew parallels between the great reforming governments of Curtin and Chifley and their modern successors. The Accord itself was presented as a model of consensus, an antipodean social contract dressed up in a corporatist style which offered non-wage compensations to the working class in the form of social-wage benefits, made large-

---

80   Jaensch, *The Hawke-Keating hijack,* pp. 46-55.

sounding promises of welfare reform ('By 1991 no child will be in poverty'—R. J. Hawke 1988) and offered the union movement unprecedented access to government.

Electorally, the mix of policies and rhetoric adopted by the ALP in government since 1983 seems on the face of it to have resolved only one of the fundamental problems traditionally confronting Labor governments: maintaining government by constructing a base of support broader than that represented by the social movement.

Yet rather than identifying some immanent 'crisis of the state' and by implication of laborism itself, laborism in the 1990s continues as always to face historically contingent issues. The origins of the contemporary question marks hanging over the labour movement are to be found in (i) the continuing radical transformation of both capitalist work processes and of its social movement base *qua* unions, (ii) the instability of Labor's modernization project which, dependent on economic growth scenarios which no longer can rely on a consensus about either the sustainability or the desirability of such scenarios, and (iii) in the discursive tensions around the figure of the state itself.

The interpretation offered here stresses the historically contingent nature of laborism and of the state. I have tried to avoid any essentialist argument which sees some immanent structural contradiction between capital and state from which a teleological/pessimistic reading of the recent history of the state can be derived. Nor do I subscribe to a structuralist reading which sees the state caught up in the logic of post-modernity and doomed to a terminal decline. As Cerny has remarked we now have:

> an infinitely more complex state than before, one not simply intervening more or getting weightier, but one also drawn into the structures of everyday life by the changes and gaps and tensions within everyday life itself ... To 'get the government off our backs' as President Reagan wished to do, often paradoxically requires more intervention not less.[81]

---

81 Cerny, *The changing architecture of the state*, p. 196.

LABORISM AND THE STATE

The pessimistic reading sees in the current dominance of economic rationalism and its prescriptions for a minimalist state the end of civilization as we have known it. To see the discursive *revanche* of bourgeois economics, which has accompanied cuts in state services and funding, as symptoms of some terminal, because structurally pre-given, 'crisis of the state' is to seriously misconstrue the historical and controversial character of the state.

The state has always been an arena of contest not least of all about the scope and intent of its activities in relation to civil society.[82] State activity and policy-making is always an outcome of political debates in which particular actors and ideas deploy ideas and power to secure their own way. Lacking that indispensable apparatus of all who would like to be able to say in ten years time, 'I told you so', there is no evidence to suggest that the will of those who are currently in charge of the fortunes of the ALP, to continue to make history, will diminish. As at any other point in the history of laborism, the ALP will continue to make sense of, or continue to shape, what is new terrain but not under circumstances entirely of its own making.

---

82 P. Beilharz, M. Considine and R. Watts, *Arguing about the welfare state*, Allen & Unwin, Sydney, 1992.

4

Greening the modern state: managing the environment

Robyn Eckersley

> '... in its mere continuity industrial society *exits the stage of world history on the tip-toes of normality, via the back stairs of side effects* ...' (his emphasis).
>
> Ulrich Beck, *Risk society*.[1]

The ecological crisis has thrown down new responsibilities and challenges for the liberal democratic state in the post-World War II period. On the domestic front, both elected governments and state officials have been forced to respond to persistent environmental concern and conflict. As one of the more enduring new social movements of the post-1960s period, the ecology movement has generated new political demands that challenge the indiscriminate economic-growth consensus of the modern welfare state. What began as agitation over the growing negative side-effects of economic development, soon transformed into a direct challenge to the industrial order itself (in both its capitalist and communist guises). This broader challenge—also taken up by the fledgling green parties—marks an historic moment. Not since the emergence of the labour movement has there been such a potentially profound realignment in political cleavages and voting patterns. However, unlike labour demands, green demands have so far proved to be a little more resistant to corporatist bargains with industry and government. Notwithstanding the recent push for sustainable development, there

---

1 Sage Publications, London, 1992, p. 11.

are few signs of a new historic compromise between the green movement and the three partners to the traditional and now eroding compromise of growth-dependent welfare capitalism (labour, capital and the government)—at least of the kind that would put to rest environmental concern and conflict.

On the international front, nation-states are the principal actors in what is shaping up to be a global morality play between North and South over the fate of the international commons. The evident need for global environmental co-operation throws down a new set of challenges for the international order based on notions of common heritage, shared responsibility and shared duties, notions that directly impinge on state sovereignty and domestic institutions and policies.[2] These challenges were brought to a head at the much-heralded United Nations Conference on Environment and Development (the Earth Summit) held in Rio de Janeiro in June 1992. Despite the international endorsement of the (ambiguous) concept of sustainable development and the growing acknowledgment that world security is increasingly acquiring an ecological dimension, high hopes for an ecological dividend arising from the end of super-power politics were dashed at the Earth Summit. Far from reordering priorities in the neo-liberal New World Order, the Earth Summit merely highlighted the obstacles in the way of redressing the striking asymmetries between North and South in terms of energy and resource-use, degree of economic development and affluence, extent of contribution to global ecological degradation, and cultural perceptions of environmental problems. If the Earth Summit achieved anything, it was to serve notice on the developed world that it must not only reduce its high per capita ecological sins but also provide the resources and opportunities to enable the South, in pursuing its legitimate development aspirations, to somehow leapfrog over the ecological mistakes of the North.

Standing at the intersection of these domestic and international green pressures, the modern state has been singled out as the pre-eminent institution to tackle the 'tragedy of the commons'. As the sovereign and supreme legal power within its territory, the state can make binding

---

2   A. Hurrell and B. Kingsbury, *The international politics of the environment*, Clarendon Press, Oxford, 1992.

rules backed by sanctions, extract monies and generally regulate the environmental decisions of consumers, investors, producers and its own agencies.

Yet singling out the state as the pre-eminent institution does not mean that it is the ideal institution. The growing global dimension of environmental problems is inextricably linked to the increasing globalization of the world economy; both developments are encroaching on the ability of nation-states to control their own destinies. Indeed, the case is sometimes made that the state is too weak, ill-equipped and nationalistic to tackle the big global ecological problems, and too big and inflexible to attend to the diversity of smaller local ecological problems. The ubiquitous, irreversible and transboundary character of many ecological problems have also highlighted an increasing lack of correspondence between those who *make* decisions, those who are *responsible* for decisions, and those who are *affected* by them. This is one facet of what Martin Janicke has referred to as the 'steady deterioration of the *control ratio* between politics and the machinery of government'.[3]

However, the ecological challenge to the liberal democratic state goes much deeper than the problem of political control and accountability. Ecological problems add a new layer of spatial, temporal and epistemological challenges to liberal democratic theory and practice. The modern liberal democratic state (whether unitary or federal) is organized to represent the interests of citizens in territorially defined political communities. When it comes to ecological accounting, the state is, in many respects, not unlike the capitalist firm insofar as it tends to externalize or pass on ecological costs in space and time to noncitizens (e.g., noncompatriots, future generations, nonhuman species) who cannot vote, participate or otherwise be formally represented in political deliberations within the polity. The recent push for sustainable development is partly a push to provide more systematic representation or consideration of the interests of this new environmental constituency of noncitizens—a push that challenges the traditional *raison d'être* of the modern state.

Yet even if the new environmental constituency were to be given

---

[3] M. Janicke, *State failure*, Polity Press, Cambridge, 1990, p. 27.

more systematic direct or vicarious representation in the processes of democratic will formation, there is the added problem of whether the administrative state is institutionally capable of providing a flexible and co-ordinated response to the complex, systemic and increasingly transboundary nature of many ecological problems. The modern bureaucratic steering system tends to break problems down into their parts, compartmentalize them, and allocate them across different departments. It works by a rationality which routinely displaces problems across bureaucratic system boundaries. Such administrative rationality, it has been argued, is considerably at odds with ecological rationality.[4] These difficulties appear to be compounded in federal systems such as Australia's, which is made up of nine distinct political authorities (plus local government) with areas of overlapping jurisdiction covering regions of enormous geographic and climatic diversity.

In short, the ecological crisis has raised a new layer of challenges to modern state sovereignty; questioned some of the basic regulative ideals and institutions of liberal democracy; and exposed limitations in the organization of government administration. This chapter will focus primarily on the domestic aspect of these ecological challenges. The discussion will begin by contrasting the conventional neoclassical economic analysis of the role of the liberal democratic state in protecting the environment with various green analyses and normative claims. This will provide a backdrop to an exploration of the ways in which the Australian federal state has responded to the new set of political demands and counter-demands generated by the ecological crisis, drawing on some key developments in Australian environmental public policy, institutional reform and federal/state conflict over the last two decades. The chapter will conclude with a brief evaluation of the impact of the ecological challenge on theories of the modern state and the lessons to be learned for both environmental management and democracy in the future.

The state and the ecological crisis: redressing side-effects

What role should the state play in managing environmental problems?

---

4 J. Dryzek, *Ecological rationality*, Blackwell, Oxford, 1987.

Many political scientists typically approach this question via an analysis of Garrett Hardin's parable of the tragedy of the commons.[5] In this oft-quoted fable of medieval herders, the individual freedom of herders to continue to graze additional cows on the (unregulated) commons is shown to bring environmental ruin to everyone. This analysis provides one particularly graphic example of the prisoners' dilemma in game theory; it demonstrates how the 'rational' pursuit of private gain by economic actors can lead to collective outcomes that make everyone worse off, even when economic actors have knowledge of the likely long-term consequences of their decisions. Pollution, land degradation, species extinction are all typical by-products of this tragic dynamic.

In terms of neoclassical theory, these by-products are taken to represent the 'negative ecological externalities' of production and consumption—the unintended side-effects of market transactions which are suffered by third parties. Capitalist entrepreneurs are only interested in those parts of the environment that can be captured, commodified and sold in ways that prevent free riders. Even under conditions of so-called perfect competition, markets generally fail to provide environmental public goods, although such goods provide the preconditions for the operation of market activity.

Both Hardin's parable, and the economic analysis of negative ecological externalities, are generally taken as providing a case for some kind of state intervention (in this case, mutual regulation or market correction respectively). The intention is to protect public environmental goods in ways that maintain the ecological basis for capital accumulation and maintain a healthy work-force. Hardin himself advocated 'mutual coercion mutually agreed upon by the majority of people affected'—a prescription that essentially represents a return to classical liberal social contract theory, but with a new ecological twist.

However, according to neoclassical environmental economics, the state only becomes an instrument for carrying out what cannot be efficiently or effectively carried out by the market. Their goal is not environmental protection *per se*, but rather the optimal allocation of resources by means of market-based instruments such as environmental taxes and charges. These instruments are intended, in theory at least,

---

5   G. Hardin, 'The tragedy of the commons,' *Science*, vol. 162, 13 December 1968, pp. 1243-48.

to correct market failure. This is done by ensuring that externalities are properly 'internalized' by economic actors so that the final price of goods reflects the full costs of production (i.e., the private costs of the firm *plus* the ecological costs to society).[6]

More full-blooded libertarians have rejected the notion of state intervention and taken up the cause of 'free market environmentalism'.[7] According to this libertarian analysis, the problem of the degradation of the commons arises from 'the lack of the very institution that lies at the heart of the free enterprise system', namely, private property.[8] That is, the solution to the tragedy of the commons is not more regulation and taxation but rather the privatization of the commons. This is an argument which rests on the highly questionable assumption that if the environment were privately owned it would be looked after. According to these theorists, we should pay more attention to state failure than to market failure.

In each of the above prescriptions, the problem of environmental degradation is approached through the lens of pre-existing liberal normative theories of the state, the market, property rights and/or democracy. That is, ecological problems have prompted ecological renovations to these theories, but no foundational critique or structural rebuilding.

It is not my intention to provide a detailed critical examination and comparison of the assumptions and claims of these normative theories. They have been briefly outlined here merely to provide a useful benchmark against which alternative green claims and theories regarding the role of the state may be compared. They are also of interest insofar as they inform mainstream environmental policy debates concerning the determination of the most appropriate policy instruments for environmental protection.

---

[6] The British environmental economist David Pearce has been in the forefront of publicizing this framework of analysis. See, for example, D. Pearce, A. Markandya and E. Barbier, *Blueprint for a green economy*, Earthscan, London, 1989 and R. Kerry Turner and D. Pearce, *Environmental economics*, Harvester Wheatsheaf, New York, 1994.

[7] A leading proponent is Terry Anderson (*Free market environmentalism*, Pacific Research Institute for Public Policy, San Francisco, 1991).

[8] P. Ackroyd and R. Hide, 'A Case Study—Establishing property rights to Chatham Islands Abalone (Paua)' in *Markets, resources and the environment*, eds A. Moran, A. Chisholm and M. Porter, Allen & Unwin, Sydney, 1991, p. 189.

What is ironical about the first two of these neo-classical theoretical models is that, despite their liberal genealogy, the rigorous implementation of their recommendations (especially the prescription for internalizing externalities) would ordain a massive greening of the capitalist economy and a significant range of added restrictions on investment decisions and private-property rights. To rephrase the opening quote by Ulrich Beck, neoclassical economic theory would ensure that capitalist society exited the stage of world history on the tip-toes of normality, via the back stairs of 'negative externalities'. This was indeed the prescription of the widely cited Pearce Report (published in 1989 as *Blueprint for a green economy*). It was commissioned, perhaps somewhat innocently, by the Thatcher government in the heyday of environmental concern in the late 1980s.

More generally, environmental policy communities in OECD countries have shown growing interest over the last decade in market-based instruments for the promise they hold of lowering the costs of environmental protection— at least when compared to the traditional regulatory approach.[9] Notwithstanding the impeccable market credentials of environmental economics, however, political leaders have been particularly slow to force producers and consumers to pay the full environmental costs of production. We saw this in Australia recently with the failure to implement a carbon tax.

Aside from the political and methodological obstacles in the way of calculating an optimal level of taxation and pollution (and the obvious inflationary consequences of such a strategy), the increasing international mobility of capital has served as a powerful discipline (sometimes constructed and imagined, sometimes real) against unilateral moves towards a concerted green taxation regime. Despite mounting charges of state failure from libertarian and neo-Marxist critics alike,[10] so-called 'command-and-control' regulatory regimes have remained the mainstay of environmental policy implementation.

---

9 *Economic instruments for environmental protection*, OECD, Paris, 1989.
10 See Anderson, *Free market environmentalism;* Janicke, *State failure*, and Dryzek, *Ecological rationality*.

The green case

Is there a uniquely green theory of the role of the state in managing environmental problems? Not quite. Green political theorists and activists have certainly earned a reputation for the novelty of their ethical and political demands (especially their defence of 'the rights of nature') and for their concerted push for a 'green economy'. However, the democratic and institutional implications of these demands remain both controversial and, in many cases, under-developed within green circles and, not surprisingly, widely misunderstood beyond such circles.

Although the themes of local autonomy, grass-roots democracy, and 'small is beautiful' have served as major rallying points for the green movement, there is still considerable disagreement over whether there is indeed an optimal scale and level of political decision making to achieve ecological reform (e.g., local, national, regional, global). Predictably, the major protagonists in this debate have been eco-communitarians and eco-anarchists on the one hand, and eco-socialists and more reformist green social democrats on the other hand. The former, represented by social ecologists such as Murray Bookchin, eco-fundamentalists such as Rudolf Bahro, and bioregionalists such as Kirkpatrick Sale, maintain that the green movement should bypass the modern nation-state and build decentralized, autonomous, and human-scaled ecological communities at the local level.[11] Included among these prescriptions are Bookchin's ecologically informed model of municipal socialism, Bahro's defence of liberated zones and the more novel case for the redrawing of political boundaries to conform to geographical bioregions, regions determined according to 'soft' ecological contours such as watersheds. As a long-term goal, bioregional theorists envisage a patchwork of economically self-reliant ecological communities within bioregions, linked together by a loose confederal structure that respects the political and economic autonomy of member communities.

The bioregional model is perhaps the most ecological of institutional designs offered by green theorists. However, as a general societal model

---

[11] M. Bookchin, *Remaking society,* South End Press, Boston, 1990; R. Bahro, *Building the green movement,* Heretic/GMP, London, 1986; and K. Sale, *Dwellers in the land,* Sierra Club Books, San Francisco, 1985.

(as distinct from a model that might be selectively applied to particular transboundary ecological problems) it has been subjected to a wide-ranging critique.[12] While eco-socialists and green social democrats accept the need for some devolution of power from the state to sub-national regional and local communities, they argue that a democratic state with a range of 'appropriate' centralized powers can act as an enabling institution that can facilitate the pursuit of broad green goals such as social emancipation and environmental protection. According to this argument, only the state is able to maintain basic standards of ecological integrity, income, health, education and welfare across different communities and regions. And only the state can tackle the ecological myopia of the market, respond to international problems, guard against local parochialism and protect basic freedoms via the rule of law.

While the themes of decentralization, grass-roots democracy and local action are indeed significant themes in popular green literature and green party platforms, their scope and application clearly remain controversial. Indeed, these popular themes are not generally reflected in the day-to-day political campaigns of environmental lobby organizations. As we shall see, the green movement in Australia has earned a reputation for urging the central government to override the wishes of local communities and state governments in relation to specific environmental controversies. In reacting to particular environmental problems, environmental organizations and green parties in Australia have, through their demands and general pronouncements about what the state ought to be doing, tended to approach the state in mainly instrumental and symbolic terms. Implicit in these demands is a plea for a 'strong state' and a 'good state'.[13]

That the state should be 'strong' arises from the need to proscribe a wide range of environmentally degrading activities and ensure that the economy operates comfortably within the carrying capacity of eco-systems. Although this view of the state supports the deployment of

---

12 See R. Eckersley, 'Linking the parts to the whole: bioregionalism in context', *Habitat Australia*, vol. 20, no. 1, 1992, pp. 34-6 and R. Goodin, *Green political theory*, Polity Press, Cambridge, 1992, pp. 147-68.
13 This posture is implicit in many of the policy documents produced by the Australian Conservation Foundation and the newly formed Australian Greens.

the regulatory and fiscal policy tools recommended by eco-social contract theorists and environmental economists, it does so on the basis of a much broader, ecologically informed notion of optimality. In terms of economic theory, greens prefer the ecological economics of Herman Daly (which seeks a steady-state economy in terms of material-energy throughput, as district from money circulation) over the environmental economics of David Pearce (which merely seeks the optimal allocation of resources in accordance with neoclassical economic theory).[14]

That the state should be 'good' arises from the belief that the state is the most appropriate (and certainly the most powerful) institution to assume the role of ecological guardian in the name of the public interest—protecting wilderness, native forests, ecosystem integrity, human health, threatened species, the global commons and future generations. Such a posture harks back to the European idea of the state as the embodiment of reason, ethics and the collective good—clearly *not* the inherently oppressive institution rejected by eco-anarchists nor the neutral umpire defended by free-market environmentalists.

Such a composite picture of the green state is clearly a very general and idealized one, and a number of important qualifications are immediately necessary. First, little understanding is to be gained from approaching the state as a unitary entity (least of all as a moral subject) that stands over and above civil society. Rather, the state is more appropriately understood as 'deeply enmeshed in all operations of social life, working increasingly as "the container of social processes", and representing a set of facilities "through which society can exercise some leverage upon itself" '.[15]

Second, it is inaccurate to equate the state with the democratic will or the collective good, both of which are especially opaque and troublesome notions. Of course, these points are not lost on green defenders of the state, very few of whom accept the liberal democratic

---

14   See H. Daly, *Steady-state economics*, 2nd edn, Island Press, Washington, 1991 and Pearce et al., *Blueprint for a green economy*.
15   M. Lacey, 'The environmental revolution and the growth of the state: overview and introduction' in *Government and Environmental Politics*, ed. M. Lacy, The Woodrow Wilson Centre Press, Washington, D.C. and the John Hopkins University Press, Baltimore, 1991, p. 2. Lacey's quotes are taken from G. Poggi, 'The modern state and the idea of progress' in *Progress, and its discontents*, eds G. Almond, M. Chodorow and R. Pearce, University of California Press, Berkeley, 1982, p. 351.

state as an unproblematic given. What can be said is that if the state is considered to be the (or simply one) appropriate institution to defend generalizable environmental interests, then liberal democratic institutions and bargaining processes have not proved to be particularly conducive to the articulation and defence of such interests. Indeed, liberal democratic institutions and practices carry some systematic anti-ecological biases.

The modern state did not evolve with complex, transboundary ecological problems in mind. Rather, it evolved to represent the interests of citizens of territorially bounded political communities. The new environmental constituency of non-citizens (non-compatriots, future generations and non-humans) receives, at best, qualified, haphazard and vicarious representation that is, in cases of conflict, invariably traded off against more immediate national human interests. Even within the territorial domain of liberal democracies, the public interest in environmental protection fares particularly badly. Environmental protection largely depends on public interest advocacy on behalf of long-term and generalizable interests, which requires a cautious and anticipatory approach to risk-assessment and to scientific complexity and uncertainty. However, liberal democracies operate on the basis of partisan political competition between selfish actors, and on the basis of very short time-horizons (corresponding, at most, to election periods).

On the basis of this critique, many green theorists have argued that the environment is likely to be better served by much stronger forms of democracy than liberal democracy. That is, more 'deliberative' forms of democracy or, following Jürgen Habermas, more 'rationalized' speech communities, have been defended as being more conducive to reaching decisions about generalizable environmental interests.[16] Attention has also been directed to broadening the discourse of rights to include environmental interests as one means of providing more systematic consideration of ecological concerns.[17]

Such a cursory ecological audit of liberal democracy and the modern

---

16 See, for example, Dryzek, *Ecological rationality,* and J. O'Neill, *Ecology, policy and politics: human well-being and the natural world,* Routledge, London, 1993.
17 R. Eckersley, 'Connecting ecology and democracy: the rights discourse revisited', paper presented to the European Consortium for Political Research Conference, Madrid, April 1994.

state provides one possible set of clues as to why the escalation of ecological degradation and the consistently high levels of general public environmental concern throughout the 1980s and, to a lesser extent, why the early 1990s have not been translated into more aggressive legislative and fiscal reforms and institutional innovations. That is, this set of clues points to a particular kind of democratic deficit in relation to ecological concerns.

However, this democratic deficit is only one part of the story. Another set of clues can be found in what might be called (to maintain the symmetry) the administration deficit, which encompasses the conflict between ecological and bureaucratic rationality discussed earlier as well as other administrative problems, such as weak resourcing of environmental agencies and less than vigilant monitoring and enforcement of environmental laws.

A third basis of explanation lies in the fact that the modern state is not only a major site of social contestation but also a highly fragmented entity with its own conflicting organizational imperatives, identities and functions. Given that states are routinely presented with more demands than can be satisfied, what is of interest is how different agencies and personnel of the state seek to appease, deflect, contain or otherwise manage environmental demands and conflicts. In this management exercise, different arms of government and different state agencies and instrumentalities of government (development departments, environment departments, independent commissions of inquiry) will often be found to be in conflict. Such problems are compounded in federal systems.

All, then, does not augur well for sound environmental management by the modern liberal democratic state—an observation that is generally borne out by the experience of the Australian federal state.

Environmental management in a federal context

A federal system of government raises vexed questions for both the environment and democracy—questions which link up with, but do not directly correspond to, debates about centralist versus decentralist (or top-down versus bottom-up) approaches to environmental management. This lack of direct correspondence may be attributed to the different legal, functional and spatial meanings which attach to the term decentralization, which may include devolution of power, delegation of power, or deconcentration of administration from the centre to the local/regional periphery.[18] Decentralization has also been interpreted as meaning privatization or the divestiture of state functions to private enterprise or voluntary non-government organizations.[19] Each of these interpretations may just as easily be carried out in federal or unitary systems of government. In other words, centralist versus decentralist tensions are endemic to both systems of governance. In each case, discerning 'that point where major areas of functional responsibility and political participation are maximised' remains elusive.[20]

In the case of Australia's federal system, it might be argued on the one hand that environmental debate has tended to be excessively focused on the rights, prerogatives and powers of the various tiers of government at the expense of the rights and duties of citizens and corporations. That is, debates concerning environmental problems or environmental management principles often become buried in jurisdictional debates, which divert attention from substantive issues and impede an integrated and bold approach to environmental problem solving.

On the other hand, it might be argued that Australia's federal system offers considerable scope for shared, multi-levelled management of ecological problems while also enabling overriding central control of those ecological problems that are seen to have a national or international dimension. Such a division of jurisdiction, which approximates the 'principle of subsidiarity' adopted by the European Community, might appear to provide one feasible compromise between democratic and ecological requirements.[21] As we shall see, the recent move towards co-operative federalism on the environment, expressed in the Intergovernmental Agreement on the Environment signed by the Australian Heads of Government in 1992, is not too far removed from this principle.

---

18   D. Rondinelli and J. Nellis, 'Assessing decentralisation policies in developing countries', *Development policy review,* no. 4, 1986, p. 5.
19   ibid.
20   M. Carley and I. Christie, *Managing sustainable development,* Earthscan, London, 1992, p. 143.
21   This principle, according to which a task should be undertaken by the lowest unit of society by which it can be effectively managed, was first proposed by Leopold Kohr in *The breakdown of nations,* 2nd edn, Dutton, New York, 1978 (first edition 1957).

The pattern of intergovernmental conflict in Australia over the environment in the last two decades has, at different times, provided support for both proponents and opponents of federalism. During this period, the strongly pro-development posture of some state governments[22] in the face of popular environmental protest, combined with the proliferation of international environmental treaties, has placed increasing pressure on the federal government to assume the mantle of environmental saviour. The federal government's increasing preparedness to respond to these demands in the 1980s—a decade of unprecedented environmental concern—served to both consolidate and extend federal environmental jurisdiction at the expense of the states. However, as we shall see, this federal environmental adventurousness has been highly selective and there are now clear signs that the high-water mark has been reached.

Most of the discussion and analysis of the state and environmental management in Australia has tended to focus on these highly visible federal-state environmental battles, many of which have concerned the preservation of native forests and other 'wilderness' areas. Indeed, these battles usually serve as the major points of reference for students of Australian environmental public policy. This modern ecopolitical narrative is now amply documented and usually begins with the unsuccessful campaign for federal intervention to prevent the inundation of Lake Pedder by the Tasmanian Hydro-Electricity Corporation in the early 1970s. The narrative then usually follows the major federal-state environmental conflicts in the which the federal government has effectively determined the outcome. Key milestones include the halting of sandmining on Fraser Island, the 'saving' of the Gordon-below-Franklin River from a hydro-electric power scheme, the preservation of Queensland's wet tropical rainforests, the Wesley Vale Pulp mill saga, the moratorium on logging in the Southern forests of Tasmania and the prevention of mining in Kakadu National Park.[23] In all of

---

22 Because of Australia's federal system the plural reference to Australia's 'state governments' should always be taken to refer to the states of Victoria, Queensland and so on. The singular reference to '*the* state' is to the generic institution. Reference to 'the Australian state' is to the entire system of Australian governance, including all tiers from local to national. In any case, it should be clear from the context of discussion.
23 For accounts of these conflicts, see D. Mercer, *A question of balance: natural resources*

these cases, the power of the federal government was wielded against private capital and/or a state government or its agencies (and in some cases, local government) in the name of environmental protection. In other cases, more co-operative strategies have been pursued, most notably the Murray Darling Basin initiative and the Landcare initiative (discussed in more detail below).

The green movement has exploited the political advantages of federalism in a significant number of these campaigns, many of which have resulted in the 'saving' of particular threatened pieces of Australian natural heritage by the Commonwealth government. However, a closer examination of the legacy of these campaigns reveals that they have not led to any major greening of the machinery of government or of the economy. Indeed, most of the celebrated environmental victories of the 1980s were very much at the margins, both in terms of population centres and degree of impact on patterns of economic development. Moreover, these environmental victories have generated a much more organised resistance to environmentalism. This has coincided with the onset of an international recession to produce a much less ecologically responsive federal state in the 1990s.

Although significant, the successful environmental campaigns of the 1980s have led to very minor institutional reforms in Australia. This suggests that to focus exclusively or excessively on the federal dimension is to deflect attention away from a more fundamental set of problems concerning the relationship between the state and the economy. After all, the argument that the state should take responsibility for its environment presupposes some measure of economic and political autonomy. On this subject, federal states seem to be no better placed than unitary states to grapple with the political tensions created by aspirations for political self-determination and environmental responsibility and the powerful trend towards integration in the world economy.

---

conflict issues in Australia, Federation Press, Annandale, NSW, 1992; K. Walker, ed., *Australian environmental policy*, New South Wales University Press, Kensington, 1992; E. Papadakis, *Politics and the environment*, Allen & Unwin, Sydney, NSW, 1993; T. Bonyhady, *Places worth keeping: conservationists, politics and the law*, Allen & Unwin, Sydney, 1993; and P. Christoff, 'Greening Australia?: the challenge of environmental politics', in eds J. Brett, M. Goot and J. Gillespie, *Developments in Australian Politics*, Macmillan, Melbourne, forthcoming.

Both federal and unitary states face the same imperatives and constraints imposed by capitalist economies, which fundamentally shape the broad negotiating margins (as distinct from the detail) of environmental politics.

As the following examination of recent key developments in Australia will reveal, although there has been a profound shift in the environmental policy discourse over the last two decades, this has not been matched by a corresponding greening of the machinery of government or of the economy. Indeed, notwithstanding the unprecedented environmental concern of the 1980s, most of the institutional innovations occurred in the 1970s.

The ecological record

Australia's environmental problems are serious. Agricultural practices introduced by European settlers have wreaked havoc on Australia's native ecosystems and resulted in severe land degradation, especially salination and erosion, in large stretches of the continent as well as nutrient pollution of major river systems. Australia also has the dubious distinction of having one of the world's worst records of species extinction.[24] Moreover, about 50 per cent of original forests and about 35 per cent of woodlands have been cleared or significantly modified since white settlement.

Australia is a highly urbanized nation, with 85 per cent of the population living in cities. Australian cities suffer from rapid urban sprawl, poor public transport and decaying urban infrastructure (such as outdated sewerage systems). Low-density settlement and urban sprawl in the cities is not only encroaching on some of the country's most fertile land and important water catchment areas, it also contributes to high per capita consumption of energy resources.[25] The Australian economy is an energy-intensive, resource-based economy with a large agriculture and minerals sector as well as energy-intensive industries such as steel and aluminium production. Australia is heavily dependent on the extraction and use of fossil fuels, and is the world's leading

---

24 Australian Bureau of Statistics, *Australia's environment: issues and fact*, ABS Catalogue no. 4140.0, Commonwealth of Australia, 1992, p. 49.
25 ibid., p. 267.

exporter of coal. This heavy dependence on fossil fuels ranks Australians as the fourth highest per capita greenhouse gas emitters in the world (after Brazil, East Germany and the USA).[26]

A key question emerging from this very cursory survey of major environmental problems in Australia is whether the Australian economy is capable of being properly greened in its present form. The state has had a considerable hand in orchestrating this energy-intensive, resource-driven pattern of economic development. Indeed, many of Australia's present ecological problems have been intensified through state-sponsored practices to boost production (notable examples include tax relief for land clearing and tree felling, the superphosphate bounty and government agricultural advice to use high chemical inputs on farms). Notwithstanding the endorsement of sustainable development, there has been a surprising reluctance on the part of governments and state agencies to search for creative links between the need for economic and ecological restructuring. As we shall see, this reluctance has constrained the negotiating margins of environmental politics in Australia—margins that are by no means as narrow as they have been made to appear.

Prior to the rise of modern environmentalism in the 1960s, the state response to environmental problems in Australia had been slow and uneven. The federal compact at the turn of the century had given no specific head of power with respect to the environment to the new Commonwealth government. The newly formed states thus retained their traditional responsibilities of controlling land-use and allocating land for development, attracting industry, managing energy supply and otherwise providing economic infrastructure. Managing the local environment in these early days essentially meant regulating the more visible and odious side-effects of local economic activity. For most of this century the states have generally preferred to see the 'wastelands' of the Crown turned over to productive use. It was assumed that environmental problems were understood and that piecemeal, ameliorative measures, such as 'end-of-pipe solutions', would suffice.

---

26 ibid., pp. 98-9. Australia's contribution is ranked at 17 in total world emissions (ibid., p. 99).

The first major wave of institutional reform

It took more than two decades of unparalleled growth and affluence in the post-World War II period before environmental problems 'emerged' in the 1960s as a persistent source of scientific and political concern. By the early 1970s, most of the states had embarked upon major overhauls to their pollution control regimes. Indeed, many of the major innovations in environmental management—such as the establishment of environmental protection agencies—were carried out during this period at both state and federal levels. These new regimes for environmental protection, which drew upon the United States model set up by the National Environmental Policy Act, were heralded as providing the foundations for a new era of environmental management in Australia—enabling the balancing of environment and development considerations. However, whereas judicial review of administrative action became a vital component of the US regime, it was accorded a shadowy status in Australia.[27]

At the national level, it was the heady period of the Whitlam Labor government that saw the establishment of a separate Department of the Environment and Conservation and the enactment of a wide range of new environmental legislation.

However, the new regulatory climate of the 1970s was, as Christoff explains, 'not necessarily one in which new environmental regulations were seen as defining new rights for citizens and the environment'.[28] For example, despite the fanfare, the aims of environmental impact assessment were essentially quite modest: merely to ensure that environmental considerations would be 'taken into account' by the relevant minister in deciding whether to confer the necessary approvals in respect of a specified class of large projects. The limited applicability of the legislation and the broad discretion conferred on the executive has largely removed the possibility for any judicial review of decisions

---

[27] As Clark and Mackay have shown, although some of the Australian regimes have followed the US model, they have operated in a different constitutional and political setting and produced very different outcomes (G. Clark and M. Mackay, 'The ideal institution of environmental regulation: an assessment of the origins, compromises and establishment of the US and Victorian (Australia) environmental protection agencies', 1993, unpublished ms).

[28] Christoff, 'Greening Australia', p. 7.

concerning the necessity for, adequacy of, and response to environmental assessment. These were essentially administrative reforms that have proved to be particularly opaque to judicial review at the behest of ecologically concerned citizens.[29]

Environmental impact assessment requirements have certainly introduced a greater environmental sensitivity to major developments in Australia. However, in the two-decade history of environmental impact assessment in Australia, cases of actual project abandonment on environmental grounds are extremely rare.[30] The ad hoc nature of individual project assessments (as distinct from regional assessment) and the requirement that impact statements be prepared by the developer (albeit subject to later public and administrative scrutiny) have been widely criticized.[31] Not surprisingly, attention has rarely been given to the question of alternative land-use options, as distinct from, say, alternative waste-treatment technologies or alternative sites for development. Environmental impact assessments, along with the new pollution control regimes, must be understood as fundamentally ameliorative; they make no attempt to redirect the pattern and character of investment decisions along ecologically sustainable lines.

Provincial intransigence

The major innovations to environmental administration in Australia in the 1970s proved unable to contain the growing environmental conflict over land-use in the following decade, particularly at the state level where the primary responsibility for regulating land-use decisions lies.

---

29 A notable exception is s.123 of the NSW Environmental Planning and Assessment Act 1979, which overcomes the limited common law rules of judicial standing by allowing any person (or class of persons) to take proceedings in the Land and Environment Court to enforce the Act, irrespective of whether a private right has been infringed.

30 At the federal level, the EIS on the Wesley Vale pulp mill undertaken pursuant to the Commonwealth Environment Protection (Impact of Proposals) Act is a lonely example of a major project that was halted on environmental grounds. Yet even this example did not involve outright proscription; rather, it was the proponent that chose not to conform to higher environmental hurdles imposed by the federal government (to the dismay of the government).

31 For a more comprehensive critique, see Ralf Buckley, 'Shortcomings in current institutional frameworks for environmental planning and management', *Canberra bulletin of public administration,* no. 62, October 1990, pp. 50-6.

Although the federal government entered the field of environmental protection in the early 1970s, the primary responsibility for attracting and regulating particular developments has remained with the states and local government.

Many state governments have been reluctant to halt or significantly compromise development activity on environmental grounds. That so many environmentalists beat a path to Canberra for relief in the late 1970s and 1980s in key campaigns must be seen as less a reflection of the special green inclinations of the federal government than of the singular unresponsiveness of certain state governments to environmental demands. Such reluctance may be attributed partly to the colonial legacy of statist development, the productivist culture of many state instrumentalities charged with regulating resource development and the narrow fiscal base of state governments. This reluctance has been further reinforced by competition between states to attract large-scale industry through such incentives as lower electricity tariffs, lower taxes and charges, less onerous (or poorly enforced) environmental regulations and specifically tailored industry agreement acts, many of which are designed to fast track development by suspending ordinary environmental procedures. The desire to minimize green tape has been especially pronounced in the most revenue hungry and most mineral dependent states, which tend also to have the highest degree of external control over their economies. Some states have been especially dismissive of environmental demands in times of recession and high regional unemployment, the political impact of which is often more keenly felt by local and state governments than by those in power in 'remote Canberra'. Under these circumstances, hints of federal intervention on environmental grounds have been met with strong states' rights rhetoric and displays of local patriotism by industry lobbies and governments alike, which have portrayed environmentalists as traitors to the economic well-being of the community.

The political economy of the Australian states and the active role played by state governments in attracting investment provide a significant backdrop to the pattern of environmental conflict in Australia. As Walker has put it, such 'broader "macro" constraints tend to predetermine the framework of government policy long before specific issues reach the agenda'.[32] Yet this general picture would not be complete without mention of the political personalities of state premiers such as Sir Charles Court, Joh Bjelke-Peterson and Robin Gray, whose belligerent and confrontational styles, enthusiasm for 'mega-projects' and dismissal of environmental concerns have helped to seed a highly organized, vocal and tactically sophisticated environment movement in specific areas such as wilderness preservation and forestry.

The waning federal resolve

Following the proliferation of international environmental treaties, it is now widely acknowledged that there are few, if any, areas of environmental management that are beyond the reach of federal power.[33] Any further encroachment on state environmental jurisdiction by the federal government is now essentially a matter for political judgment rather than constitutional power.

The current signs are that the federal government is unwilling to take any decisive action to consolidate or extend its expanded environmental jurisdiction. Although Australia signed Agenda 21 (the international strategy for sustainable development) and the Framework Conventions on Climate Change and Biodiversity at the Earth Summit in June 1992, the federal government has declined to adopt an assertive environmental posture *vis-á-vis* the states. Instead, it has pursued a conciliatory approach through the Intergovernmental Agreement on the Environment (IGAE), concluded in 1992. The IGAE is in large measure a response to the federal-state conflicts of the 1980s. The Agreement seeks to reduce disputes and foster a more co-operative approach to environmental management. It is also intended to provide a clearer definition of the responsibilities and interests of the three tiers of government in order to provide greater certainty for business, minimize duplication of government decision making and improve environmental protection. The general principles of the IGAE effectively

---

32 K. Walker, 'Conclusion: the politics of environmental policy' in *Australian environmental policy*, ed. Walker, p. 241.
33 See, for example, J. Crawford, 'The constitution and the environment' in *Our common future: environmental law and policy workshop papers and proceedings*, eds J.M. Behrens and B.M. Tsamenyi, Faculty of Law, University of Tasmania, Hobart, 1991, pp. 8-24.

endorse the current position: the states and territories have responsibility for the majority of environmental issues within their borders while the federal government's responsibilities are to be confined to those areas where it has demonstrated responsibilities and interests, such as implementing treaties, regulating offshore and interstate environmental problems, controlling Commonwealth land and territories and facilitating the development of national ambient environmental standards and guidelines.[34] These standards and guidelines are to be set by a new intergovernmental ministerial council to be called the National Environmental Protection Authority, recently renamed the National Environmental Protection Council (NEPC).[35] Although one of the professed aims of the IGAE is better environmental protection, most of the provisions in the agreement concentrate on streamlining approval processes, creating greater certainty and resource security, and providing more opportunities for consultation. Although decisions by the NEPC are to be made by a majority vote of ministers (rather than by consensus), it is unlikely that this departure from the usual decision-making practice of ministerial councils is likely to provide much of a counterweight against the inherent conservatism of collective decisions made in such intergovernmental councils. That is, the decision-making process is more likely to lead to the lowest common denominator than to world's best practice.

Closing ranks: resource security

Even before the signing of the IGAE, there were already clear signs of a closing of intergovernmental ranks against environmental demands, partly in reaction to mounting industry pressure. Threatened by the possibility of further restricted access to mineral and timber resources, organizations such as the Australian Mining Industry Council and the National Association of Forest Industries have mounted campaigns for their own form of resource security. Both the federal and some state governments responded to these demands by drafting legislation for the forestry industry, which sought to guarantee access to a specified

---

34 *Intergovernmental agreement on the environment,* Department of Arts, Sport, the Environment and Territories, February 1992, p.6.
35 ibid., 23.

volume of timber over specified time periods. The federal response was unveiled by the Hawke government in its March 1991 Industry Statement, which declared that investment security would be provided for major new wood processing projects involving value-added investments of $100 million or more (where the state government also agreed to enact resource security legislation).[36] In seeking to demonstrate to the forestry industry the sincerity of his government's commitment to providing investment security, Hawke took the unprecedented step of agreeing to bind the federal government *not* to exercise any of its legal powers to stop major projects involving 'downstream' processing of forest products (e.g., pulp and paper manufacturing). This included an effective promise not to make any decision or enact any legislation that might impede states from making wood available for such resource projects.[37] Although the Forest Conservation and Development Bill 1991 was defeated in the Senate by the Opposition and minor parties, the Commonwealth has pursued its commitment to resource security by administrative means, following general agreements reached with the states in the IGAE and the Draft National Forestry Statement.[38]

The resource security saga marked an important turning point in federal-state relations concerning the environment. Instead of the environment movement turning to a sympathetic federal government to overrule an intransigent state, the federal and state governments, with the support of industry, combined to head off possible future campaigns by the environment movement by closing any possible legal opportunities that might have provided a future lever for federal intervention on environmental grounds.[39]

---

[36] Statements of Prime Minister Bob Hawke, Treasurer Paul Keating and Industry Minister John Button, *Building a competitive Australia,* Australian Government Publishing Service, Canberra, 12 March 1991. A key objective of resource security was 'to phase out woodchip exports by the year 2000 or soon after, and replace them with value-added products' (p. 1.16).

[37] ibid., p. 5.58.

[38] For a detailed discussion see R. Fowler, 'Implications for resource security for environmental law' in *The challenge of resource security,* ed. A. Gardner, Federation Press, Sydney, 1993, pp. 51-88.

[39] See P.R. Hay and R. Eckersley, 'Green politics: lessons from Tasmania's Labor-green accord, 1989-1991', *Current affairs bulletin,* vol. 69, no. 11, 1993, pp. 10-15.

From EIA to ESD: an elusive consensus

At the same time as the federal government offered resource security it sought to move away from what had largely been an ad hoc and reactive approach to environmental decision making towards a more integrated and consensual approach. The foundations for this move were laid in 1989 in the Prime Minister's environment statement, which endorsed the concept of sustainable development as a basis for future policy making.[40] Just as environmental impact assessment was hailed as ushering in a new era in environmental management in the early 1970s, so too was the Ecologically Sustainable Development (ESD) consultation process and the resulting National ESD Strategy hailed as providing a new era for the 1990s. However, whereas the 1970s EIA rhetoric focused on *balancing* environment and development considerations—on the assumption that environmental protection and economic development were essentially competing objectives—the sustainable development rhetoric of the early 1990s had shifted to the language of *integration*, language that acknowledged the interdependencies between a sustainable economy and a sustainable environment. In terms of environmental management principles, this was indeed a major sea change that followed key shifts in the international environment and development debate in the wake of the publication of the influential Brundtland Report in 1987.[41] Instead of merely tacking on environmental considerations to particular development projects (the EIA approach), the ecologically sustainable development discourse promised to build enduring bridges between environment and development objectives.

In the hope that a common language might open up a space for the discovery of a greater measure of common ground between hostile parties, the government established an Ecologically Sustainable Development (ESD) consultation process.[42] Predictably, the alleged 'community'

---

40 R.J.L. Hawke, *Our country our future: statement on the environment,* Australian Government Publishing Service, Canberra, 1989.
41 *Our common future*, Aust. edn, Oxford University Press, Melbourne, 1990.
42 Ecologically Sustainable Development Steering Committee, *National strategy for ecologically sustainable development,* Australian Government Publishing Service, Canberra, 1992; National Greenhouse Steering Committee, *National greenhouse response strategy*, Australian Government Publishing Service, Canberra, December, 1992.

ESD consultation process drew criticism from many quarters for being unrepresentative and more than once it seemed likely that the process would either lose legitimacy or founder, especially during the official taskforce phase, when many of the Working Groups' recommendations were watered down. Many states complained to the Department of Prime Minister and Cabinet (which co-ordinated the exercise) about not being invited to participate in the initial planning stages of the process. Two of the key environment groups in Australia, the Wilderness Society and Greenpeace Australia, declined to participate at all in the ESD process on the ground that the federal government's commitment to resource security legislation made a mockery of the ESD process. The Australian Conservation Foundation (by a close vote) and the World Wide Fund for Nature opted to stay in the process and together they provided the major green representation on the ESD committees, aided by federal funding which enabled the establishment of an ESD Policy Unit staffed by officers of the Australian Conservation Foundation and the World Wide Fund for Nature.

The change of Labor Prime Minister from Hawke to Keating in the final phase of the ESD exercise resulted in a significant loss of momentum. (Indeed, Keating has arguably been more successful in marginalizing environmental demands than Hawke was in incorporating them into government policy.) Unlike the federal government's Accord exercise with the unions in the early 1980s, the ESD exercise in the late 1980s attracted surprisingly little publicity—even when industry joined green groups in accusing federal and state bureaucrats of hijacking the operation and watering down the Working Groups' recommendations during the final stages of preparing the strategy. The final ESD Strategy was largely couched in permissive (rather than mandatory) terms with few commitments to targets and timetables or specific legislative and fiscal initiatives.

The upshot was that the ESD exercise produced a range of useful and uncontroversial recommendations for incremental reforms in certain areas (especially energy efficiency). However, the process did not deliver any historical compromise between the state, capital, labour and the environment movement that might usher in the sorts of deep-seated structural changes that would put the Australian economy on an ecologically sound footing.

Nor did the Greenhouse Strategy provide any basis for any deep-seated economic or ecological innovation.[43] Australia's interim planning target of stabilizing greenhouse gas emissions at 1988 levels by the year 2000, and reducing these emissions by twenty per cent by the year 2005, has been made subject to a proviso that effectively reverses the precautionary principle that forms part of the Framework Convention on Climate Change. According to this proviso, Australia will not implement 'response measures that would have net adverse economic impacts nationally or on Australia's trade competitiveness, in the absence of similar action by major greenhouse gas producing countries'.[44]

One striking feature of the ESD process is the minor role played by politicians and the central role played by state officials, particularly Commonwealth bureaucrats.[45] Having initiated the process, the executive entrusted senior level bureaucrats with the task of bringing the major stakeholders to the table, steering the deliberations and producing a formal document which did not require any government commitment. Moreover, the ESD process was not a simple case of the state mediating between a range of conflicting stakeholders to produce a new environmental policy consensus to guide government. Rather, it was a case of certain key development departments finding ways of incorporating environmental concerns into a pre-existing consensus in favour of economic development. As McEachern explains, 'It was possible to use corporatist forums because the debate occurred in the embrace of that preceding and prevailing consensus.'[46]

---

43   R. Eckersley, 'Re-interpreting "no-regrets": a green economic critique of the greenhouse response strategy', in *Greenhouse and the energy regions: proceedings,* eds S.L. Pfueller, M.A. Hooper and D.H.P. Harvey, Monash Distance Education Centre, Churchill, Victoria, 1993, pp. 55-68.

44   The target and proviso were adopted by the Commonwealth, state and territory governments in October 1990 and reaffirmed in the Intergovernmental Agreement on the Environment (Schedule 5) and the National Greenhouse Response Strategy.

45   C. Hamilton, 'Ecologically sustainable development: implications for governance', paper presented at the international workshop on 'Sustainable development—implications for the policy process' hosted by the Royal Australian Institute of Public Administration, Canberra, 12 December 1991, p. 2; D. McEachern, 'Environmental policy in Australia 1981-91: a form of corporatism?', *Australian journal of public administration,* vol. 52, no. 2, June 1993, p. 177.

46   ibid., p. 182.

Whither innovation in Australia?

By the 1980s (even before the influential Brundtland Report appeared) the intellectual premises of environmental policy were changing, particularly in western Europe where green parties had gained a foothold. It was increasingly acknowledged by the environmental policy community that environmental problems were not fully understood and could not be adequately handled discretely by specialized branches of government. The new approach also recognized the limitations of 'end-of-pipe' solutions and adopted a longer-term assessment of costs and benefits and a more cautious approach to risk assessment and scientific uncertainty. It became evident that the so-called balanced approach to environmental management, which pulled back from charging producers and consumers the full environmental costs of their activities, did not avoid costs—it merely passed them on in space and time. This new approach highlighted the costs of failing to act as much as the costs of taking action. As the notion of integration challenged the traditional notion of balance in relation to economy-environment relations, increasing attention was directed to the use of market-based instruments as tools of environmental policy (such as taxes, charges and marketable emission permits) in addition to, or sometimes in lieu of, the traditional regulatory approach. Gradually shifting the burden of taxation away from profits and labour and towards energy, resources and wastes has also become one of the cornerstones of a new green fiscal policy.[47]

Moreover, strict environmental regulation became a means of developing a new competitive advantage in environmental technologies, while also catering for a rising green consumer demand.[48] In Europe, the argument that stringent environment policy (at least in the area of pollution control) might actually provide a boost to (rather than a burden on) the economy has become known as 'ecological modernization'.

---

[47] R. Repetto, R.C. Dower, R. Jenkins and J. Geoghagen, *Green fees: how a tax shift can work for the environment and the economy,* World Resources Institute, Washington D.C., 1992.

[48] M. Jacobs, 'Growth, industrial policy and regulation-led innovation: some thoughts on macro-environmental economics', occasional paper no. 6, Institute of Ethics and Public Policy, Monash University, November 1993.

As we have seen, the new policy discourse of ecologically sustainable development, which incorporates the precautionary principle, has now been officially adopted in Australia. However, there has been no corresponding restructuring of the economy or the machinery of government of a kind that would steer the Australian economy along a more ecologically sustainable path. Indeed, one of the major institutional initiatives of the late 1980s—the Resource Assessment Commission—has recently been dismantled.

On the economic front, the Australian ESD strategy provides no concerted attempt to follow the path of ecological modernization, which capitalizes on environment-economy synergies and represents the minimalist integration interpretion of sustainable development. Rather, while the Prime Minister's Department was overseeing the ESD initiative, the Treasury was busy overseeing the completion of a set of major economic restructuring initiatives that increasingly forced environmental protection back into the category of luxury-item on the political agenda.[49] Instead of developing a green fiscal framework, major initiatives such as *One nation* sought to fast-track resource developments and perpetuate Australia's dependence on resource-based exports, albeit with a slightly higher value-added component.

In view of the significant shift in environmental policy discourse in the 1980s, we have to ask the question, 'Why have economic and industry policy remained at serious cross-purposes with environment policy in Australia?'

Implications of the ecological challenge for theories of the state

There are some who might wish to challenge the alleged newness of environmental problems—at least in terms of their effect on debates about the modern state and its relationship to the economy. According to neo-Marxist analyses (offered by theorists such as Habermas and Offe), environmental problems simply represent another example of 'legitimation crisis', which can be theorized in the same way as, say, welfare problems. On the one hand, the modern state has an institutional

---

49 P. Christoff, 'Ecological modernisation and Australian dilemmas', paper presented at the Australian Political Studies Conferences, Monash University, September 1993.

self-interest in safeguarding the interests of capital, not because of any conspiracy but rather because of its functional dependence on the flow of resources that private capital provides. On the other hand, the state must redress the negative social and ecological externalities generated by private capital accumulation (or, in some cases, the activities of its own instrumentalities). However, any concerted attempt to regulate private investment and management decisions to a point where negative ecological externalities are eliminated (as distinct from merely ameliorated) would be deeply inimical to the interests of private capital and likely to lead to a capital strike or flight. Governments simply cannot risk serious economic dislocation or a cessation of growth, as either of these is likely to bring about their demise.

These contradictory imperatives—to appease public concern over ecological degradation and maintain private capital accumulation—are not resolvable. They can only ever be managed, and usually only at the margins through incremental change. Successful management requires cultivating at least the semblance of consensus while effectively maintaining policies and institutions that appease those groups (capital, labour) whose support is vital for ongoing capital accumulation.

These generic accounts of the contradictions facing the modern welfare state help to set the broad parameters of political manoeuvrability for the state *vis-á-vis* the economy. However, they pay insufficient attention to conflicts within the state apparatus. They do not explain the particular compromises forged by political leaders and bureaucrats, or particular arrangements forged by bureaucrats and their clientele. Nor do they pay sufficient attention to bureaucratic rivalries, which are often reproduced in Cabinet in the pecking order of ministerial portfolios. Moreover, recents shifts in the environmental policy discourse indicate that the economy-environment contradictions are not as deep-seated as this generic analysis suggests, at least if ecological modernization is taken seriously.

Ecological versus bureaucratic rationality

Ecological problems have thrown down new challenges to the rationality of bureaucratic organization and decision making. Indeed, it has been argued that the environmental crisis has given rise not only to a political crisis but also to an institutional crisis.[50] There is now a growing theoretical literature pointing to a fundamental incompatibility between traditional bureaucratic rationality and ecological rationality. Ecological problems are 'inherently complex, nonreducible, variable, uncertain, spontaneous, and collective in nature'.[51] According to Dryzek, to be ecologically rational (i.e., to be able to maintain consistently ecological life-support systems) a social steering system must be able to respond effectively to negative feedback, co-ordinate across all system boundaries to prevent problem displacement, and be flexible and resilient in order to cope with unexpected changes.

As raised earlier, modern bureaucratic organization and rationality has been concerned to devise efficient means for achieving stated ends through problem decomposition and allocation, rule-bound behaviour, specialization and routinization, and a top-down chain of command.[52] The rigid nature of traditional bureaucratic structures does not allow for sufficient interactions across the boundaries of administrative subsets, which often leads to problem displacement and an inability to respond swiftly and creatively to changed circumstance. Traditional forms of inter-agency communication and co-ordination (interdepartmental committees, Cabinet discussion and informal liaison among civil servants) are too ad hoc and infrequent to anticipate and prevent systematic problem displacement.

While modern government departments and agencies in Australia do not necessarily all conform exactly to this traditional Weberian ideal-type of bureaucracy, they nonetheless approximate it in varying degrees. Many of Australia's ecological problems have been intensified through the narrow compartmentalization of agency roles. Budgeting difficulties can also exert pressure on certain agencies to maintain short-term cash flows at the expense of longer-term considerations. In the case of forestry agencies, this has led to the encouragement of more intensive methods of resource extraction such as woodchipping. As we have seen, part

---

50 R. Bartlett, 'Ecological reason in administration: environmental impact assessment and administrative theory', in *Managing leviathan: environmental politics and the administrative state,* eds R. Paehlke and D. Torgerson, Broadview Press, Peterborough, Ontario, 1990, p. 82.
51 Dryzek, *Ecological rationality*, pp. 26-33.
52 ibid., chapter 8.

of the failure of the ESD exercise may be attributed to the fact that the committees were organized along traditional departmental and industry lines.

The problem of agency compartmentalization is also exacerbated by the problems of agency capture and inter-agency competition. Both sets of problems can generate crises of political accountability and supervision. The upshot has been an increasing gap between those who decide and implement, and those who carry responsibility for decisions. The influence and control of parliament over the machinery of state must pass through what Janicke has aptly referred to as 'the needle eye of ministerial responsibility'.[53] In Janicke's assessment, the 'countervailing power of the weakly organised public interest' cannot match the power of the bureaucratic-industrial complex.[54] Many environmental battles in Australia, particularly at the state level, have been pitted against particular resource instrumentalities (e.g., forestry commissions) that have been more or less captured by their clients and have consequently shown a notable reluctance to recognize nonproduction values.

The state orchestration of ecologically sustainable development clearly requires a more flexible, collegial and consultative administrative arrangement than the present one. Such an arrangement would need to include, yet go beyond, simply reordering the current ministerial and departmental pecking order to give environment agencies more status and resources *vis-á-vis* agencies such as trade, industry, finance and treasury. In the *absence* of such a re-ordering, new initiatives may backfire. For example, notwithstanding the shift in policy discourse from 'balance' to 'integration', merely amalgamating environment and development agencies into larger mega-agencies carries considerable dangers, especially where there are pre-existing power and resource disparities in the former agencies. In such circumstances, environmental advocacy is likely to be diluted rather than strengthened.

In many cases of environmental management, the problem is to be found less in the 'organs' of the state and more in the 'connective tissue', which encompasses both the style and direction of communicative

---

53 Janicke, *State failure*, p. 27.
54 ibid., p. 14.

pathways and particular organizational cultures. Carlie and Christie have outlined one promising response to the challenge of environmental policy formulation, integration and co-ordination, called 'action centred networks'.[55] These are flexible, open and task-oriented interdisciplinary networks that cut across traditional industry and administrative boundaries. In relation to ecological problems, action-centred networks are made up of partnerships between relevant stakeholders, broadly defined to include government agencies, business, research and grass-root community groups. They are concerned with problem identification, consensus building, and policy co-ordination and integration. Moreover, different 'nested networks' would need to be developed to tackle different levels of a particular problem (i.e., local, national, regional).

Such action-centred networks are considerably different in structure and function from the ESDs discussed above. Following Carlie and Christie's model, they demand stakeholder equality and some relinquishment of control by government and state agencies. They would be given particular management and research tasks, grounded in real problems, and be required to engage in a regular, critical review of their function and organizational learning.

It is perhaps no coincidence that two of the most promising environmental management initiatives in Australia—the Landcare initiative and the Murray-Darling Basin Management Initiative—have loosely approximated this reflexive, action-centred network approach. The Landcare initiative, or National Soil Conservation Strategy, was launched in 1989 partly as a response to local community landcare initiatives and to an historic partnership and joint proposal made by the National Farmers Federation and the Australian Conservation Foundation.[56] Committing $320 million to the following Decade of Landcare, the federal government has become the facilitator of much more systematic inter-agency communication and co-ordination (most notably between the CSIRO, and the departments responsible for primary industry, the environment, relevant state agencies and local government) and much more extensive community-based research and participatory

---

55 *Managing sustainable development*, pp. 171-3.
56 See R. Farley and P. Toyne, 'A National Land Management Program', *Australian journal of soil and water conservation*, vol. 11, no. 2, 1989, p. 609.

planning, at the district and catchment levels rather than at individual property level.[57] The Murray-Darling Basin (MDB) Natural Resources Management Strategy (approved by the MDB Ministerial Council in 1990) provides a similar example of the virtues of transcending formal geographical, constitutional and administrative boundaries with catchment-wide planning and management with a strong community participation focus (the river basin spans four states and the Australian Capital Territory and covers one-seventh of the continent).[58] Although significant social, economic and cultural constraints still remain, the initiative provides the most ambitious model of integrated bioregional governance in Australia.

Green lessons

This chapter has highlighted the ecological challenges to the modern democratic state, focusing on the interrelated democratic and administration deficits in environmental policy formulation and implementation. The picture would be incomplete without mention of the international pressures that work against a more widespread and concerted greening of the economy and the machinery of government. In an increasingly 'borderless' economic world, there appear to be few incentives for states to orchestrate a thoroughgoing greening of the domestic economy in the absence of international regulation or, failing that, comparable environmental regulation (and taxation) by relevant trading partners. This is reflected in the ongoing contradiction between macro-economic policy and environmental policy at the national level, notwithstanding the rhetoric of sustainable development. The need for international co-operation is evident, but the proliferation of international environmental treaties in the post-World War II period has been far too modest and slow to keep pace with the growing scale and rate of ecological problems. Strategic rivalries, an unwillingness on the part of national leaders to forego short-term economic welfare, and doubts

---

57 A. Campbell, 'Landcare in Australia: spawning new models of inquiry and learning for sustainability', paper presented to the International Symposium on Systems-Oriented Research in Agriculture and Rural Development, Montpellier, France, 21-25 November 1994.

58 J. Burton, 'Community involvement in the management of the Murray-Darling basin', *Canberra bulletin of public administration*, no. 62, October 1990, pp. 76-80.

and conflicts concerning the funding, monitoring and enforcement of environmental treaties all serve to impede seriously environmental co-operation or else serve to reduce treaty provisions to 'lowest common denominator' standards and practices.[59]

In light of these problems, many believe that a radical shift in the institutions of domestic, regional and international governance is required to ensure that the modest gains achieved by the growing number of environmental treaties are not overwhelmed by the magnitude of the ecological crisis. The need for such a shift has been acknowledged by the thirty signatories to the revolutionary but short-lived Hague Declaration, which recognized 'that a requirement of unanimity is tantamount to a prescription for impasse'.[60] It is in this context that federal states, and other politically and economically integrated regions (such as the European Community), have acquired a new importance as possible models of environmental governance. In such cases of pooled sovereignty, the centre or larger co-ordinating unit of government is given power to override the periphery or member unit in certain circumstances in the name of national or regional environmental protection.

However, the Australian experience (and, indeed, the recent European experience) suggests that the political and economic integration of different tiers of government makes little difference in the absence of firm political commitments to environmental reform and profound changes to the organization and culture of government administration and state-economy relations. It is at this point that the argument becomes somewhat circular. That is, we have seen that firm political commitments to environmental reform are hard to come by in liberal democracies —partly because of the difficulties associated with defending long-range, generalizable interests, partly because of bureaucratic rigidities, and partly because of international capital mobility and the general 'discipline

---

59 The problem of environmental treaty compliance has been partially offset in some instances by a growing array of transnational non-government organizations (NGOs) that have taken on the mantle of international environmental watchdogs. Major examples include Friends of the Earth, the World Wide Fund for Nature, Greenpeace and many aid and charitable organizations.

60 H. French, *After the earth summit: the future of environmental governance,* Worldwatch Paper 107, Worldwatch Institute, Washington, 1992, p. 35.

of the market', which severely constrain the negotiating margins of environmental policy.

Yet we have also seen that there are ways of breaking down this deadlock. The discussion has identified some of the changes that are needed to many of the links in this circular chain, both in terms of substantive policy and institutional design. Most importantly, we have seen that redressing the 'democratic and administrative deficits' also requires a much more concerted reconnection between the processes and institutions of democratic policy formulation and administration in ways that break down the growing gap between those who possess 'relevant knowledge', those who decide, those who carry responsibility, those who implement and those who are affected. This is indeed a daunting task, but the significance of this process of political reconnection is amply borne out in the more successful environmental management initiatives in Australia—initiatives that also reinforce the green support for more reflexive, pedagogical, 'communicatively rationalized' forms of democratic deliberation. Many outstanding problems remain, not the least of which is how to extend the time horizons of deliberation, how to provide more systematic consideration of the new environmental constituency and how to cope with environmental complexity and uncertainty. The modern state may not be up to this task. But, for the moment, there seems to be little alternative but to test and reform it as major changes assert themselves 'via the back stairs of side effects'.

5

The poverty of the welfare state: managing an underclass

Rob White

In the area of welfare support and social intervention a shift has occurred in Australia which suggests that the state has moved its emphasis from activities of social provision to those of social control. The changed emphasis has been accompanied by significant changes in the ways in which the state has constructed and intervened in the lives of the poor, so much so that in this area it now makes sense to talk of a shift from a social state to a repressive state.

The aim of this chapter is to explore the idea of an underclass in the Australian setting and to indicate the political character of the debates surrounding the economic position and behavioural features of certain sections of the population. The chapter begins by examining briefly the nature of welfare in Australian society—the allocation, targets and administration of goods and services. This is followed by an extended discussion of the definitions of and relationship between poverty, unemployment and the underclass. The chapter is premised upon two key assumptions. The first is that there is an abiding pressure on the state in capitalist society to facilitate the process of capital accumulation, the principle element of which is to control labour. The second assumption is that a primary role of the welfare system under capitalism is to manage and control those people who are outside of the labour-market. In the light of these two assumptions I want to argue that in the present period of capitalist restructuring on a world scale, the role of the state in Australia is becoming even less that of apparent welfare provider than that of enforcer of a particular kind of social order.

It is not that we are seeing the death of the welfare state, but that it is changing. From a broad structural perspective, welfare has classically operated to placate the claims of workers and specific sectional interest groups, and to reproduce via education, health and welfare measures a particular kind of labour force and citizenry. In other words, from its inception and through its continuing development the welfare state has immediately and inevitably been implicated in the maintenance and reproduction of the capitalist societies within which it has emerged. There are, of course, many different state forms possible under capitalism, from liberal democracies to dictatorships to fascist regimes, with considerable variation within each of these categories. Similarly there are very different systems of welfare provision depending upon the particular nation-state in question. The precise shape and form of the welfare state varies not only depending upon national context, but also according to specific historical or conjunctural trends. It is the nature and direction of these conjunctural trends in the Australian context which forms the substance of this chapter.

The phenomenon of widespread unemployment constitutes the biggest single factor, but by no means the only factor, in the current relationship between the market, the state and the community. This in turn has placed considerable pressure on governments to balance the demands of the economy expressed in fiscal, monetary and wages policies with social-policy demands, demands stemming from the continued decline in living standards which have accompanied the movement of people out of work and into the welfare queue, or into work of a low-paying nature. One consequence of this tension at the policy level has been a combination of increasingly selective welfare provisions targeted at families, a shift in support responsibilities from the state to the family, and increasing regulatory action by the state in relation to the claiming of benefits. These trends are creating a cash crisis for many households, especially for low-income households and individuals living in poverty.

A crucial issue confronting the state is how, in the face of increasing disparities of wealth and income in Australia, can the legitimacy of the capitalist system and of the state itself be maintained while, at the same time, resource-allocation favourable to capital accumulation is continued. One answer has been to extend the possibilities of control and regulation over individuals, particularly those who are most marginalized in society, and to do so in ways which shifts the focus of political debate away from structural questions of inequality and oppression. As will be seen, this takes the form of legitimating coercive measures under the guise of protecting the citizenry from the intrusions and threatening presence of the underclass.

Welfare, well-being and the state

Generally speaking, debates about welfare provision under capitalism reflect two main approaches or paradigms. On the one hand, there are those who subscribe to the views of economic liberalism. They see the state as providing only minimal welfare support: welfare is thus something that should be carried by private-sector agencies.[1] The focus is on the concept of scarcity, and social policy is seen mainly as a means to channel limited resources in the most efficient manner.[2] Politically, the state is seen to have a minor role in welfare matters. A strong state may be required in terms of maintaining public order, but a free economy is stressed in terms of the de-regulation of market transactions (including the labour-market) and minimal state intervention in the lives of citizens.[3] Welfare is ultimately seen as an individual responsibility.

On the other hand, social liberalism or social democratic conceptions see welfare as enabling wider human and social development, and as intimately linked to one's rights as a citizen. The state is seen as an instrument of reform, and social policy as a quest after social improvement. The goals of such a welfare system are the maximization of welfare, the elimination of poverty and the pursuit of equality. The focus therefore is on benefits that should accrue to a wide spectrum of citizens, and the equitable distribution of community resources.[4]

The allocation of welfare

The difference between these two broad perspectives is apparent when we consider questions such as who should be eligible to receive benefits,

---

[1] For a critical discussion and critique of 'economic liberalism' see P. Beilharz, M. Considine and R. Watts, *Arguing about the welfare state: the Australian experience*, Allen & Unwin, Sydney, 1992.

[2] For a discussion on divergent approaches to welfare support, see A. Graycar and A. Jamrozik, *How Australians live: social policy in theory and practice*, Macmillan, Melbourne, 1989.

[3] A. Gamble, *The free economy and the strong state*, Macmillan, London, 1988.

[4] See Beilharz et al., *Arguing about the welfare state*, and Graycar and Jamrozik, *How Australians live*.

how much they should receive and who should deliver the benefits. 'Selectivity' refers to the idea that services, benefits and programmes should be available selectively—that is, to only those people deemed to be in real need. In this framework, social welfare is seen as a safety net, available as a last resort for the less fortunate in Australian society. 'Universality' refers to the notion that services, benefits and programmes should be available universally—that is, to everyone in society, simply by virtue of their status as citizens or residents of Australia. In this framework, social welfare, including such things as pensions, schools and health services, is seen as a right for all, regardless of income or position.

While the theoretical underpinnings of welfare appear to diverge greatly from each other, in practice this may not be the case. That is, public expenditure is not always guided by these general considerations, though they may be drawn upon to justify specific policy developments. Graycar and Jamrozik, for example, point out that as well as including a range of universal provisions available to all income groups, current government policy is selective both in favour of low-income groups and high-income groups.[5]

The allocation of welfare resources is itself determined by wider structural imperatives, and is contingent upon the uneasy relationship between the capital accumulation functions of the state and its welfare component. As Gough pointed out several years ago, the welfare state is contradictory in nature: first, because of its 'repressive, capital-oriented side', and because it embodies real gains won through social conflicts that do, in part, 'enhance welfare'; and second, because the 'very scale of state expenditure on the social services has become a fetter on the process of capital accumulation and economic growth itself'. It means that 'advanced capitalist countries both require but cannot afford a growing level of state intervention in the welfare fields'.[6]

Translated into the concrete practices and the historical vagaries of welfare provision, these contradictions crystallize into the questions of how best to manage state welfare given certain empirical conditions. The issue is often how best to manage welfare and poverty, rather than

---

5   Graycar and Jamrozik, ibid., p. 70.
6   I. Gough, *The political economy of the welfare state*, Macmillan, London, 1979, p. 14.

how to effect structural change or redistribute community resources on egalitarian grounds. To put it differently, the institutionalization of welfare in Australia has been based upon a residual concept of welfare with attempts to temper the deficiencies of the capitalist market by compensating those who cannot get by or who are excluded from the market.

In contemporary Australia constraints on social expenditure are assumed as given because the private market sector is seen as the linchpin of the economy, and is not seen as a proper or desired site for extensive state intervention, control and ownership. For economic rationalists and economic liberals, welfare is constructed in terms of the most disadvantaged in society, and welfare is provided only as a last resort. A hallmark even of social liberalism is that the prized values of universalism and equality are, in practice, always subject to external economic criteria. In either case, the development of social policy tends to be both pragmatic (in that it reflects concerns with immediate, practical problems rather than with wide-scale social change) and contingent (in that it is linked to immediate economic and political circumstances rather than to ideological principles *per se*).

Thus, in a period of economic recession what were seen as universally available services and benefits will usually be, and in the 1990s are being, re-defined in ways that make welfare provision more selective in nature. One of the consequences of a shift from universality to selectivity in particular areas of welfare allocation is that such changes affect the level of popular support for state-provided welfare in general. The legitimacy of the welfare system rests to a certain extent upon universal provision where everyone, including middle-income taxpayers, experience some form of benefit. When this is withdrawn, through more selective targeting of benefits and services, the danger is that resentment and disillusionment with welfare provision will subsequently increase.[7]

The need for and dependency on welfare assistance, and the greater importance of institutional services and facilities (such as schooling) as a means to attain an economic livelihood, are themselves shaped

---

7   F. Castles, 'The economy: Australia's reversible citizenship', *Australian society*, September 1989, pp. 29-30.

by the state's intervention in the economic sphere. Decisions made in these areas have a major impact on the economic well-being of workers, on the level of employment in particular industrial sectors and on the resources available for allocation to social welfare. The agenda of governments in recent years has been to emphasize economic growth rather than full employment, free trade rather than protectionism, and enterprise bargaining or individual contracts rather than centralized wage fixation. Additionally, changes in the amounts of money and the social responsibilities transferred from the federal government to the states have had a marked impact on the nature, accessibility and quality of publicly provided social welfare institutions such as schools, hospitals and transportation systems.

State and territory governments have recently been presented with severe fiscal pressures emanating from reduced federal allocation of grants, transferral of social service responsibilities to the regional level, and longer-term in-house financial mismanagement. The dilemma has become one of how best to manage the costs of historically defined or expanding social need, while simultaneously establishing the localized means to control the likely outcomes of regressive economic policies. The 1993 Victorian budget was notable in this regard: its answer was to engage in significant cuts to health and education, while boosting the monies spent on the police force. Some subsequent financial drawbacks in 1994 in police funding were accompanied by extraordinary extensions of police powers including provisions for taking body samples and using 'reasonable force' on unwilling detainees. Clearly, in this period, business interests and the coercive institutions of the state have taken priority over allocation to developmental social institutions.

The targets of welfare

The welfare state caters to a wide spectrum of social interests through a combination of universalistic and selective service and benefit provisions. If we exclude tax concessions and the like, benefits oriented to the more affluent and the business sector, and public institutions such as education and health which are meant to serve a general constituency, then welfare can, in effect, be seen as a provision for those who are for various reasons excluded from the waged labour-market. The different categories of the out-of-work can be conceptualized in terms of differing degrees of connection with the labour-market, and different levels of responsibility *vis-á-vis* their relationship to paid work.

The state has long identified those people who are defined by their incapacity or diminished capacity to work. Historically this group included the so-called impotent poor, those who because of age, invalidity, illness or situation were deemed to be less responsible for the fact that they cannot participate in the work-force. Those with incapacity to work include (a) the long-term unemployed and those living in chronic or life-cycle poverty such as the aged, widows and invalids, and whose main form of state assistance is the pension or allowance; (b) the short-term unemployed and those people temporarily experiencing a form of crisis poverty (migrants, victims of natural disasters and illness) and who likewise receive pensions or short-term benefits; and (c) those people entrusted by the state with caring for others, for example sole parents and guardians, and those whose assistance takes the form of family allowances, child-disability payments and the like.

A second category of welfare recipients includes those people who do have the capacity, but not the opportunity, to engage in paid work. The response of the state in this instance is to provide benefits and re-entry programmes for those deemed to be more responsible for their own welfare and work prospects. Programmes and benefits are, in turn, differentiated according to the length of time one is outside the labour force (for example, short-time allowances such as Job Search, long-term payments such as Newstart), and are structured to facilitate skill development, motivation and ready insertion back into the paid labour-force. The individual is held responsible to take advantage of any training programmes on offer, and to show that they are indeed diligently trying to find work.

The sexual division of labour also has a bearing on the position and composition of welfare recipients. In particular, women tend to be concentrated in a narrow range of occupations, are over-represented in part-time paid work, and structurally occupy the lower rungs of the workplace and career hierarchies. Simultaneously, the inadequacy of child-care services, the reinforcement of traditional gender roles through various welfare measures, and the tasks socially imposed upon women with regard to caring for the elderly, the young and the sick, structure women's role in society in such a way as to make them less responsible in the sphere of waged work, but more responsible in the sphere of unpaid welfare work. The relationship between the sexual division of labour in the paid and unpaid spheres has a direct bearing on the fact that in Australia women and their dependents are the main beneficiaries of state welfare payments.

A further category of welfare recipients is that of the underclass, those who are defined as having the capacity to work, but who for various reasons cannot find work or lack the motivation to do so. These people are often presented as being irresponsible. The state may assist this category of the out-of-work, but generally assistance is provided through non-government welfare agencies, with indirect financial assistance from the state. It is this category of people which tends to also be most subject to state intervention via such developments as the 1994 Jobs Compact or through its coercive arms—namely, the criminal justice system. Here the issue often has less to do with welfare *per se*, than with social control.

Importantly, the different categories of the out-of-work are fluid from the point of view of changing state definitions of capacity, need and responsibility. This is apparent, for example, in recent changes to the Workcover Scheme in Victoria which in effect reduces the number of people eligible for workers' compensation, and which thereby has implications for the social security system. Similarly, recent 'reforms' regarding disability pensions have been directed at restricting the definitions used for eligibility purposes, partly in order to stem the apparent flow of recipients from one category of the out-of-work (the unemployed) to another (the unemployable). The notions of capacity and responsibility are subject to ongoing negotiation, with the tendency being for the state to define and re-define need primarily in relation to fiscal rather than social criteria.[8]

What I am arguing is that the categorization and management of the out-of-work is contingent upon, and varies according to, long-term economic trends and general employment patterns. The content of welfare

---

8   See, for example, the review of reforms relating to social security payments for people who are ill or have disabilities in a special lift-out 'New disability reforms', *Social welfare impact*, vol. 21, no. 9, 1991.

provision, especially those programmes directed at labour-market re-entry such as the 1994 White Paper, is not merely concerned with meeting the individual needs of the welfare recipient. It is intended to provide a particular kind of work preparation, one which emphasizes the work ethic, compliant attitudes and behaviour, and constant 'busyness' in everyday activities. The targets of welfare are, in essence, meant to comply with the dictates of the welfare provider in terms of how they organize their lives and their daily routines.

Marginalization and the administration of welfare

One of the features of the way in which welfare has been institutionalized in Australian society is that it is frequently linked to the systematic exclusion or marginalization of the out-of-work from the mainstream of social life. Poverty, unemployment and dependency upon welfare 'handouts' involves complex processes of stigmatization and social regulation. Chapman and Cook describe marginalization as:

> a process which ineluctably creates groupings of people who become somehow 'detached', and who feel themselves excluded, from mainstream society. The marginality of certain groups is most plainly expressed in terms of their role in the socio-economic relations of production and reproduction, and their role in the consumption of the goods and services generally available.[9]

To understand fully the processes of marginalization, and the particular groups most likely to experience marginalization collectively and individually, it is necessary to analyse changes in state policy regarding work and industry, family and social services including transportation, and education and training provision. The making of the marginalized is invariably linked to both the structure of community resource allocation (via the market and the state), and the prevailing conceptions of worth and meaning associated with specific modes of activity and lifestyle choices. Importantly, the marginalization of people is also at one and the same time a political marginalization. That is,

---

9   T. Chapman and J. Cook, 'Marginality, youth and government policy in the 1980s', *Critical social policy*, no. 22, 1988, p. 43.

the targets of welfare also tend to be marginal to political power and processes, with little direct access to political parties and trade unions which could provide a forum for the pursuit of organized political and economic objectives.

Marginalization is built into the administration of welfare in a number of ways. Specifically, the conditions of dependency and subordination are reinforced through the methods of resource allocation and the regulatory objectives of the welfare state. The selectivity of welfare assistance is apparent in the wide range of detailed eligibility criteria covering each pension, benefit or allowance. Age, residence, marital status, degree of incapacity, steps taken to find employment, income level and assets held, are variously used in assessing the eligibility and rate of payment.[10] The more stringent tests are those pertaining to unemployment allowances. To be eligible for welfare (in the narrow sense of the term) therefore, one has to be prepared, at the point of application, for a high and increasing level of state testing of eligibility, involving a willingness to provide personal information freely and in documented form.

It also often means a fairly heavy state intrusion into private affairs, depending upon the programme in question. As part of eligibility criteria the welfare recipient tacitly agrees to an unprecedented level of bureaucratic surveillance in their life. Practically speaking, this can manifest itself in requirements that some 'clients', such as the unemployed, have to constantly prove their 'responsibility' through undertaking assigned training programmes and providing proof of active search for jobs. In recent years, the introduction of the Newstart scheme has been accompanied by significant concerns over the power placed with Commonwealth Employment Service officials to stop payments, determine the 'needs' of clients (including personal grooming, residential location and general attitudes), and to demand a 'respect for authority' as part of the benefit criteria. The imposition of obligation, and the intrusion into personal lifestyle, is also seen in recent changes to the Sole Parent benefit. Here a number of assumptions relating to the role and position of women in society—as dependent and responsible for

---

10 P. Hanks, 'Social security pensions and benefits', in *Rights and freedoms in Australia*, eds J. Wallace and T. Pagone, Federation Press, Sydney, 1990.

child care—have been ingrained in the relevant legislation. Significantly, the eligibility rules hinge upon whether or not the recipient is living in a de facto relationship or not. Further, it is presumed that:

> the sole parent is 'guilty' of living in a *de facto* relationship and it is their responsibility to convince the Department otherwise. The result is that the onus of proving the existence or otherwise of a *de facto* relationship has shifted from the DSS to the person in receipt of the sole parent's pension. Clearly, such a shift in the onus of proof discriminates against sole parents.[11]

Once the hurdles of eligibility have been surmounted the level of payment is well below the poverty line in any case. This is because the principle of 'less eligibility' underpins the allocation of welfare payments. That is, it is believed in Australia that people needing welfare assistance, regardless of reason or circumstance, should receive less money than the lowest paid full-time worker. The low level of payment in turn circumscribes the quality of life available to the recipient of state welfare. Social functioning, as Jamrozik explains, 'depends on the provision of, and access to, an adequate quantity and quality of material resources sufficient for the achievement of a certain minimum standard of living and a certain quality of life'.[12] The exclusion of some people from mainstream work, and the powerlessness and lack of status in society associated with this, is compounded by a reduction in their status as consumers and in their ability to improve their life-situation over time. The quality of services available to welfare receivers, their access to such services and the constraints involved in claiming services such as, for example, legal aid, also have consequences for the physical and psychological well-being of those forced into dependency upon the state.

The focus of the welfare system, particularly in recent years, is on administrative efficiency rather than on questions of well-being.

---

11 J. Cabassi, 'Caught in the poverty trap', *Legal service bulletin*, vol. 15, no. 2, 1990, p. 74.
12 A. Jamrozik, 'Winners and losers in the welfare state: recent trends and pointers to the future', in *Social welfare in the late 1980s: reform, progress or retreat?*, eds P. Saunders and A. Jamrozik, Social Welfare Research Centre, Sydney, 1987, p. 48.

The objective of the governmental bureaucracy is to operate within strict financial and regulatory guidelines, as informed by the tenets of economic rationalism.[13] The imposition of new managerial forms in the human services, usually revolving around particular, quantitative performance indicators, and reinforced by extensive procedural rules and regulations regarding who gets what and how, has rendered the system highly selective and overridingly concerned with how best to manage scarce resources. One consequence of this has been to institutionalize the notion that welfare is a privilege, not a right; another has been to reinforce the elements of compulsion and supervision in the allocation system. Further to this, the move to introduce active components such as compulsory training schemes into the system makes it clear that welfare provision is to be based on a deficiency model which focuses blame and responsibility on the individual for their inability to participate in the work-force.

These trends I suggest signal a major change in the nature of the welfare state itself in the Australian context. Specifically, the object of welfare is no longer tied into a project of legitimizing the system as a whole; nor is welfare intended, in the terms of a social liberal perspective, to enhance the well-being and developmental opportunities of citizens. Rather the objective appears simply to be one of holding out against the rising tide of destitution, a condition which has accompanied capitalist restructuring over the last decade or so. While the welfare state has not in the past been associated in any meaningful way with transformative politics, in particular with a socialist programme of social transition, it has at least been grounded in the reformist traditions of social democracy. The last decade, however, has seen the dismantling of both the ideology and practice of the social democratic welfare state. The result has been a leaner, meaner form of welfare provision, one devoid of any pretence to societal enhancement generally. Welfare is no longer something provided for citizens; it is something done to them when they have no other place to go to for help.

---

[13] See M. Considine, 'The costs of increased control: corporate management and Australian community organisation', *Australian social work*, vol. 14, no. 3, 1988, pp. 17-25; M. Sawer, *Sisters in suits: women and public policy in Australia*, Allen & Unwin, Sydney, 1990; and M. Pusey, *Economic rationalism in Canberra: a nation-building state changes its mind*, Cambridge University Press, Melbourne, 1991.

THE POVERTY OF THE WELFARE STATE

The institutional tendency toward a victim-centred focus is very much related to broader systemic imperatives and the creation of poverty itself. The residual nature of welfare, plus state attempts to balance economic and social policy resource-allocation demands, leads to a narrow construction of the poverty problem. For instance, as Jamrozik argues, the current institutional tendency is to relate the existence of inequality to the characteristics of certain population groups rather than to identify the sources of inequality in the market economy and the structures of power in a class-divided society. Jamrozik also points out that the effect of both government and non-government services is not so much one of alleviating poverty but of socializing people into living in poverty.[14] To put this slightly differently, marginalized groups are the objects of state policy, and welfare exacerbates their sense of inferiority and exclusion at the very same time as it enforces a certain kind of dependency and reliance upon the state.

In summary, it can be said that the role and impact of welfare policies and practices need to be evaluated critically insofar as they are designed not to eliminate poverty, but to attempt to accommodate it within the existing political-economic system; not to deal with the causes of poverty, but to attempt to contain it by focussing on the poor themselves and managing the consequences of poverty.

Poverty, unemployment and the underclass

It has been argued to this point that the welfare system itself represents an institutionalization of inequality, and that it does not, and cannot, respond adequately to the needs of people under the existing system of resource allocation. This section looks more closely at the issue of poverty, and in particular the position of the underclass in the structural and ideological context of late-twentieth-century capitalism.

Poverty and unemployment

To be a recipient of welfare is to be poor. But to be poor one does not have to be in receipt of state welfare. The category 'the poor' extends

---

14 A. Jamrozik, *Class, inequality and the state*, Macmillan, Melbourne, 1991.

beyond the welfare system *per se* to include many people who are currently in the waged labour-market. The condition of poverty is centrally defined by one's relationship to the labour-market in terms of employment, under-employment, level of wages, and full-time or part-time work. Just as there are variations in the employment situation of the poor, so too there are important distinctions to be drawn between different sections of the poor, differences in the processes of stigmatization, conceptions of deviancy and the social sanctions directed at them.

At a general level, the position of the poor is subject to much academic debate centring on the measurement of poverty. Less attention appears to be given to the actual experiences of living in poverty, or to the ideological role of the poverty line in separating out the poor from the rest of society.[15] Frequently the issue of poverty is framed in terms of the problem of 'the poor', rather than in the problems of being poor. Disadvantage is seen as a property of the group, rather than a consequence of structural imperatives. Such an attribution misses out on seeing how much the nature and extent of poverty in Australian society at any point in time is both a reflection and consequence of labour-market activity and the development of state policy.

At the heart of the issue of poverty is the relationship between the rich and the poor. This is as much as anything a matter of how the society as a whole allocates community resources and tasks, about who owns and controls the means of production and consumption in society. Within this framework, which in this instance consists of a small number of individuals and groups determining the shape of Australian industry and government policy, there are also variations in the allocation of total community resources. For example, in recent years in Australia there have been significant shifts in the distribution of wealth and income. Lombard found a marked widening of the income gap between 1983 and 1989: the top one per cent of income earners earned as much as the bottom eleven per cent in 1983–84, but in 1989 they earned as much as the bottom 21 per cent. Lombard also found that the gap was further increased by government taxation policy through the lowering of marginal, and hence average, tax rates. The female share of national

---

15 See ibid.

income, relatively low compared with males, had remained stationary.[16] Further evidence of the emergence of a category of the working poor is provided by union statistics on the rates of pay of young workers, and by analyses of the disappearance of middle-income earners accompanied by substantial increases in the number of low-paid workers. Youth wages in the 1980s in fact declined to the extent that the ratio of junior male to adult male wages was the lowest since 1964, and for females it was the lowest since figures were first recorded in 1962.[17] In terms of wage distributions within the work-force, Gregory comments that:

> The rich are getting richer and the poor are getting poorer and not just because of the high rate of unemployment. Since 1976, the highest-paid workers (the top 20 per cent) have had a 6 per cent real-wage increase while the lowest-paid workers (the bottom 20 per cent) have experienced a 10 per cent fall in their real wages.[18]

The last decade has seen a further concentration of wealth in Australia into fewer and fewer hands.[19] One outcome of this redistribution of community resources has been a rise in the overall poverty rate as officially measured. Meanwhile, research based on Morgan Gallup poll results shows that the Henderson poverty line is well below what is considered to be the minimum income required to make ends meet.[20] The main point to be made here is that poverty is a persistent and inherent feature of the current socio-economic structure in Australian society. Poverty levels may fluctuate, but overall the level of chronic, rather than simply temporary, poverty in recent years has burgeoned.

---

16 M. Lombard, *Income distribution in Australia 1983-89*, Macquarie University, Sydney, 1991.
17 Australian Council of Trade Unions, *Youth strategy*, ACTU, Melbourne, 1989.
18 B. Gregory, as quoted in R. Markey, 'New poor emerges as wage gap widens', *West Australian*, 11 June 1992, p. 11. See also M. Eaton and F. Stilwell, 'Ten years hard labor', *Journal of Australian political economy*, no. 31, 1993, pp. 89-105.
19 See A. Dilnot, 'From most to least: new figures on wealth distribution', *Australian society*, July 1990, pp. 14-17; and Australian Catholic Bishops' Conference, *Common wealth for the common good: a statement on the distribution of wealth in Australia*, Collins Dove, Melbourne, 1992.
20 P. Saunders and B. Bradbury, 'Galluping poverty', *Australian society*, September 1989, p. 27.

The unemployed constitute a particular sub-category of those living in poverty. The 1990s have seen official unemployment rates hover around the eleven per cent mark nationally, with regional variations seeing extremely high levels in country areas and in the manufacturing sector of the major urban centres. Unemployment is distributed unevenly and unequally on the basis of class background, ethnicity and race (for example, about 50 per cent of Aboriginal people are unemployed), age (disproportionately affecting young people and older workers), sex (especially in terms of full-time and part-time jobs) and geography. It has been estimated that in 1992 over 300 000 children lived in families dependent on unemployment benefits, and that about one-third of unemployed families lived in poverty.[21]

The novel development of the last couple of decades is that unemployment rates, and hence poverty rates, have remained high, even in periods of job growth. It has been pointed out, for example, that even though in the mid-1980s there was a massive growth of 1.6 million jobs in Australia, the 'seasonally adjusted unemployment rates did not dip below 7 per cent of the labour force for the greater part of the 1980s; despite the growth of job opportunities over this period'.[22] The level and extent of unemployment has thus proved to exhibit a particularly entrenched character, with no real prospects for change on the horizon. The problem of unemployment, while having cyclical dimensions, both in terms of seasonal employment patterns and up-turns and down-turns in the business cycle, is structurally linked to long-term changes in the methods of production (especially as affected by microchip technology) and the globalization of production. This has had a major impact on class relations, and on economic and social conditions for large numbers of workers, in Australia as elsewhere.[23] And it places new pressures on the state.

In the context of very high levels of unemployment, the emerging issue in political circles is that of the duration of unemployment and

---

21 Australian Council of Social Services, 'A day of action on unemployment', special insert, *Social welfare impact*, vol. 22, no. 4, 1992, p. 2.
22 V. Sheen and J. Trethewey, *Unemployment in the recession: policies for reform*, Brotherhood of St. Laurence, Melbourne, 1991, p. 11.
23 See B. Probert, 'Restructuring and globalization: what do they mean?', *Arena magazine*, April-May 1993, pp. 18-22.

THE POVERTY OF THE WELFARE STATE

the consequences this may have on things such as the work ethic, maintenance of social order and effective use of human resources. For example, government ministers have been recently expressing concern about an estimated 500 000 people who would have been out-of-work for over one year.[24] If we take the case of young people specifically, it is significant that the average length of time a young person is unemployed has increased from 2.9 weeks in 1966 to 25.1 weeks in 1991.[25]

In addition to the question of duration of unemployment, there is the issue of the discouraged unemployed worker. It was reported in February 1993 that more than two million Australians who wanted to work were without a job.[26] The Bureau of Statistics survey also recognized the status of some 146 000 people who were classified as 'discouraged job-seekers', those who had given up looking for work because they were convinced that they would not get a job. In general, the survey found that the number of women, usually low-skilled and mothers, who were discouraged from seeking paid work had doubled during the recession period; that the number of males had likewise doubled; and that a disproportionate number were migrants from English and non-English-speaking countries alike. Issues such as being rejected for being too old or too young, no jobs in suitable hours, being caught in poverty traps, and no jobs in their line of work were cited as reasons for becoming part of the 'hidden jobless'.

As in the case of poverty and the poor, state and public concern over the presence and activities of the unemployed has been conditioned by, but lagged significantly behind, the extent and distribution of unemployment. Changes occurred as unemployment affected many households via their children, and as retrenchments cut across all

---

[24] From an economist's viewpoint, Chapman estimated that if unemployment rose to 12.4 per cent by the end of 1994, the number of long-term unemployed would reach 530 000. See B. Chapman, 'Long-term unemployment: the dimensions of the problem', *The Australian economic review*, 2nd quarter, 1993, pp. 22-5.

[25] Australian Youth Policy and Action Coalition, *A living income: income support for young people*, Youth Action and Policy Association (NSW), Sydney, 1992, p. 15. See also, K. Larwill, *Unemployed Australia: a resource book*, Brotherhood of St Laurence, Melbourne, 1992.

[26] See T. Colebatch, 'Two million want jobs', *The age*, 23 February 1993, p. 1.

industrial sectors, occupations and skill-divides.[27] In this context the ordinary unemployed person is no longer seen in the pejorative terms of the dole bludger. Rather, the category of the ordinary unemployed is seen to be made up of respectable people going through tragic or extraordinary circumstances. Nevertheless, there are an increasing number among the unemployed, particularly among the long-term unemployed, who are being defined as outside of the ordinary and are being seen as problematic or troublesome. It is these people who will most overtly experience the emerging state of social control.

The visibility of the problem of long-term unemployment coupled with the sheer economic costs to the government have generated varying responses on the part of the state. After years of sustained high levels of unemployment, the Labor Government finally moved in 1993 to instigate a public investigation and analysis of the issues in the form of a White Paper on (Un)Employment. The thrust of the White Paper was evident in government policy at least a year before it was published. The government began using the rhetoric of the work ethic and the 'social divide' between worker and non-worker as a means to justify a tougher approach to benefit provision. As the former Minister for Employment, Education and Training, Kim Beazley, stated in September 1993:

> We're moving toward the concept of obligation. That is, after a period of time out of work there is an obligation on the government to provide training and work-related opportunities and an obligation on those receiving benefits to take them. We're getting to identify the great deal of work that is available there in the community which will never be done unless active measures are taken to ensure it's done. Increasingly, unemployment benefits will be a wage subsidy for participation in this type of work. We're not talking about digging holes and filling them in again. We're talking about things that will be useful for the community—both on the physical side and the white-collar side. Underpinning these considerations is the need to make the long-term unemployed competitive for getting back into the work-force.[28]

---

27 Sheen and Trethewey, *Unemployment in the recession*.
28 K. Beazely quoted in D. Macken, 'Benefit of the doubt: rethinking the dole', *Good weekend*, 18 September 1993, p.38. See also Commonwealth of Australia, *Working nation: policies*

THE POVERTY OF THE WELFARE STATE

Translated, this means that the long-term unemployed will not be allowed an 'easy' road in terms of the claiming of benefits or choice in how or where they will use their labour-power. Interestingly, some of the provisions of the 1994 White Paper were hinted at in the 1993 Budget papers. Without much fanfare or media attention we saw the introduction of tougher work-test arrangements. As one newspaper report commented: 'The tougher measures are part of a broader push by the Government to save more than $40 million a year by getting 80 000 benefit recipients, off the dole.'[29] Thus, a fiscal imperative to reduce expenditure is at the heart of attempts to reduce the number of claimants via more rigorous testing and surveillance procedures. While such measures may be presented as being neutral from the point of view of bureaucratic organization and administrative logic, other attacks on the long-term unemployed have been constructed ideologically in more overt fashion. Here the direction of state intervention is not only towards the reactive management of need, but is pro-active, moving towards the control of the needy. In particular, it is the underclass which is presented as a problem crying out for a special kind of solution.

The 'underclass'

At least initially, the underclass can be conceived as a further sub-category of the unemployed. It can be seen to involve a combination of an objective position of exclusion from the labour-market and/or state welfare provision, and a subjective dimension of experience in terms of general social attitudes, values and behaviour which are deemed to be disrespectful or anti-social.

The underclass has been created by a series of inter-connected factors and trends. These include most prominently factors which relate to the state:
- inadequacies at a macro-economic policy level: namely, the failures and limitations of state action with regard to industrial policy and job creation;

---

and programs, AGPS, Canberra, 1994.
29 D. McKenzie, 'Tougher work tests to slash dole payments', *The age*, 24 August 1993, p. 1.

- inadequacies at a social policy level: namely, the low current level of benefits and allowances, cuts in and limited access to social support services, and the adoption of remedial rather than preventive social and economic measures;
- the repressive or coercive aspects of welfare provision: the multitude of work, income, asset, lifestyle and attitude tests required to establish eligibility and the level of state welfare support, the stigmatization and moralizing that can accompany government and non-government welfare provision;
- the effect of social reaction on behaviour and attitudes: for example, being treated with suspicion by police and others because of one's status as non-consumers.

The objective and subjective dimensions of the category underclass can be illustrated by contrasting different categories of unemployed people on the basis of their relationship to the labour-market.[30] Where the unemployed do not, for whatever reason, see themselves in terms of labour-market preparation and possible insertion back into the dominant relations of production, they will often be seen in terms of underclass terminology. The unemployed can broadly be divided therefore into two main groups: those who are marginal to the labour-market and those who are excluded from it.

The first group includes those people who by virtue of their age, skills or disability are ineffective in competing for jobs, who are outside the labour-market because they lack marketability. These people suffer systematic disadvantage in the market. At an experiential level, they nevertheless maintain an interest in getting jobs and thus state policies relating to education and training are central to their lifestyle and efforts to become part of the employed.

The second group, comprising those excluded from the labour-market, includes people who are excluded through a combination of long-term unemployment, inadequate work histories and declining motivation to compete in apparently hopeless circumstances. The people in each of these groups have a different relationship to the state.

---

30 See L. Morris and S. Irwin, 'Employment histories and the concept of the under-class', *Sociology*, vol. 26, no. 3, 1992, pp. 401-20.

Stringent hurdles in the claiming of state support, for example, the Newstart Allowance which demands active job search and active job preparation, constitute rules of inclusion and exclusion in relation to state welfare provision. For those who play by the established rules of the game the reward is a meagre sum with which to achieve a modicum of physical survival. However, for those who persistently find it difficult to succeed within the terms of the policy agenda, those who, for example, find that more training does not necessarily guarantee greater employability, who refuse to accept the notion that welfare resources exist principally as a 'privilege' rather than a right, or who exhibit high degrees of alienation, resentment and loss of faith in themselves or the system, the status of being part of the underclass is an increasing reality in Australia. For it is the 'habitual' and long-term unemployed who are seen as a threat to the economic fibre of the nation; it is the 'culturally impoverished' and 'socially deviant' unemployed who are seen to threaten the standards of decency and respectability in society. As a sub-grouping of the poor and the unemployed, the underclass thus appears as a highly visible blight on the social landscape and an unnecessary drain on public and private resources.

The state is organized around institutions primarily defined in terms of development (for example, education, health) and coercion (for example, police, courts, prisons). What distinguishes each is the use or threat of force in the exercise of its functions. The use of state repression against the underclass is symbolically important in terms of keeping the dissatisfied and dispossessed in line, in fragmenting the working class politically, and in deflecting attention from the structural role of both the state and of capital in reproducing poverty and marginalization. Hence, the demise of the social state is intertwined with the increasing prominence of the repressive state. Justificatory defences of the adoption of tougher welfare approaches and law and order politics as a solution to social marginalization are woven into the discourses used to define, describe and categorize the underclass. A complex ideological self-justification is currently in train—one which is aimed at winning consent ideologically for the use of coercion institutionally. And the underclass is at the centre of this project.

In popular terms the underclass has been described as the permanent poor. In its inclusive formulation, the term has included a very wide spectrum of people, from urban street-kids and the homeless through to single mothers and middle-aged unemployed family men. The wide definition sees the underclass as exhibiting characteristics such as severe income deprivation, unstable employment, low skills, persistent and often intergenerational poverty, limited access to social institutions, high incidence of health problems, crime, and drug abuse. Very often the key criteria is simply that of exclusion from the paid work-force.

However, there is another type of description which over-lays the general category.[31] Here membership of the underclass is defined politically, with an emphasis on both agency and structure. Left perspectives on the underclass, for example, emphasize the status of certain people as caught up in structural processes and dislocations. The underclass is seen as part of, not separated from, the wider class structure. It is conceived as a disposable reserve army of labour, as relative surplus population to the needs of capital. The activities of the underclass stem from the alienation and restricted choices associated with transformations in the wider political-economic structure.

The view from the Right concentrates less on structural position than on the behaviour of members of the underclass. This is a narrower definition of underclass, close in some ways to the distinction made above with respect to groupings within the unemployed. The emphasis here is on the 'choices' made by these people, their destructive anti-social behaviour and the fact that they are largely undeserving of state support and unwanted in society. It is argued that members of the underclass have a dependency culture, that they are trapped by welfare. From this perspective the underclass is to be criticized for its behaviour, and its members penalized for the fact that they are chronically out-of-work. In essence, this position sees the underclass as largely responsible for its own plight. It is a blame-the-victim perspective.

Ideologically, recent portrayals of the underclass have functioned, inadvertently or otherwise, to shift public opinion against the most marginalized, dispossessed sections of the population. For example, in an article written for an Australian audience regarding the Rodney King case and the Los Angeles riots, Murray argued that two things have happened since the 1960s:

---

31 F. Robinson and N. Gregson, 'The "underclass": a class apart?', *Critical social policy*, vol. 12, no. 1, 1992, pp. 38-51.

First, blacks began to behave in ways that scared and angered whites. Some of these ways of acting affected whites only second-hand, creating a festering irritation that made whites less sympathetic towards blacks—the rise in illegitimacy, black youths dropping out of work, inner-city fads and customs and sexual norms that many adult whites found distasteful, immoral or both. But the tangible and pervasive change that quite directly affected whites was the skyrocketing black crime rate. It was not just the increase in numbers of crimes, it was the nature of the increase: violent crimes. Robbery. Assault. Rape. Homicide. White crime climbed, too, but remained at a much lower absolute level and was much less violent.[32]

The article went on to argue that blacks had been given a number of advantages over the last twenty years, to no avail. It finished with the comment that 'it is not the old style of racism to conclude that the present problems of the black community owe more to black behaviour that to white oppression'.[33]

The themes of dangerousness, irresponsibility, immorality and self-blame run through popular accounts of the Australian underclass as well. For example, in a major piece in the *Bulletin*, Crisp informed the reader that the problem is not simply one of being poor, but of values and behaviour:

> What is intriguing, and even more worrying, is the gradual emergence of a new substratum: a breed of young people who expect society to provide them with the lifestyle of their choice without giving anything back. They feel no obligation to work and thumb their noses at most traditional social structures: they are a problem for society but not for themselves.[34]

After a discussion of issues ranging from mutilation murders and drugs to the culture of poverty, Crisp quotes at length the views of Annie Crowe and Ian Hood who run the Kings Cross Youth Resources Ltd. The main message is of the bad attitudes, and the choices that young people make to be part of the underclass. According to Crowe:

---

32 C. Murray, 'Underclass: from liberal guilt to awkward questions', *Weekend Australian*, 16-17 May 1992, p. 21.
33 ibid.
34 L. Crisp, 'The underclass: Australia's social time bomb', *Bulletin*, 3 April 1990, p. 48.

The underclass is not a question of money or background. Opportunities have been there, are there. It's a question of attitude, some people like to live on the edge: a very risky lifestyle, where they've got fingers in a bit of prostitution, drugs, bit of dealing, bit of crime. They'll be fairly footloose, moving round from place to place, take on a series of casual relationships, get themselves involved in all sorts of peculiar and nefarious activities. Marry a Chinese for the money. It means nothing to them.[35]

For Crowe, young members of the underclass are on the street because their personalities are predisposed to the lifestyle. Again, the element of 'choice' is foremost in this type of description:

If these young people wanted to, it would be easy for them to make it in a straight world. They're very good manipulators, con people, they know how to use their physical assets to great advantage and are often highly seductive in their behaviour. They are intelligent with an insight to human nature that can floor you. With these qualities they could not only survive in the business world but do well. They just don't want to.[36]

So, the underclass is characterized by lack of control, engagement in violent crime, laziness and lack of motivation to participate in paid work or the world of straight society.[37]

From such perspectives the notion of underclass is constructed as a moral category. Members of the underclass are presented as morally corrupt and as a group to be disciplined and reformed. A distinction is being made, therefore, between the virtuous poor—those who have healthy attitudes toward self-improvement and a conventional lifestyle, and who submit easily to state criteria for welfare assistance—and the vicious poor, those who lack industry and the work ethic, who are idle, wanderers and display little respect for authority. It is the deserving poor who are the objects of state welfare; the undeserving are left to

---

35 ibid., p. 51.
36 ibid., p. 52.
37 For a more in-depth discussion of media portrayals of the 'underclass' in the Australian context, see I. Watson, 'The ideology of the underclass and the reality of the working poor', in *Theory and practice in Australian social policy*, (vol. 3), eds Peter Saunders and Sheila Shaw, SPRC, Sydney, 1993. On the 'underclass' and the welfare system, see J. Rodger, 'The welfare state and social closure: social division and the "underclass"', *Critical social policy*, no. 35, 1992, pp. 45-63.

fetch for themselves or to search out assistance from non-government charitable institutions. It is a familiar theme through the history of the Australian welfare state: the difference now is that the underclass is becoming a significant structural category in Australian society.

The marginalization of this section of the working class also brings them into the purview of a state which has extended its means of surveillance to new levels. It is the perceived behavioural threat from the emerging underclass which has informed various law and order policies and which partly shapes the way in which law enforcement agencies operate in relation to the unemployed. This kind of approach to dealing with members of the underclass focuses on kinds of behaviour rather than on social conditions giving rise to or providing meaningfulness to that behaviour. The strong arm of the state is precisely aimed at the new 'dangerous classes' of late capitalism. Everywhere they go, members of the underclass are treated with suspicion and fear. This reaction manifests itself in the form of increased regulation of public space and public activity, and calls for increased police powers to move the 'riffraff' from the streets, shopping centres and malls.[38]

The impact of pervasive and strong official intervention into the lives of members of the underclass, plus the prior difficulties of economic hardship, low self-esteem, few social resources and general boredom, associated with exclusion from the spheres of production and consumption, makes for an explosive mix of creative survival skills and rebelliousness, desperation and anger. The existential dilemmas of many of those on the margins of society reduces the probability that they will care for either the 'legitimate' institutions of society or those who wield the sanctions designed to protect the interests of the propertied and the respectable.

Concluding remarks

Recent years have seen a marked shift in the orientation and objectives of the welfare state. The agenda is no longer focussed upon political

---

[38] See, for example, R. White, 'Street life: police practices and youth behaviour', in *The police and young people in Australia*, eds R. White and C. Alder, Cambridge University Press, Melbourne, 1994.

legitimation and social redistribution, but is characterized by greater allocation of community resources to capital accumulation and an emphasis on managing more efficiently those who have been excluded from the structure of work. Within the orbit of welfare provision, the system has become ever more selective and regulatory. The compulsory aspects of the Newstart contract, the monitoring of welfare beneficiaries via Social Security review teams, the periodic interrogation of sole parent claimants and so on, constitute ongoing harassment for many of the poor and unemployed. The precarious nature of survival means that many people will be loathe to jeopardize their welfare income through bringing themselves to the attention of state officials.

The regime of state welfare and private-charity selectivity also means that many recipients are forced into artificial 'busyness'. Furthermore, as the relief work programmes of the 1890s and 1930s have shown, and as reflected in talk of 'work for the dole' and 'compulsory national service' today, the state will intervene to organize the labour and activity of the unemployed in ways which are meant to minimize potential disruption of the social order.

The state, usually at the provincial and local council level, has had to deal also with the deficiencies of the market by attempting to deal with those outside official welfare provision. This has been spearheaded by various ideological campaigns which scapegoat the marginalized. The movement from welfare to the criminalization of the poor is evident in vigorous efforts to 'clean up the streets' and to impose order in the urban landscape. A general climate of moral panic and public fear contributes to the further ostracizing the underclass. Simultaneously the brutalization and dispossession of greater numbers of people in Australia will undoubtedly give rise to a wide spectrum of anti-social and self-destructive behaviour.

The marginalization of a growing proportion of Australians economically, socially and politically stems from the effects of capitalist restructuring on a global scale and deep transformations in the form of the state. State power itself has been steadily centralized in recent years through a combination of corporatist political arrangements involving trade-union bureaucracy, government and business, and the adoption of corporate management administrative models in the running

THE POVERTY OF THE WELFARE STATE

of public services and agencies.[39] These kinds of developments have been described by Poulantzas as aspects of a trend toward authoritarian statism.[40] According to Poulantzas, trends involving the capitalist state include such phenomena as a growth in repression and the use of real and symbolic violence, the playing up of authoritarian themes such as law and order, the concentration of real power in government and administrative structures, and the shift in formal state power away from parliament to unelected bodies. He also points out the growing distance between political democracy and socio-economic democracy. That is, large sections of the population are not only disenfranchised from the economy and adequate living conditions, but their participation in the institutions of political democracy is increasingly fragile as well.

The marginalization and disenfranchisement of sizeable and identifiable groups of people in Australian society raises big questions about the long-term stability of the social system. The stigmatization and systematic interventions into the lives of the most vulnerable sections of the working class carries with it the seeds of potential social explosion and unrest, as well as alienated behaviour at a personal level. The examples of Los Angeles, Tyneside and Redfern—all sites for recent 'riots'—provide an indication of the tensions brewing in particular neighbourhoods and among specific groups of people.[41] In each case the triggering agents have been similar: poverty, police abuse and racial marginalization. Addressing the issues and problems of the underclass is fundamentally a matter of political choices. At the level of principles and practical proposals, the answers to issues such as poverty, unemployment and the formation of an underclass are fairly straightforward. A realistic, humane and positive response to marginalization would have to be built upon a series of interrelated

---

39 R. White, 'Corporatism, social welfare and the state', in *Social policy in Australia: what future for the welfare state?*, (vol. 3), ed. A. Jamrozik, Social Policy Research Centre, Sydney, 1990.
40 N. Poulantzas, *State, power, socialism*, Verso, London, 1978.
41 See M. Davis, *City of quartz: excavating the future in Los Angeles*, Verso, London, 1990; C. Cunneen, *Aboriginal-police relations in Redfern: with special reference to the 'police raid' of 8 February 1990*, Human Rights and Equal Opportunity Commission, Sydney, 1990; and E. Conway, 'Digging into disorder: some initial reflections on the Tyneside riots', *Youth and policy*, no. 37, pp. 4-14.

planks which included the active role of the state. Briefly, these might include:

- Greater action in the area of re-distribution of community resources. The right to the means of life should not be contingent upon activity but be based on need. For both the working poor and the unemployed, there is a greater need to increase social resources such that physical survival and enhanced social functioning are guaranteed institutionally.
- Concerted action on employment and job creation. The right to work can be concretely grounded in policies which recognize the transformation of paid work in the late twentieth century, the essential creativity and necessity of labour in the self-worth of human beings, and the necessity to involve all members of society in the carrying out of tasks essential to preserving and improving the social and natural environment.
- Acknowledgment of the importance of community space in the construction of social life. The right to space of one's own means that there needs to be greater community control over privately owned areas which have a high public usage, such as shopping centres.
- Greater community input and involvement in local neighbourhood decision-making, and in public service provision. The right to accountability is crucial in the case of institutions and agencies such as social services and the police.
- Greater protection from state intrusion and denial of human rights. The protection and expansion of civil and human rights is vitally important in terms of due process procedures in welfare administration and policing practices, and in guaranteeing freedom from coercive state programmes based upon forced labour.

Such demands are, however, clearly strategic in nature. That is, each challenges the logic and direction of present trends relating to the operation of the welfare state in Australia. They provide a platform to contest ideas at a political level, and to make problematic the issues of democracy, power and class interests in the creation and maintenance of social division and inequality.

THE POVERTY OF THE WELFARE STATE 137

It is working-class men and women of many ethnic backgrounds who are suffering the brunt of economic restructuring and welfare cuts and reconstruction. The key debates over welfare in the 1990s will ultimately have to make reference to the demands of those who want to build a society that is inclusive rather than exclusive of people, and which sees the meeting of social needs, under collective control, as more important than sustaining a system based upon private profit for the few. Sustained attempts to socialize people to live in poverty, and attempts to control those who refuse to abide by the rules of the system, will in the end make for a society where, for many, life will be short, nasty and brutal—and the rest will gain little comfort from the knowledge that, from behind the security of their urban fortresses, they at least will not have to rely upon welfare handouts for their livelihood.

6

Australian feminism and the state: practice and theory

Ann Curthoys

> If we change the norms of political behaviour it could help overthrow the system; if we play with the boys but refuse to play by their rules, the game may suffer a severe change.
>
> Eva Cox, 1974

> To put it simply, while women are unlikely to achieve equality through the operations of the state, they are even less likely to buy it through the marketplace.
>
> Sara Dowse, 1984

> It is both a paradox and a liability for women that what rights they enjoy are conferred by the State.
>
> Anna Yeatman 1994[1]

Many people have remarked on one outstanding feature of Australian feminism: its close interaction with the agencies of the state as a means of achieving its ends, a much closer interaction than in otherwise comparable societies like the USA and Great Britain. This significant engagement has meant not only fighting politically for appropriate reform legislation, but also direct feminist involvement in state bureaucracies as policy advisers and implementers. Books and articles attempting

---

1. Eva Cox, 'Politics aren't nice', *Refractory girl*, no. 7, Summer 1974-75, p. 30; Sara Dowse, 'The bureaucrat as usurer', in *Unfinished business: social justice for women in Australia*, ed. Dorothy Broom, George Allen & Unwin, Sydney, 1984, p. 143; Anna Yeatman, 'Women and the state', in *Contemporary Australian feminism*, ed. Kate Pritchard Hughes, Longman Cheshire, Melbourne, 1994, p. 187.

to assess and theorize this history have been appearing since the early 1980s, with something of a flood around 1989–91. In this debate, only some aspects of 'the state'—those to do with social justice, redistribution, and protection from violence—generally come under close feminist scrutiny. Feminist interest has been very much focused upon questions of social policy, and rather less upon questions of democratic process and representation, though this is now changing rapidly as feminists take up other questions, from women's representation in parliament to the gendering of the military state.[2] My discussion addresses three themes: the successes and failures of modern feminism's engagement with the state; the relationship between feminism, liberalism and democracy; and the ways in which recent preoccupations with postmodernism, republicanism and colonialism have affected feminist political and theoretical discourse.[3]

Feminists enter the state 1970–94

The women's liberation movement, when it came to prominence in early 1970, did not initially seek to influence the state from within. Based on a far-left socialist tradition, its ideas and organizational skills were honed in the anti-Vietnam-war movement, and its prevailing philosophy and rhetoric were revolutionary. Early women's liberation

---

[2] For an excellent discussion of the question of women and the military, see Eleanor Hancock, 'Women, combat, and the military', in *Women and the state: Australian perspectives*, ed. Renate Howe, La Trobe University Press, Melbourne, 1993, pp. 88-98.

[3] This essay is the product of a long-standing interest, and as a consequence some of the ideas mentioned here are developed somewhat differently in earlier publications. Some of the ideas in this chapter were first expressed in a review article in *Arena*, no. 93, 1990, pp. 153-61. Other related earlier essays include 'Doing it for themselves: the women's movement since 1970' in *Gender relations in Australian history: domination and negotiation*, eds Kay Saunders and Raymond Evans, Harcourt, Brace, Jovanovich, Sydney, 1992, pp. 425-48; 'Feminism, citizenship, and national identity', *Feminist review*, no. 44, 1993, pp. 19-38; and 'Australian feminism since 1970' in *Australian feminism: questions for the nineties*, eds Ailsa Burns and Norma Grieve, OUP, Melbourne, 1994. For their assistance in the process of developing these ideas, I wish to thank the following: Judith Brett, editor of *Arena*; the Australian Historical Association, at whose conference on 30 September 1992 I delivered an earlier version of this paper, and especially the people who contributed to the valuable discussion after the paper; and the Monash University Politics Department, to whom I delivered a seminar on some of these issues in May 1993. I particularly wish to thank Carol Johnson for her valuable and dissenting comments on earlier drafts.

theory was strongly influenced by Marxism, but quickly developed some rather non-Marxist characteristics. There was a tension within women's liberation theory between, on the one hand, an awareness derived from the Marxist and New-Left influence in the movement of the class (and to some extent, ethnic) differences between women, and on the other hand, a feminist assertion of their unity in oppression.

The new movement engaged in direct forms of public protest, seeking to influence the state from *without*. A major political campaign was initiated for women's right of access to safe and cheap abortion. Other forms of activity included 'consciousness-raising' (small-group discussion), cultural expression through writing and other media, and political theorizing, debate and argument. The main aim was to change consciousness; party and parliamentary politics were not, for most, an appropriate or effective option.

The movement itself changed, however, within a very short time. Within two years of the establishment of women's liberation groups, the first serious inroad into parliamentary politics was made with the establishment of the Women's Electoral Lobby (WEL). Through its participation in the federal election campaign in 1972, it placed feminist demands on the wider political agenda. WEL grew directly from women's liberation groups in Victoria, but quickly developed a far more direct emphasis on attempting to achieve change through pressure on the existing political parties. It was able to place pressure most successfully on the Australian Labor Party, and seems to have assisted its success. The newly-elected Whitlam Labor government knew it had to take on board the demands that WEL had made during the campaign.

With an active women's movement and a reforming Labor government, there was a period of rapid change in relation to the feminist agenda in the years 1973 to 1975. Some of these changes, such as Commonwealth provision of child care, had been in train before the Labor government was elected, but it consolidated and extended them. Others were genuine Labor government initiatives. The Whitlam government had several aspects to its approach: it set up new systems of policy advice, tackled entrenched forms of sexual discrimination through legislation, and provided significant public funding of women's services.[4]

It began by instituting new policy advice structures. In April 1973, amid much publicity, Elizabeth Reid was appointed to assist the Prime Minister on women's issues, and with this appointment the modern femocrat phenomenon was born. As Marian Sawer points out, in the decade that followed Reid's appointment, the number of femocrats rose markedly, many of those who had been short listed for the women's adviser position in 1973 subsequently entering the bureaucracy in a range of departments. When in July 1974 a Women's Affairs section was established in the Department of Prime Minister and Cabinet, feminists such as Lyndall Ryan and Sara Dowse were appointed.

The Government's policy of providing funds for community initiatives in setting up new services could, feminists soon realized, include women's services—refuges for battered women, health and rape crisis centres, and so on. This sudden opportunity to gain government funds for feminist projects posed some tricky problems. For those in WEL, or from an active Labor Party background, it was relatively easy to adapt to the new situation and seek government funding for feminist purposes. But for those from further to the left, suspicious of the Labor Party from the anti-war movement of the 1960s and averse to any kind of involvement with the capitalist state, the contradictions were sharper. One might be sacrificing long-term independence and critical distance for short-term gain; one might be 'co-opted', made too moderate or prepared to compromise. Worse still, there was the danger that feminists in the refuges and health centres that sprang up all over the country were providing cheap, or even free, dedicated labour for services that ought to be fully government-funded. These agonizings found expression in the pages of the Sydney-based feminist journal *Refractory girl*, and are still being debated today.[5]

But such doubts soon affected only a minority. Most feminists, whether of socialist or social democratic persuasion, came to feel that real change towards a feminist direction was indeed possible through the agency of the state. The state came to be seen as a means to

---

4   Carol Johnson, 'Whose consensus? women and the ALP', *Arena*, no. 93, 1990, pp. 85-104.
5   For a detailed discussion of this debate, see Marian Sawer, 'Feminism and the state', in *Refracting voices: feminist perspectives from Refractory girl*, special issue, Refractory Girl Publications, Sydney, 1993.

supplement women's access to market-earned income, especially through additional and better employment rights and access to child-care services, and to a lesser extent through the provision of direct welfare benefits.

Despite the Whitlam government's pro-feminist initiatives, feminist concerns were an easy victim to the government's agenda of public-sector restraint when the economy deteriorated in 1974–75. As Carol Johnson argues, gender issues were seen as not relevant to the problems of a capitalist economy in recession, and the prime focus was maintaining class harmony in difficult circumstances.[6] The fall of the Labor government in November 1975 led to a further slowing down of change and reform at the federal level. Nevertheless, most of the major gains of the Whitlam years were consolidated, and there were some important developments in several states. The process of creating women's, indeed feminist, policy positions continued under the new coalition (Fraser) government, which in 1976 made the Women's Affairs Branch the nucleus of a network of women's policy units in various departments. The pattern emerged that the women's movement made most headway under Labor governments, at either state or federal level, and, while experiencing some setbacks when Liberal governments came in, was frequently able to maintain and at times extend gains even under less sympathetic governments.[7]

To take just one example, this pattern is strikingly evident in the case of equal employment opportunity. After the achievement of the Arbitration Commission's Equal Pay decision in December 1972, the women's movement increasingly attempted to achieve, through the agency of the state, equal opportunity in employment. And indeed it did make real headway in changing both attitudes and practices connected with employment within the public sector.[8] Progress was made more easily at the state than federal level, especially, but not only, in states with Labor governments: Labor-led South Australia led off with a Sex Discrimination Act in 1975, and Labor-led New South Wales and Liberal-led Victoria followed in 1977 with an Anti-Discrimination Act and Equal Opportunities Act respectively. The New South Wales Act

---

6 Johnson, ibid., pp. 94–5.
7 For more detailed discussion of this point, see my 'Doing it for themselves'.
8 Hester Eisenstein, *Gender shock*, Allen & Unwin, Sydney, 1990, chapter 5.

was amended in 1980 to give it more teeth, establishing the Office of the Director of Equal Opportunity in Public Employment, an office with considerable powers. Many feminist activists became the equal opportunity officers required by the Act, while countless more served on equal opportunity committees within their places of work. Queensland, under National Party governments during the 1980s, did not follow suit until the election of the Goss Labor government in November 1989. An Anti-Discrimination Act and an Equal Opportunity in Public Employment Act brought Queensland into line with other states, with indeed a broader mandate.[9]

In both Thatcher's Britain and Reagan's United States, two important reference points for Australian feminism, the 1980s was a difficult decade for feminist reform. It prompted the thesis of a 'backlash', articulated for a mass audience in 1992 by Susan Faludi in her best-selling book *Backlash: the undeclared war against women*.[10] In Australia during the same period, however, the feminist agenda fared reasonably well. A major political change was the growing importance of women in extra-parliamentary and parliamentary politics. Women became better represented in parliament, including at ministerial level, their representation between 1979 and 1990 in state parliaments rising from 4.8 to 11 per cent, and in federal parliament from 3.2 to 12.5 per cent.[11] It came to be assumed there should be at least one woman in cabinet, and at the end of the decade women even became state premiers in Western Australia and Victoria, although for fairly short terms. Women became more significant at the extra-parliamentary level as well: in local government, in the mass peace movement of the early 1980s, and in the growing environmental movement.

Labor regained power federally with the election of the Hawke government in 1983 on a platform of social harmony, an Accord between business and trade unions, and economic restructuring with trade union

---

9   Barbara Sullivan, 'Women and the current Queensland state government', *Hecate*, vol. 19, no. 1, 1992, pp. 8-26.
10 I discuss the inapplicability of Faludi's backlash thesis to Australia in 'Women with attitude: the feminisms of Faludi and Wolf', *Arena magazine*, no. 2, January 1993, pp. 48-51.
11 Office of the Status of Women, Department of the Prime Minister and Cabinet, 'National agenda for women: mid-term implementation report on the 1988-92 five year action plans', August, 1990, p.87, quoted in Anne Summers, *Damned whores and god's police*, revised edition, Penguin, Ringwood, 1994, p. 48.

participation and consent. An emphasis on the 'social wage' was to lay the basis for wage restraint, and hence increased investment and greater competitiveness on world markets. In keeping with this notion of a social wage harnessing social-justice issues to economic restructuring and development, the Hawke Labor governments sought to mainstream the feminist agenda. In the early years of the Hawke era a number of developments occurred: annual Women's Budget Statements were developed to assess economic and budgetary policy against feminist criteria; the Office of the Status of Women was upgraded in status and power by its return to the Prime Minister's Department from which it had been relegated by the Fraser government in 1977; the number of publicly assisted child-care places was substantially upgraded; and the national Sex Discrimination Act and Affirmative Action (Equal Opportunity for Women) Act were passed.

Yet by 1987 the Hawke government was moving very fast in the direction of economic rationalism. The conjunction of a social-democratic commitment to using governmental power to redress sexual and other inequality with an increased emphasis on reducing economic protection and regulation posed new problems for feminist strategy. One response was to harness feminist arguments to economic rationalist causes, as in the case of the child-support scheme. The scheme collects maintenance payments from non-custodial parents through the tax system, thus applying, as Anna Yeatman puts it, a 'user pays' principle to parenting.[12] More generally, a feminist economic rationalism sought to argue that sex discrimination is economically inefficient: a healthy capitalist economy requires not patriarchy but sexual equality. An alternative feminist response was to argue against economic rationalist principles on social and ethical grounds. There must continue to be a place, feminists like Marian Sawer argue, for visions of social justice, fairness and equality secured by the state against the relentlessly inegalitarian market. A society based on a free market alone will feel no accountability to women or anyone else.[13]

With the replacement of Bob Hawke by Paul Keating late in 1991

---

12 Yeatman, 'Women and the state', p. 179.
13 Marian Sawer, 'Reclaiming social liberalism: the women's movement and the state', in *Women and the state*, ed. Howe, p. 21.

and the re-election of the Keating government in 1993, the process of economic restructuring, deregulation and participation in a global economy continued apace. Given continuing recession, the economic gains for many women were few; high unemployment undermined many earlier gains. Nevertheless, the Keating Labor government took some action in the areas of child care, women's health and domestic violence; the federal parliament sponsored a bipartisan enquiry into equal status and equal opportunity for women; and women participated even more than men in the growth in access to higher education. Keating shifted the ground with a new emphasis on symbolic national questions—national identity and multiculturalism, economic and cultural orientation to Asia, constitutional reform, Aboriginal land rights and republicanism. At the level of public rhetoric, at least, women were to be firmly included in the concept of the multicultural outward-looking nation. There was also a renewed debate on women in the military forces. Feminist concern began to shift from a traditional focus on the provision of social services and legislative guarantee of equality of opportunity to a broader perception of the state as a political entity managing a wide range of cultural and international interactions.

Feminist political analysis

1970s

There have been many attempts to theorize the Australian feminist and especially femocrat experience, lasting now over twenty years. In the 1970s, these analyses occurred in a range of small political groups, and through their pamphlets, conferences and magazines. They were influenced not only by direct Australian political experience but also by what Australian feminists read in American, British or French discussion. Overseas debates were not imported or reproduced blindly; some British and American arguments were taken up with interest, while others had little or no resonance here. But this intellectual traffic tended to be one-way with Australian feminist work rarely being read anywhere else. The model of 'overseas theory' and 'Australian experience' continued to underlie Australian discussion.[14]

---

14 These issues are discussed at greater length in my 'Australian feminism since 1970', in

Early interest in British debate can be seen when we take a closer look at the arguments during the 1970s over whether the state could indeed be an arena for feminist action. The attempt to develop a simultaneously Marxist and feminist account of the state was largely a British one, the most quoted British Marxist feminists being Michele Barrett, Elizabeth Wilson and Mary McIntosh. In Marxist debate, the state had traditionally been construed as a tool of the dominant classes, and therefore as necessarily all-powerful and repressive. This pessimistic tradition, however, was coming under critique from within Marxism itself. These feminist writers were influenced especially by the Marxist Nicos Poulantzas, who began to oppose both the Marxist notion of the state as an agent of the ruling class, and the liberal notion of the state as neutral. Poulantzas put forward the influential idea of the state as a site of contestation, internally contradictory, rent by both class and intra-class conflicts. In his view, while the state is not neutral, its legitimacy and effectiveness in maintaining social order rest on its appearing to be so—and therein lies the opportunity for contest.[15]

Wilson and McIntosh attempted to adapt these formulations to address the relationship between men and women conceived as distinct groups and the state. Wilson used Poulantzas to argue that in order to ensure the maintenance of its own power, the state is indeed forced to make concessions to the dominated classes in the form of economic sacrifices. But she then modified his theory to suggest that these economic concessions are made mainly to the male half of the dominated; the state concedes little if anything to women.[16] Mary McIntosh argued that the state oppressed women through its support for a family household, itself needed by capitalism to guarantee the protection, maintenance and reproduction of labour power. Where the family failed, the state stepped in directly to achieve these ends.[17] Despite their gloomy picture of what could be expected from the state, they did conclude that as an alternative to the (oppressive nuclear) family, it had become for women an important site of struggle.

Australian feminism, eds Grieve and Burns.
15   Nicos Poulantzas, *Political power and social classes*, New Left Books, London, 1973.
16   Elizabeth Wilson, *Women and the welfare state*, Tavistock, London, 1977.
17   Mary McIntosh, 'The state and the oppression of women', in *Feminism and materialism*, eds Annette Kuhn and Anne Marie Wolpe, Routledge and Kegan Paul, London, 1978.

Similar ideas were developed in the Australian context in the mid to late 1970s by Ann Game and Rosemary Pringle. In the article 'Labor in power: the feminist response' (1976), they had argued against the radical feminist conception of a 'male power structure', and emphasized the class basis of the state. Two years later, in 'Women and class in Australia: feminism and the Labor government', they argued that while male power had a relative autonomy, no government in a capitalist state could do more than 'touch upon the symptoms of sexism'. Feminism, attracted to the idea of women as a structural group, had become 'absorbed into a subtle hegemony of the outlook and interests of middle-class women'.[18]

1980s

By the early 1980s, Australian feminists were increasingly producing their own substantive and theoretical accounts based on a combination of feminist theorizing drawn from a range of international sources with sustained reflection on the specifically Australian political context. For reasons of political commitment and individual careers, a significant number of feminist academics, political scientists, sociologists and historians had spent a period themselves as femocrats, and some of the analysis came from women who had had a dual academic-femocrat experience. Others had had a more traditional academic career. There were some notable discussions in several collections of essays, such as those edited by Cora Baldock and Bettina Cass, *Women, social welfare and the state* (1983); Dorothy Broom, *Unfinished business: women and social justice* (1984), and Marian Simms, *Australian women and the political system* (1984). Discussion papers written by academics-turned-femocrats, such as Lesley Lynch, Eva Cox and Marian Sawer, were carried in the journal *Refractory girl* in the mid 1980s, and in further collections such as that edited by Jacqueline Goodnow and Carole Pateman, *Women, social science and public policy* (1985).[19] By the

---

18   Ann Game and Rosemary Pringle, 'Women and class in Australia: feminism and the Labor government' in *Critical essays in Australian politics*, ed. Graeme Duncan, Edward Arnold (Australia), Melbourne, 1978, pp. 116, 134.
19   *Women, social welfare and the state*, eds Cora Baldock and Bettina Cass, George Allen & Unwin, Sydney, 1983; *Unfinished business: women and social justice*, ed. Dorothy Broom,

end of the decade, the pace of discussion increased, as feminist political scientists and sociologists set out to assess and understand feminism's engagement with the state. Major books include Suzanne Franzway, Di Court and R.W. Connell's *Staking a claim: feminism, bureaucracy, and the state*, appearing in 1989. There were three books in 1990 alone: Marian Sawer, *Sisters in suits: women and public policy in Australia*; Anna Yeatman, *Bureaucrats, technocrats, femocrats: essays on the contemporary Australian state*; and Sophie Watson's collection *Playing the state: Australian feminist interventions*. There were at least two more the following year: Gretchen Pointer and Sue Wills, *The gifthorse: a critical look at equal employment opportunity in Australia*, and Hester Eisenstein, *Gender shock*. The discussion continues, with major articles by Rosemary Pringle and Sophie Watson, Marian Sawer, Eleanor Hancock and Anna Yeatman.[20]

Positive and negative assessments

After the extensive soul-searching of the early Whitlam years, most Australian feminists concluded that feminists could indeed use the state to achieve feminist ends. Sara Dowse, head of the Women's Affairs Branch in the middle to late 1970s, articulated in 1984 what had become the prevailing Australian feminist view. The state, she argued, *did* respond to feminist political action, providing jobs, benefits and services for women far beyond those the private sector ever provided. The state

---

Allen & Unwin, Sydney, 1984; Marian Simms, *Australian women and the political system*, Longman Cheshire, Melbourne, 1984; Lesley Lynch, 'Bureaucratic feminism: bossism and beige suits', *Refractory girl*, no. 27, 1984, pp. 38-44; Eva Cox, 'Women and the state', *Refractory girl*, no. 23, 1982, pp. 28-31; *Women, social science and public policy*, eds Jacqueline Goodnow and Carole Pateman, Allen & Unwin, Sydney, 1985.

20 Suzanne Franzway, Di Court and R.W. Connell, *Staking a claim: feminism, bureaucracy, and the state*, Allen & Unwin, Sydney, 1989; Marian Sawer, *Sisters in suits: women and public policy in Australia*, Allen & Unwin, Sydney, 1990; *Playing the State: Australian feminist interventions*, ed. Sophie Watson, Allen & Unwin, Sydney, 1990; Anna Yeatman, *Bureaucrats, technocrats, femocrats: essays on the contemporary Australian state*, Allen and Unwin, Sydney, 1990; Gretchen Poiner and Sue Wills, *The gifthorse: a critical look at equal employment opportunity in Australia*, Allen & Unwin, Sydney, 1991; Rosemary Pringle and Sophie Watson, ' "Women's interests" and the post-structuralist state', in *Destabilizing theory: contemporary feminist debates*, eds Michele Barrett and Anne Phillips, Polity Press, London, 1992.

apparatus provided a glimpse of a future state of affairs, containing within itself its own challenge, a society organized on something other than greed. Feminists, she felt, could set about transforming the state from within.[21] The collection in which her essay appeared, Baldock and Cass's *Women, social welfare and the state*, aimed more generally to show the ways in which the state could and at times did act to benefit women.

Feminist historians made a distinctive contribution to this discussion, suggesting that the suspiciousness of socialist feminists in the early 1970s and since had derived from their socialism, not their feminism. Most feminists, the historians suggested, have long regarded the state as a political ally, looking to it in various periods for help in redressing gender-based inequalities, and playing an active part in its activities. The feminist strategies of the 1970s and since were new, but in their scale, ambition and above all their relative success rather than in their fundamental approach. The suffrage movement of the nineteenth (and in some states early twentieth) century was a demand for direct political participation, though even before then some women had sought influence in some of the bureaucratic agencies of the state, and women had long been professional providers of social services. Once the vote had been gained, feminists became in the twentieth century lobbyists for motherhood and child endowment, child-care services, legal reform and non-discriminatory education. They worked tirelessly to promote women's representation within the public services, statutory authorities and other public bodies, seeking to influence all aspects of economic and social policy.[22]

In the 1980s and after there was also a growing comparative interest

---

21 Sara Dowse, 'The bureaucrat as usurer'.
22 Carolyn Allport, 'The princess in the castle; women and the new order housing', in *All her labours*, vol. 1, eds Women and Labour Publications Collective, Hale and Iremonger, Sydney, 1984, pp. 129-31; Marilyn Lake, 'A revolution in the family: the challenge and contradictions of maternal citizenship in Australia', in *Mothers of a new world: maternalist politics and the origins of welfare states*, eds Seth Koven and Sonya Michel, Routledge, New York, 1993, pp. 378-95; Kerreen Reiger, *The disenchantment of the home: modernising the Australian family 1880-1940*, Oxford University Press, Melbourne, 1985; Susan Magarey, *Unbridling the tongues of women: a biography of Catherine Helen Spence*, Hale and Iremonger, Sydney, 1985; Patricia Grimshaw et al., *Creating a nation*, McPhee Gribble, Melbourne 1994.

from feminist scholars and activists elsewhere. Feminists migrating to Australia from North America and the United Kingdom were often struck by Australian feminist success as policy advisers within the public service. To their surprise, they found that it was not only liberal feminists who were so at home with various state bureaucracies; many radical and socialist feminists were fairly comfortable as well. Two of those who wrote about their impressions were Sophie Watson and Hester Eisenstein, both of whom had developed their feminism elsewhere, Sophie in England and Hester in the United States. Both later wrote about their feelings of surprise when observing the Australian femocrat phenomenon, Hester writing in *Gender shock*: 'When I arrived in Sydney, I was dazzled by the highly political feminists I encountered. They seemed utterly at ease with the structures of power at state and national levels. They understood the mysteries of bureaucratese, of applying for senior positions in government...'. She contrasted such ease with American feminist institutional marginality.

Sophie Watson's impressions appeared in the introduction to her collection *Playing the state*, in which she also asked: 'Have feminist demands been diluted or co-opted through engagement with the institutions and discourses which constitute the state?' It was a question especially designed for a British socialist and feminist audience, but it had underlain the Australian debate as well. The answers in her collection, and outside it, varied. Some academic commentators who had experience as femocrats argued that no, feminist demands had not been diluted or co-opted. Lyndall Ryan, one of Watson's contributors, saw the state's potential to liberate women from dependency on husbands and fathers as enormous, and femocrat successes thus far as highly significant.[23] Eisenstein in *Gender shock* saw significant gain through Equal Opportunity legislation, and especially in the femocrat 'contestation of the masculinist character of the state'. *Gender shock*, with its play on the idea of 'culture shock', is, however, a revealingly contradictory text. The author's very different American and Australian experiences are hard if not impossible to reconcile, and her long-range socialist-feminist pessimism sits uneasily with a more liberal-feminist pragmatic

---

23 Lyndall Ryan, 'Feminism and the federal bureaucracy 1972-1983', in *Playing the state*, ed. Watson.

optimism.[24]

Marian Sawer was much more decisive and confident. In *Sisters in suits* she praised the nature and quality of services delivered, describing the level of government-funded resources run by women for women as 'remarkable by global standards and far above that in Britain or the United States'.[25] As success stories she included government recognition of feminist analyses and programmes on issues such as domestic violence, child sexual abuse, women's health issues, community-based child care, re-entry confidence-building, training and education programmes for women who have been out of the workforce, the dramatic rise of women's participation in higher education, and the achievement of greater rights and participation (but not earnings, she says, rather questionably) in the workplace.

Even greater, in Sawer's estimation, was Australian feminist achievement in the realm of bureaucratic innovation. The principle of policy advice within departments linked to a central co-ordinating unit forms, Sawer argues, is one of the major enduring achievements of Australian feminism's engagement with the state: 'Over the last fifteen years Australian women have created a range of women's policy machinery ... which is unrivalled elsewhere ... By 1988, Australian women had won a growing international reputation for the kind of policy mechanisms they had developed.'[26] She praises Australian feminists for developing mechanisms which were consistent with feminist philosophy; a centre-periphery model with the hub in the major co-ordinating government department and spokes in functional departments, a network of policy units rather than a separate, vertically-integrated, women's policy department.[27] This very positive achievement, she later argued, meant that feminists in the late 1980s took some time to realize the extent of the threat posed by an 'ideologically coherent and aggressive form of market liberalism'.[28]

Other commentators have been more critical. A common thread in more negative analyses is that feminism's apparent successes have

---

24 Eisenstein, *Gender shock*, p. 35.
25 Sawer, *Sisters in suits*, p. 251.
26 ibid., pp. xiv-vi.
27 ibid., p. 30.
28 Sawer, 'Reclaiming social liberalism', p. 19.

involved an increase in the powers of the state in individual lives, a decrease in family and collective power, and a giving of benefits favouring some rather than all women. Gretchen Poiner and Sue Wills in *The gifthorse* offer a very sober assessment indeed of Equal Employment Opportunity legislation in these terms. Bob Connell, Suzanne Franzway and Di Court, in *Staking a claim*, agree that the reforms that have been achieved are not trivial, and that femocrats do have some degree of power. But they go on to emphasize the immense powers of the state, and say that the state cannot deliver what feminism wants of it.[29] Anna Yeatman's *Bureaucrats, technocrats, femocrats* sees the fundamental femocrat dilemma as being the way in which the strategies they propose will tend, whatever their intentions and class sympathies, to suit the interests of middle-class women like themselves. Ideas such as affirmative action and equal opportunity, for example, are helpful only for those already with education and recognized skills. Further, femocrat successes operate in firmly circumscribed aspects of state activity. Within the middle and upper levels of the public service, where feminists claim most advance, women are more readily employed in the 'soft' areas such as education and human and community services like child care, health services, social security and social welfare, while men continue to dominate the 'hard' areas of economic and financial policy, foreign affairs, immigration, trade, defence, and labour and industrial relations.

In a later essay, 'Women and the state' (1994), Yeatman emphasizes the power and penetration of the state in everyone's lives. The state is the 'pre-eminent organisational power in respect of the lives of women as all other subjects', and it works to confirm women's status as subordinate to men. Yet she also emphasizes the state's need to command belief in the legitimacy of its authority from a majority of its subjects, thus making it susceptible to claims and demands for social justice from various groups. The state must sometimes enter into a reform mode, in the process constituting new rights for women, or at least some women, especially, but not only, those privileged by ethnicity, race or class.[30]

---

29 Connell, Court and Franzway, *Staking a claim*, p. 158.
30 Yeatman, 'Women and the state', pp. 177-97.

Feminism, liberalism, and democracy

Liberalism

The feminist literature on the state does not confine itself to assessing feminist successes and failures. It also addresses theoretical issues, such as whether there can be a distinctively feminist conception of the state, politics and democracy. Most if not all contributors to the current debate attempt to see the state as more internally contradictory than earlier Marxist or liberal theory appeared to allow. In *Staking a claim*, sociologists Franzway, Court and Connell suggest that we must see the state as constituted by gender as well as class relations, as an *agent* in sexual politics acting in a public realm culturally marked as masculine. The joint chapter by Sophie Watson and Rosemary Pringle in Watson's *Playing the state* describes the state not as an agent but as a 'set of *arenas*', a 'collection of *practices*', which cannot occupy the whole field of actual power relations, and operates on the basis of already-existing power relations.

A major focus of continuing debate has been the relationship between liberal and feminist conceptions of the state. Is feminism a form or liberalism, or one of its most powerful modern critics? In *Staking a claim*, Franzway, Court and Connell reply that it is both, pointing to liberalism's provision on the one hand of a basis for the claiming of rights and opportunities additional to those which women are traditionally thought to have, and on the other hand liberalism's foundation in the notion of the abstract rights of the individual, derived from the Enlightenment, where the individual is supposed to be sexless yet is really male.[31] The possible limitations of liberalism for feminist theory have been most thoroughly pursued by Carole Pateman who moved from Australia to the US in the late 1980s. Pateman has authored several major works, most notably in this context *The sexual contract* (1988). Of the authors I am concerned with, hers is the least affected by Australian feminist political practice, though her work has been influential within Australian feminist discussion of liberal theory and

---

31 See also Pauline Johnson, 'Feminism and liberalism', *Australian feminist studies*, no. 14, 1991, pp. 57-68.

the state. In particular, a shift away from a Marxist-Poulantzian notion of the capitalist state to a notion of the patriarchal state, most noticeable in the work of Game and Pringle, was strongly influenced by her 1983 essay on feminism and political theory.[32]

Liberalism and feminism, Pateman wrote in this essay, are closely related. Both rely on a conception of individuals as free and equal beings, emancipated from the ascribed, hierarchical bonds of traditional society. The paradox is that feminism inevitably challenges liberalism itself.[33] In a 1988 essay, 'The fraternal social contract', she argued that the social contract of liberal theory was made not by individuals, as usually supposed, but by brothers, a fraternity, by men who share a bond *as men*. The contract guarantees the rule of men over women; through the contract the brothers appropriate women's ability to give birth: 'The social contract is the point of origin, or birth, of civil society'.[34] For Pateman, liberalism is profoundly and permanently tainted by its origins, theory and practice: 'The history of liberal feminism is the history of attempts to generalise liberal liberties and rights to the whole adult population; but liberal feminism does not, and cannot, come to grips with the deeper problems of how women are to take an equal place in the patriarchal civil order'.[35]

In *The sexual contract* Pateman closely examines the notion of the social contract in order to explain the patriarchal character of societies such as Britain, Australia and the United States. Women, she maintains, are still excluded from the central category of 'the individual', the bedrock on which contractarian doctrine is constructed. Feminists have often tried to respond to patriarchal insistence on women's natural difference from men by constructing a non-sexed individual, insisting on the elimination of all reference to sexual difference in political life, and seeking gender-neutral laws and policies.[36] The desire is to *include* women by making gender irrelevant. Yet for feminists to argue for the elimination of sex or biological difference from political debate

---

32 See Barbara Sullivan, 'Women and the current Queensland state government', p. 157.
33 Carole Pateman, 'Feminist critiques of the public/private dichotomy', reprinted in Carole Pateman, *The disorder of women*, Polity Press, Cambridge, 1989, pp. 118-40.
34 Reprinted in Pateman, *The disorder of women*, p. 45.
35 ibid., p. 51.
36 Carol Pateman, *The sexual contract*, Polity Press, Oxford, 1988, p. 16

is to accept patriarchal society as it is.[37] Her solutions are for sexual difference to be addressed openly and politically, rather than repressed in the name of a hypothetical illusory non-sexed individual. The achievement of legal equality and freedom becomes then not the end of feminism but rather the precondition for the development of women's autonomy, where women become free as women, rather than as like men.

Marian Sawer argues that Pateman identifies liberalism with a very specific American contractarian liberal tradition, rather than with the forms it has taken in Australia. Sawer emphasizes the differences between late nineteenth century 'social liberalism', important in Britain and Australia, and its contractarian predecessors. Social liberalism provided the philosophical basis of the welfare state, emphasizing the role of the state in social reform through ameliorating the inequalities produced by the market. The femocrat strategy belongs in this social liberal tradition, though it departs from it in seeing government activity as affecting men and women differently. In Sawer's argument, while forms of liberalism based on the rights of the individual and notions of laissez faire in economic policy are inimical to feminism, other forms of liberalism can serve feminist ends very well: 'it is only social liberalism which can provide a basis for the moral claims of feminism'.[38]

Democracy

Feminist political desires since the 1970s have been mainly for new social policies, pushing the state to reduce or eliminate social and economic barriers to full sexual equality and liberation. As long as significant participation in government itself seemed hopelessly unrealizable, it seemed far better to concentrate on achieving influence as femocrats and lobbyists. More recently, in the first half of the 1990s, however, there has been an important shift back to those general questions of political rights and duties which so pre-occupied the women's organizations of the nineteenth and early twentieth centuries. The forms and meaning of democratic participation and process have, through a revival of the Enlightenment concept of citizenship, returned

---

37 ibid., p. 224.
38 Sawer, 'Reclaiming social liberalism', p. 21.

to the centre of feminist theorizing and argument. British feminist Anne Phillips has outlined the current debate, and her work is gradually being taken up by Australian feminists.[39]

There has, for example, been renewed interests in questions of women's under-representation in state and national parliaments. In rising during the 1980s from 3.2 to 12.5 per cent in the national parliament, Australian women's parliamentary participation rates moved from the bottom to the top of the international range of between 2 and 12 per cent. (This international range does not include the Nordic countries, where formal party quotas ensuring a 40 per cent minimum for either sex has dramatically raised the proportion of parliamentary members who are female.)[40] The problem of women's under-representation has been addressed in a number of ways. One way, currently under discussion within the Labor Party and advocated for some time by feminists, is to propose affirmative action to boost the preselection of women parliamentary candidates, seeking the Nordic-style quota of 40 per cent.

Another is to advocate a shift away from single to multi-member electorates, on the basis that in multi-member electorate systems, or proportional representation, women, along with minority ethnic groups and political parties, tend generally to do very much better. Marilyn Lake argues that where people can vote for more than one candidate, they are more likely to vote for a male-female mix, whereas when they can vote for only one person, women, like Aboriginal people, will be more likely to be seen as representing a sectional interest; only (white) men are perceived as standing for the electoral population as a whole.[41] Helen Irving opposes this argument, seeing the pre-selection of women candidates as depending on changes in political culture more than electoral systems. Multi-member electorates, in enhancing the influence of minority groups and parties, who may equally be thoroughly reactionary as progressive and reforming, are not necessarily to be

---

39   Anne Phillips, *Democracy and difference*, Polity Press, Cambridge, especially chapter 6, 'Must feminists give up on liberal democracy?', pp. 103-22. See also her *Engendering democracy*, Polity Press, Cambridge, 1991.
40   Summers, *Damned whores*, p. 48; Phillips, *Democracy and difference*, p. 106-15.
41   Marilyn Lake, 'A republic for women?', *Arena magazine*, March 1994, pp. 32-3, reprising arguments put forward in *The Australian*, 15 June 1993.

AUSTRALIAN FEMINISM AND THE STATE

preferred. We may be better off with our (Lower House) single-member constituencies, which favour the major parties which at least offer a package of policies rather than standing for 'a single-minded commitment to single issues'.[42] Lake in turn replies that the two-party system is repressive and based on a binary divide between capital and labour, unable to give political expression to multiple identities based on race, ethnicity, nationality, gender, age and sexuality.[43] The debate is still in its early stages, raising fundamental questions concerning women and democracy that had been tackled only very lightly in the sustained debate on 'feminism and the state'.

Postmodernism, colonialism and republicanism

Also impacting on the 'feminism and the state' debates in recent years has been the challenge of postmodernism, embraced enthusiastically in some feminist circles, and strongly criticized and rejected in others. The divergence in feminist response to postmodernism is related, I think, to a long-standing conflict within feminism over whether or not it seeks equality or difference. These divisions of belief and desire are sometimes characterized as providing the distinction between liberal feminism and radical feminism, the former stressing the gaining of formal and practical rights through the agency of the state, the latter stressing women's search for the social and cultural conditions which respect women's difference from men.

Postmodernism intersects with the history of these internal feminist debates.[44] At first glance it seems to strengthen the radical feminist position. Both radical feminism and postmodernism are critical of the Enlightenment ideals of universal and equal human rights, ideals for so long called upon by liberal feminists to support their demands for equal political and social rights, and assuming Western male reason as mode and model for humanity. Against this illusory universalism, postmodernism and radical feminism stress difference; though postmodernism adds culture and identity to radical feminism's emphasis

---

42 Helen Irving, 'Boys' own republic', *Arena magazine*, December 1993, pp. 24-6.
43 Lake, 'A republic for women?', p. 33.
44 See Pauline Johnson, 'Feminism and the enlightenment', *Radical philosophy*, 63, 1993, pp. 3-12.

on gender. Despite these convergences, radical feminists are often the most critical of postmodernism. In stressing the multiplicity, relativity and contingency of all speaking positions, including that of woman, postmodernism is sometimes seen to be undermining the ground from which radical feminism speaks. Radical feminists find it suspicious that just as women are finding a public voice from which to speak as women, rather than as substitute men, postmodernist discourse denies the authenticity and validity of a speaking position which claims to speak on behalf of women.[45]

This debate over the category woman intersects with another debate, that over whether racial categories invalidate gender categories. Can *anyone* speak 'as a woman' when women are so divided from one another by the experiences of colonization and dispossession? Western feminists are slowly coming to terms with the idea that their own project, their own history, has been intertwined with colonization, orientalism, even racism.[46] The critique from Aboriginal women of Australian feminism's Eurocentric and sometimes racist assumptions has left many feminists feeling uncertain about the meaning and value of feminism itself. Especially after the Mabo decision and subsequent debate and legislation, Aboriginal peoples' demands for land rights and sovereignty are presenting a profound challenge to non-Aboriginal Australian feminists' conceptual view of the world. Feminists are starting to realize that Aboriginal demands cannot be contained within existing feminist politics, and that the entire political framework within which they have traditionally operated is under question and liable to change.[47] The constitutional

---

45 For further discussion, see Suzanne Moore, 'Postmodern paralysis', in her book *Looking for trouble: on shopping, gender and the cinema*, Serpent's Tail, London, 1991; Nancy Fraser and Linda Nicholson, 'Social criticism without philosophy: an encounter between feminism and postmodernism', in *Theory, culture and society*, vol. 5, no. 2-3, June 1988, pp. 373-94; and Tania Modleski, *Feminism without women: culture and criticism in a postfeminist age*, Routledge, London, 1991.
46 For just one example, see Joyce Zonana, 'The sultan and the slave: feminist orientalism and the structure of *Jane Eyre*', *Signs*, vol. 18, no. 3, Spring 1993, pp. 592-617.
47 For a fuller discussion, see my 'Feminism, citizenship, and national identity: Australian debates', and 'The three body problem: feminism and chaos theory', *Hecate*, 17/1, Autumn 1991, pp. 14-21. Other discussions of these issues include Jan Larbalestier 'The 1980 women and labour conference: feminism as myth; Aboriginal women and the feminist encounter', *Refractory girl*, nos. 20-21, October 1980, pp. 31-39; Fay Gale, ed. *We are bosses ourselves: the status and role of Aboriginal women today*, Australian Institute of Aboriginal Studies,

and ethical bases of the nation-state may need to be rethought by feminists along with everyone else.

This theoretical shift is starting to affect the long-standing debates on feminism and the state. Both Sawer and Pateman, despite their differences, rested their analysis on an 'autonomous femininity', a set of definable female interests and demands that will be different from men's. A key question confronting feminists seeking political change —namely, will the reforms they seek benefit women generally, or some women at the expense of others?—cannot be adequately addressed in this framework. Rosemary Pringle and Sophie Watson, in their 1993 essay ' "Women's interests" and the post-structuralist state', provide a welcome critique of the unitary notion of women's interests. Feminist theory is increasingly coming to terms with the problem and dilemma that gender may not always be *the* most important and fundamental difference, and that the category woman is continually created, and then undone.[48]

Feminist debate has changed in another way, too. It has begun to engage with certain questions of nation and state that were earlier considered rather taboo. Whereas talk of the state was important for debating and theorizing feminist political strategy, talk of the nation and more specifically for the Australian case of a republic had been seen as unacceptably caught within male nationalist discourse.[49] Chilla Bulbeck, for example, says 'for women like me, white Anglo-descended, middle class by training if not birth, whether we are a republic or a monarchy hardly matters. In approaching the issue of national identity I can forget everything but my gender...'[50] Other feminists, however,

---

Canberra, 1983; Heather Goodall and Jackie Huggins, 'Aboriginal women are everywhere: contemporary struggles', in *Gender relations in Australia*, K. Saunders and R. Evans; and Jan Pettman, *Living in the margins: racism, sexism and feminism in Australia*, Allen & Unwin, Sydney, 1992.

48 See Anna Yeatman, 'Voice and representation in the politics of difference', in *feminism and the politics of difference*, eds Sneja Gunew and Anna Yeatman, Allen & Unwin, Sydney, 1993, pp. 228-45.

49 For an example, see Gail Reekie, 'Contesting Australia', in *Images of Australia*, eds Gillian Whitlock and David Carter, University of Queensland Press, St Lucia, 1992.

50 Chilla Bulbeck, 'Republicanism and post-nationalism', in *The republicanism debate*, eds David Carter and Wayne Hudson, UNSW Press, Sydney, 1993. Quoted by Meaghan Morris, 'The very idea of a popular debate, or, not lunching with Thomas Keneally', to be published in *Papers from communal/plural 2*, eds Lesley Johnson and Ghassan Hage, University of

gradually began to hope they could help shape, rather than simply critique, the continuing debate over constitutional and national questions. Helen Irving, drawing attention to the near-absence of women from both public and scholarly debate on the idea of an Australian republic, calls for feminist input. 'Republicanism', she argues, 'is historically significant in the way we know now that Federation was (although many people then, as now, shrugged their shoulders at it for many years).'[51] And, Stephen Muecke and I have jointly argued for an approach to questions of national identity and the republic which tries to combine feminist perspectives on Australia's past and future with a recognition of Aboriginal claims for sovereignty, recognition of prior occupation, and cultural identity.[52]

The contemporary feminism that is negotiating these difficult questions of Aboriginal sovereignty, national identity and republicanism is not the same feminism that debated the ethics and desirability of seeking funds from the Whitlam government for women's refuges and health centres. In between is a wealth of experience as femocrats, academics, teachers, trade-unionists, film-makers, journalists, and especially as political activists. That experience has, however, led not to a settled body of knowledge or received wisdom on feminism and the state. In reading and re-reading these feminist writings in the course of preparing this chapter, I was struck again and again by how complex, hesitant, nuanced, fence-sitting and contradictory the debate has become. Anne Phillips' excellent and lucid accounts explore the debates, both laying bare and participating in the indecision. (Readers may feel my own account here could well be described as fence-sitting, which indeed in many ways it is.) Feminist political theory and debate, it seems to me, is at a crossroads, looking for a way to combine a postmodernist awareness of difference, ambivalence and fragmentation with a coherent political philosophy capable of sustaining the important political struggles yet to come.

Western Sydney, forthcoming.
51 Irving, 'Boys' own republic', p. 25.
52. Ann Curthoys and Stephen Muecke, 'Australia, for example', in *The republicanism debate*, eds Wayne Hudson and David Carter.

7

Beyond foreign policy: state theory and the changing global order

Christian Reus-Smit

The modern state was born in the late eighteenth century, the product of a fundamental transformation in the European social order. Sovereign states existed for at least two centuries before then, but they were Absolutist states, political dinosaurs sustained by a predominantly mercantile and agricultural economy and legitimized by their role in the preservation of an organic, rigidly hierarchical social order. During the eighteenth century mutually reinforcing revolutions in thought and practice undermined the foundations of Absolutism. Scientific, economic and political theorists abandoned traditional holistic ways of conceiving the natural and social order, favouring instead the disaggregation of natural and social entities into their most primary components. The nature and purpose of larger combinations—be they of atoms or humans—was no longer assumed; only experience could reveal connections between elements. For scientists this involved controlled experimentation to demonstrate causal relations, for economists it meant the creative division of labour and the test of efficiency, and for political theorists it entailed political individualism and democratic, or quasi-democratic, decision-making. The crucial blow to Absolutism came from the resonance and articulation of these ideological developments with the concrete social and material transformations which swept late eighteenth-century Europe. The economic dislocations and upheavals of the industrial revolution uprooted the rigid, hierarchical social order, undercutting long-standing patterns of social organization and affiliation. The turmoil of the French Revolution sounded the death knell of the

Absolutist political order and heralded the birth of a new distinctly modern state, a state which drew its identity and realm of legitimate action from the augmentation of individuals' economic and political purposes.

We are now in the midst of another great transformation in the international social order, but this time it is the foundations of the modern state which are in flux. Globalization is the catchword of our times. Increasingly complex financial, trading and manufacturing networks in the world economy have eroded the boundaries of national economies, making national economic planning frustratingly difficult. The end of the Cold War has thrown the post-1945 political order into disarray and sparked a search for new institutional mechanisms and arrangements to preserve international order. Yet these recent events obscure the fact that a deep-rooted and far-reaching process of international institutionalization has been under way for the best part of three decades, a process that post-Cold War imperatives merely serve to hasten. Parallel to these economic and political developments is the rise of so-called 'new agenda' issues—such as human rights and environmental protection. These have spawned new transnational social movements and demanded international, if not global, supervision and management. All of these processes have been accentuated and exacerbated by the communications and information revolution which blurs the boundaries between the local and the global.

The impact of globalization on the modern state is now the subject of widespread debate among international relations scholars. Some argue that the state's sovereignty is at an end, citing its severely eroded capacity to control activities within and across its borders. The 'theory and practice of sovereignty', Camilleri and Falk argue, 'are facing profound challenges from a world in a process of rapid change'.[1] For such scholars, the world is entering a postmodern era, a world populated by multiple actors with overlapping jurisdictions and responsibilities embedded in a network of globalized processes. This view is countered by those who assert the continued centrality and power of the modern state. From this latter perspective the state remains the dominant form

---

1   Joseph A. Camilleri and Jim Falk, *The end of sovereignty? the politics of a shrinking and fragmenting world*, Edward Elgar, London, 1992, pp. 8-9.

of political organization and the primary focus of human loyalty. The state, they argue, retains its traditional monopoly on the legitimate use of force, it is still the principal agency for the satisfaction of human needs and aspirations, and processes of globalization are themselves dependent on the state for the maintenance of order and the provision of basic infrastructure.

While these competing narratives of besieged and defiant states define the parameters of current debate, neither adequately captures the relationship between contemporary patterns of global change and the modern state. End of sovereignty arguments place too much emphasis on the intrusive and corrosive processes of globalization, presenting the once autonomous and powerful state as a passive victim of change, an increasingly marginal and impotent anachronism. Statist arguments go to the other extreme, blindly denying the undeniable, ignoring processes that are touching the everyday lives of people and which are clearly transforming the social and political terrain. Handicapped by their respective blind spots, both perspectives miss the most important and interesting feature of contemporary change: the mutually constitutive relationship between states and emerging global structures and processes. This relationship has three principal dimensions. As we have suggested, the forces of globalization are transforming the state, making it difficult for governments to fulfil their traditional roles while driving them into new and challenging spheres of social, political and economic action. This is not to say, however, that states are passive actors. They have been crucial agents in the construction of many global processes and structures, especially in the political and institutional domains. Finally, to the extent that these new structures entail a redefinition of the state's identity and sphere of legitimate action, the state itself is actively engaged in this reconstitution. The state, in other words, is reconstructing itself. Only by acknowledging this three-dimensional process of mutual constitution can we accommodate, if not reconcile, our contradictory intuitions that the present international order is characterized by both change and continuity, by the forces of globalization and by the persistence of the system of states, however transformed.

This interactive process of mutual constitution has exerted a profound influence on the nature and objectives of recent Australian foreign policy. To begin with, globalization is now considered the primary dynamic and organising feature of the contemporary international environment.

According to Gareth Evans and Bruce Grant, 'globalisation is unquestionably now a primary factor for change in international affairs, generating its own issues on the international agenda as well as a greater capacity to solve them'.[2] Faced with such an environment, the Hawke and Keating governments have adopted an activist posture, attempting to mould emerging global structures through their 'new internationalist' foreign policy, a programme of 'middle power diplomacy' designed to create new international institutions and strengthen existing ones. Such a posture, Evans and Grant argue, is part of 'an emerging worldwide recognition that a great many problems can be dealt with effectively only by co-operation on a multilateral, and in some cases global, scale'.[3] This policy of international construction is inextricably connected with an explicit campaign to reconstruct the identity and role of the Australian state itself. On one level this entails the redefinition of Australia's external persona, the face it shows the world. 'In this respect,' Evans and Grant contend, 'Australia's foreign policy is presently acting as an important catalyst in building a new Australian identity—one which is much more internationalist, and regionally focused, than before'.[4] Renovating the facade, however, is not considered enough. Republicanism and multiculturalism, with all their complexities and contradictions, represent the domestic face of the government's reconstruction of the Australian state's identity and rationale to meet the demands of the new economic, political and normative global order.

This chapter develops two lines of critique. First, it argues that existing international relations theories are poorly equipped to comprehend the mutually constitutive relationship between the state and emerging global structures and processes. The dominant realist and Marxist theories of international relations conceive of the state from material-structuralist standpoints which obscure the three-dimensional mutually constitutive relationship between states and global structures. This leads them to conceive of foreign policy as a strategic action through which states pursue their interests within a given set of structural constraints and incentives. As such they ignore, if not

---

[2] Gareth Evans and Bruce Grant, *Australia's foreign relations in the world of the 1990s*, Melbourne University Press, Melbourne, 1991, p. 12.
[3] ibid. p. 11.
[4] ibid. p. 322.

deny, the crucial constitutive dimension of foreign policy: its role in the construction of global structures and in the constitution of the state itself. Secondly, because prominent interpretations of Australian foreign policy analysis have until now been informed by the assumptions of these competing international relations theories, they lack the conceptual apparatus to grasp the relationship between contemporary global processes and structures and the Australian state.

After a detailed examination of prevailing theories of international relations, their respective conceptions of the state, and their impact on the study of Australian foreign policy, I explore recent attempts to develop an alternative 'constructivist' theory of international relations. Such a theory, I shall argue, not only captures the interactive relationship between states and global structures, it also treats foreign policy as a constitutive, not merely a strategic, action. As such, constructivism provides a more fruitful conceptual basis for understanding contemporary changes in the nature and purpose of the modern state, and in turn offers a more appropriate analytical framework for the study of current Australian foreign policy. Adopting a constructivist perspective, however, stretches the very notion of foreign policy to its limits. If 'new internationalism' entails a deep reconstitution of the nature and identity of the Australian state itself, of which republicanism and multiculturalism are part, then the traditional quarantining of external policy from domestic policy becomes increasingly untenable. From a constructivist standpoint, foreign policy must be considered one dimension of a larger policy of global adaptation in which the domestic and the international are inextricably intertwined.

The following discussion of how the state has been conceived in rival theories of international relations is divided into sections on realism, Marxism, and constructivism. I will argue that the first two perspectives define the state as a strategic actor, adopt materialist conceptions of the structure of the international system, and argue that the structure of the system determines the nature and identity of the state. In contrast, constructivists define the state as a system of rule, emphasize the normative as well as the material dimensions of international structure, and treat the state and international structure as mutually constitutive. At the end of each section I show how the theoretical framework in question has influenced the analysis of Australian foreign policy, or how it might do so in the constructivist case. I will argue that conventional realist and Marxist perspectives on international relations and the state obscure important dimensions of this policy, dimensions revealed by constructivism. In other words, these three interpretive standpoints yield progressively deeper readings of Australian foreign policy, with only constructivism illuminating both its constitutive and strategic aspects.

Realism

Up until recently, realism has been the dominant mainstream account used in Australia to understand international relations. Realists assert that states are the principal actors in international politics and are the primary units of analysis. This does not mean that realists deny the existence or relevance of other actors, they simply contend that 'the nature of the state and the pattern of relations among states are the most important determinants of the character of international relations at any given moment'.[5] In the light of this emphasis, it is paradoxical that realists fail to provide a systematic theory of the state, nor do they claim to.[6] The reason for this is that realism purports to be a system-level theory, not a unit-level theory. For classical realists and neorealists alike the character and behaviour of states are determined by the nature and dynamics of the international system of states. Because sovereign states refuse to allow a common authority to regulate their interactions, the international system is anarchical. The logic of anarchy in turn places a premium on self-help, for security co-operation remains precarious so long as promises rest on nothing more than goodwill. In their quest for self-reliance states assume similar qualities and functions: that is, they become 'like-units'. Driven by the security dilemma and the principal of self-help, states seek to maximize their relative power, prompting realists to depict international relations as a perpetual struggle for power and advantage. It is thus the anarchical structure of the international system—not the historical and social circumstances and

---

5   Robert Gilpin, *War and change in world politics*, Cambridge University Press, Cambridge, 1981, p. 18.
6   For an explicit denial that realist theory requires a systematic theory of the state, see Kenneth Waltz, 'A response to my critics,' in *Neorealism and its critics*, ed. Robert Keohane, Columbia University Press, New York, pp. 337-341.

characteristics of individual units—which determines the form, function and behaviour of states.

This perspective on the state is most cogently stated by neorealists. Within the international system, Kenneth Waltz claims, each state 'is the equal of all the others. None is entitled to command; none is required to obey. International systems are decentralized and anarchic'.[7] Such systems impede cooperation, forcing states to stand alone and rely on their own resources. 'Self-help', according to Waltz, 'is necessarily the principle of action in an anarchic order.'[8] As a consequence, states are functionally similar:

> States perform or try to perform tasks, most of which are common to all of them; the ends they aspire to are similar. Each state duplicates the activities of other states at least to a considerable extent. Each state has its agencies for making, executing, and interpreting laws and regulations, for raising revenues, and for defending itself ... One has to be impressed with the functional similarity of states and, now more than ever before, with the similar lines their development follows.[9]

Waltz does not deny that states exhibit different cultural, economic and political features, rather he argues that international relations theory must abstract from these particularities to isolate those differences which are truly salient. He concludes that differences in the capabilities of states constitute the only relevant axis of variation. In an anarchical system governed by the principle of self-help, states' relative strengths and weaknesses determine political outcomes.[10] For this reason, states are preoccupied with their position within the hierarchy of capabilities, which compels them to maximize their power in comparison to other states.[11]

Critics frequently observe that the neorealist abstraction and reification of the state represents a departure from the more nuanced tenets of its classical forebear.[12] The classical realism of E.H. Carr,

---

7   Kenneth Waltz, *Theory of international politics*, Random House, New York, p. 88.
8   ibid. p. 111.
9   ibid. pp. 96-7.
10 ibid. p. 97.
11 See Joseph Grieco, 'Anarchy and the limits of cooperation: a realist critique of the newest liberal institutionalism,' *International organization*, vol. 42, August 1988, pp. 485-507.
12 See, for example, Richard Ashley, 'The poverty of neorealism,' in *Neorealism and its critics*,

John Herz, Hans Morgenthau and Raymond Aron, it is argued, was sensitive to history, practice and particularity, considerations deliberately bracketed by the sparse economism of neorealist social science. Classical realism gave the state and state practice an autonomy, or more correctly a life and individual agency, denied by the systemic imperatives of neorealism. Neorealists, according to Richard Ashley, abandoned those elements of classical realism that were 'too fuzzy, too slippery, too resistant to consistent operational formulation, and, in application, too dependent upon the artful sensitivity of the historically minded and context-sensitive scholar'.[13]

Without denying classical realism's greater practical and historical sensibilities, its differences with neorealism should not be overdrawn, especially when it comes to the relationship between the structure of the international system and the nature and behaviour of states. Waltz certainly condemned classical realism for being reductionist, for attributing the state's quest for power to the aggressiveness of human nature and not to the imperatives of the anarchical system of states. And at times Morgenthau indeed claims that the international struggle for power stems from the innate human desire to dominate.[14] Nevertheless, a closer reading of Morgenthau's *Politics among nations*—arguably the most important statement of classical realism—suggests that he considered structural determinants, not human nature, to be paramount. This is clearly apparent in the logic behind his key analytical concept: the idea of 'interest defined as power'. 'Whatever the ultimate aims of international politics,' he argues, 'power is always the immediate aim.'[15] This may seem like a restatement of his notion that humans are inherently domineering, but it is actually a claim about what constitutes rational state policy and action in a world lacking central authority. In other words, the insecurity generated by the anarchical state system promotes uniform state interests defined as power and patterns of behaviour defined as struggle. That these interests and behaviour patterns are driven by systemic pressures and not human

---

    ed. Keohane, pp. 268-73.
13 ibid. pp. 260-61.
14 Hans J. Morgenthau, *Politics among nations: the struggle for power and peace*, fifth edition, Alfred A. Knopf, New York, 1972, p. 35.
15 ibid. p. 27.

nature is evident in the classical realist fear of irrational state behaviour, such as Carr's condemnation of interwar appeasement and Morgenthau's attack on idealist foreign policies. This fear of irrationality not only admits that non-power-oriented foreign policies are possible, it also asserts that power-maximizing foreign policies are rational responses to international anarchy, not the product of universal human nature.[16]

To sustain the argument that structural imperatives dictate state behaviour, realists must adopt a distinctive conception of the state: the state as a unitary, strategic actor. If they relax the assumption of unity, then the idea of a single national interest and a single calculating stance toward the external world of systemic pressures no longer holds. To admit that the state might be fragmented, buffeted by a variety of competing domestic interests, or to recognize the multiplicity of autonomous or quasi-autonomous governmental and non-governmental linkages between states, would be to acknowledge non-systemic determinants on state behaviour. Realism thus demands singular, coherent and rational actors capable of interpreting and responding to the vicissitudes of the international system. Not surprising therefore, the assumption that the state is a unitary, strategic actor undergirds both classical realism and neorealism, even if they arrive at this assumption in different ways.

The classical realist conception of the unitary state consists of two linked ideas: the image of the state as territorially bounded political community, and the notion that such a community is united by a central authoritative and coercive agency capable of expressing and enforcing common interests and goals. The state, as F.S. Northedge writes, is an 'hereditary territorial organization ... consisting of a people organized by a single focus of authority'.[17] The link between national unity and common purpose, on the one hand, and authority and coercion, on the other, is central to the classical realist formulation. As Carr argues, the 'state, like other societies, must be based on some sense of common interests and obligations among its members. But coercion is regularly

---

16 As Morgenthau writes, 'given the conditions of the [international] power pattern, the independence of the respective nations can rest on no other foundation than the power of each individual nation to prevent the power of other nations from encroaching upon its freedom'. ibid. p. 174.
17 F.S. Northedge, *The international political system*, Faber and Faber, London, 1976, p. 134.

exercised by a governing group to enforce loyalty and obedience ...'[18] This emphasis on unity through compulsion defines Morgenthau's conception of the state. The state, he argues, 'is but another name for the compulsory organization of society—for the legal order that determines the conditions under which society may employ its monopoly of organized violence for the preservation of order and peace'.[19] Thus, although classical realists at times suggest that communitarian impulses provide the foundations for state unity—as in Carr's genealogical description of the evolution of human societies from families to states[20]—their principal case for state unity stresses the authority and coercion wielded by administrative and governing elites.

The idea that states are unitary actors because elites have the capacity to formulate and impose a single conception of the national interest is, of course, empirically questionable. In many if not most states, what constitutes the national interest in a given issue-area is highly contested, often undermining the capacity of governments to develop and pursue coherent international policies and strategies. Acknowledging this, neorealists cast their argument about state unity in theoretical not empirical terms. As Waltz argues, '[w]e can freely admit that states are in fact not unitary, purposive actors. States pursue many goals, which are often vaguely formulated and inconsistent. They fluctuate with the changing currents of domestic politics, are prey to the vagaries of a shifting cast of political leaders, and are influenced by the outcomes of bureaucratic struggles'.[21] For neorealists, state unity constitutes a Lakotosian style core assumption, the value of which depends more on its heuristic power than its empirical validity. 'A theory', Waltz contends, 'contains assumptions that are theoretical, not factual.'[22] The assumption that states are unitary, strategic actors should be retained, neorealists argue, so long as it remains 'useful'. That is, so long as it continues to generate testable hypotheses that explain more about international politics than propositions based on competing assumptions.

---

18   E.H. Carr, *The twenty years' crisis: 1919-1939*, Harper and Row, New York, pp. 95-6.
19   Morgenthau, *Politics among nations*, p. 485.
20   Carr, *The twenty years' crisis*, p. 95.
21   Waltz, *Theory of international politics*, p. 119.
22   ibid.

Confident in the heuristic power of their structural theory, neorealists thus proceed 'as if' states are unitary, purposive actors.

This conception of the state reduces foreign policy to a strategic action, a technique designed to maximize state power and realize national interests.[23] Behind this understanding lies a radical separation of the factors constituting the identity and interests of states on the one hand and their foreign policies on the other. In realist theory, particularly of the neorealist variety, state identity and interest are treated as given and their construction and formulation are effectively bracketed. Since overriding importance is attached to structural imperatives, it matters little what specific interests states have; their immediate goal will be to maximize their power in relation to other states. In this respect, foreign policies vary, not according to the social, political or cultural complexion of particular states, but rather according to their relative power. The foreign policies of great powers, be they communist or liberal-democratic, are thus said to share a common strategic logic, a logic which differs from that of middle powers and in turn that of small powers.

The realist idea that the structure of the international system determines the nature and behaviour of states, and the concomitant notion of the state as a unitary, strategic actor pursuing exogenously determined interests by maximizing power, have so shaped the field of international relations that arguably the most influential theoretical alternative—neoliberal institutionalism—also takes these assumptions as its starting point. Despite the fact that leading neoliberals such as Robert Keohane once called for the abandonment of 'the state-centric paradigm',[24] they subsequently embraced the view that the state constitutes the principal actor in international relations.[25] They also

---

23 See F.S. Northedge, 'The nature of foreign policy,' in *The foreign policies of the powers*, ed. F.S. Northedge, Faber and Faber, London, 1968, p. 9.

24 Joseph S. Nye Jr, and Robert O. Keohane, 'Transnational relations and world politics: an introduction,' in *Transnational relations and world politics*, eds Keohane and Nye, Harvard University Press, Cambridge, 1970, pp. xxiii-v.

25 This shift was first apparent in Keohane and Nye's work *Power and interdependence: world politics in transition*, Little, Brown and Company, Boston, 1977. From then on state-centrism defined the foundations of neoliberal theory. See Robert O. Keohane, *After hegemony: cooperation and discord in the world political economy*, Princeton University Press, Princeton, 1984, p. 25.

accepted the paradigmatic realist proposition that the anarchical structure of the international system is the primary determinant of state behaviour. Neoliberals, Keohane observes, 'agree with neorealists that by understanding the structure of an international system, as defined by neorealists, we come to know "a small number of big and important things" '.[26] Once they have made this structuralist move, the image of the state as a unitary, strategic actor follows. Beginning with the theoretical assumption that states are coherent rational-egoists, neoliberals describe international politics in game-theoretic terms, portraying states as self-interested utility-maximizers responding to the imperatives of the international system.[27] They part company with realists, however, when it comes to the question of international co-operation. For realists, the primacy of self-help under conditions of anarchy severely impedes cooperation between states. Because states are concerned with their relative power, it is often rational for them to go it alone even when all participants stand to gain from co-operation. Neoliberals, in contrast, argue that anarchy does not necessarily imply the absence of interstate co-operation. States engage in co-operative social relations, and create international institutions, to achieve goals that autonomy and self-help cannot provide. 'From the deficiency of the "self-help system",' Keohane contends, 'we derive the need for international regimes.'[28] The debate between neorealists and neoliberals is thus primarily about whether states are concerned with relative or absolute gains, not about the primacy of structural determinants or the image of the state as a unitary, strategic actor.[29]

The above propositions about the primacy of structural determinants, about the unitary state, and about foreign policy as an externally oriented strategic action have provided the basic analytical framework for the traditional 'realist school' of Australian foreign policy analysis. However, one important qualification is necessary here. In moving from the realm of general theory to that of specific foreign policy analysis one is forced

---

26 Robert O. Keohane, *International institutions and state power*, Westview, Boulder, p. 8.
27 Keohane, *After hegemony*, pp. 25-30.
28 ibid. p. 88.
29 The major contributions to this debate are found in the following collection: David A. Baldwin ed., *Neorealism and neoliberalism: the contemporary debate*, Columbia University Press, New York, 1993.

to address domestic factors—such as factionalism, electoral politics, interest group bargaining and bureaucratic decision-making—which necessarily complicate, if not obviate, the image of the state as a unitary actor. Realist foreign policy analysis is thus compelled to admit the very factors bracketed by realist theory. This having been said, these factors have nevertheless been incorporated in a way that upholds the primacy of systemic imperatives and retains the idea of foreign policy as strategic action. Realist scholars treat Australian foreign policy as a dependent variable (the subject to be explained) with structural considerations acting as the independent variable (the primacy source of explanation). Under this schema, domestic factors are generally introduced as intervening variables, forces which modify and condition the Australian government's responses to largely external incentives and challenges.

Without denying the distinctive characteristics of their scholarship, Henry Albinski, Coral Bell, Harry Gelber and T.B. Millar, among others, have all interpreted Australian foreign policy from a realist standpoint.[30] Among these, Bell's work is most clearly structured by the analytical principles outlined above.[31] To begin with, she treats prevailing geopolitical conditions as the primary determinant of national policy. The international environment is understood as a shifting array of threats to Australian security, and these threats are understood primarily in military-strategic terms. Australian foreign policy is in turn interpreted as a set of responses to the changing strategic environment, so much so that Bell explicitly narrows the definition of foreign policy to exclude economic determinants and reactions. Hers is 'a work of foreign policy analysis not of economic history'.[32] Realist theory predicts that lesser powers deal with the insecurities of their

---

30 See, among other works, Henry Albinski, *The Australian-American security relationship*, University of Queensland, St. Lucia, 1982; Coral Bell, *Dependent ally: a study of Australian foreign policy*, Oxford University Press, Melbourne, 1988; H.G. Gelber, *The Australian-American alliance*, Penguin, Ringwood, 1968; and T.B. Millar, *Australia in peace and war*, Australian National University Press, Canberra, 1978.
31 In addition to her work cited above, see Coral Bell, *Negotiation from strength: a study in the politics of power*, Chatto and Windus, London, 1962; *Agenda for the eighties*, Australian National University Press, Canberra, 1980; and *Agenda for the nineties*, Longman Cheshire, Sydney, 1991.
32 Bell, *Dependent ally*, p. 2

geostrategic environment by aligning with great powers, and not surprisingly Bell's analysis is primarily concerned with Australia's search for alliances. To the extent that there has been variation in Australian foreign policy, it has come from Australia's changing position within the geopolitical hierarchy of states and from the shifting configuration of international power. As it evolved from a minor power to a medium power Australia has gained greater independence, allowing domestic factors such as changing leadership, party differences and electoral forces greater sway.[33] And as the structure of the international system has shifted from bipolarity to multipolarity, Australian policy has faced new constraints and incentives.[34] When it comes to evaluation, Bell assesses Australian foreign policy in terms of whether or not it constituted a rational response to real or perceived systemic imperatives, reaching generally approving conclusions.[35]

Before the end of the Cold War, realist assumptions may well have provided an appropriate framework for the analysis of Australian foreign policy. Military and political competition between the superpowers undeniably structured the post-1945 international order, and the need to construct, maintain and service the alliance with the United States indeed dominated Australia's foreign policy agenda. Nevertheless, the analytical utility of these assumptions has rapidly declined with the advent of a more multipolar, institutionalized and globalized international order, and with the formulation of Labor's 'new internationalist' foreign policy. This is not to say, of course, that the geopolitical dynamics of the international system no longer influence Australian policy or that foreign policy now lacks a strategic dimension. Rather, it is to suggest that focusing on these systemic determinants and aspects of policy yields a particularly thin reading of contemporary Australian practice. While systemic pressures still exert a determining influence on Australian foreign policy, these now extend well beyond the configuration of geopolitical power between states emphasized by realists. As mentioned in the introduction, Australian policy-makers are beginning to take account of systemic pressures that encompass the dynamics

---

33 ibid. pp. 199-200
34 See Coral Bell, 'The changing central balance and Australian policy', in ed. Bell, *Agenda for the nineties*, pp. 1-23.
35 Bell, *Dependent ally*, p. 197.

of the world economy, environmental protection, the politics of human rights, as well as traditional military and political considerations.[36] And although policy-makers admit that Australia's options are determined by its status as a middle power—that is by its position within the hierarchy of states—these options are no longer narrowly dictated by the alliance imperative stressed by realists. In fact, middle powers are now said to be uniquely placed to shape the institutional structure of the international system itself.[37] Finally, Australian policy-makers now emphasize the role that foreign policy plays in the reconstruction and reconstitution of the Australian nation-state, a self-constitutive role obscured by the realist conception of foreign policy as primarily a strategic action.[38]

Marxism

It is common wisdom that realism and Marxism exist at opposite ends of a wide spectrum of international relations thought. Realists, it is argued, emphasize the political-military aspects of international life, while Marxists stress economic dynamics; realists focus on relations between states, whereas Marxists concentrate on competition between classes; realists hold a cyclical view of history, while some Marxists have a linear view; and, finally, realists advance an ethic of stability, in contrast to the Marxist ethic of emancipation. Notwithstanding these differences, however, there are important similarities between realist theory and the dominant Marxist perspective on international relations, namely world systems theory. Like realism, world systems theory offers a structuralist account of international politics which emphasizes systemic determinants over unit-level phenomena.[39] Just as realists attribute the nature and behaviour of states to the logic of the anarchical system

---

36 Evans and Grant, *Australia's foreign relations*, p. 33.
37 ibid. pp. 322-326. For a comprehensive discussion of the opportunities and constraints facing Australia as a middle power, see Andrew F. Cooper, Richard A. Higgott and Kim Richard Nossal, *Relocating middle powers: Australia and Canada in a changing world order*, Melbourne University Press, Melbourne, 1993.
38 Evans and Grant, *Australia's foreign relations*, p. 322.
39 For an excellent comparison of realist and world systems theories, see Alexander Wendt, 'The agent-structure problem in international relations theory', *International organization*, vol. 46, no. 3, Summer 1987, pp. 335-70.

of states, world systems theorists impute the characteristics and functions of states to the logic of the capitalist world economy. And just as realist structuralism leads to a conception of the state as a unitary, strategic actor, so does this variant of Marxist structuralism. State interests are broadly aligned with ruling-class interests and these are externally oriented and reactive, singularly responsive to the wider imperatives of the capitalist world-economy over and above domestic social, cultural and political determinants. This again means that foreign policy is understood as a strategic action, a technique by which the 'national' interests of ruling elites are pursued within an array of external systemic constraints and incentives.

World systems theory is founded on the assumption that social change and development can be understood only by examining social systems in their entirety. According to Immanuel Wallerstein, a social system is defined by 'the existence within it of a division of labor, such that the various sectors or areas within are dependent upon economic exchange with others for the smooth and continuous provisioning of the needs of the area'.[40] Given this definition, tribes, communities and nation-states are not considered valid units of analysis, for none of them constitute total social systems.[41] Since the sixteenth century, these 'non-systems' have all become progressively embedded within a single modern world system, a globalizing social order structured by the dynamics of the capitalist world economy. Sovereign states, Wallerstein contends, are functional institutions within this capitalist world system. They first emerged in Europe in response to the needs of new capitalist classes. The 'local capitalist classes—cash-crop landowners (often, even usually, nobility) and merchants—turned to the state, not only to liberate them from non-market constraints ... but to create new constraints on the new market, the market of the European world-economy'.[42] Once established, the fragmented political order of the system of sovereign states greatly enhanced the development of capitalist enterprise. 'Capitalism has been able to flourish', Wallerstein

---

40 Immanuel Wallerstein, *The capitalist world economy*, Cambridge University Press, Cambridge, 1979, p. 5.
41 Immanuel Wallerstein, *The modern world system*, Vol. 1, Academic Press, New York, p. 348.
42 Wallerstein, *The capitalist world economy*, p. 18.

BEYOND FOREIGN POLICY

argues, 'precisely because the world-economy has had within its bounds not one but a multiplicity of political systems ... [C]apitalism as an economic mode is based on the fact that economic factors operate within an arena larger than that which any political entity can totally control. This gives capitalists a freedom to maneuver that is structurally based.'[43] Overall, therefore, the state is thought to serve local capitalist interests by employing 'non-market devices' to increase short-term profitability, and the decentralized system of states facilitates the constant expansion of the capitalist world economy. 'The interstate system', in Wallerstein's words, 'is the political superstructure of the capitalist world economy and was a deliberate invention of the modern world'.[44]

Like realists, world systems theorists stress the uneven distribution of power between states, but instead of emphasizing military-strategic differences, they attribute this inequality to the logic of the capitalist world-economy in which the system of states is embedded. According to Wallerstein, states are functionally differentiated in terms of the role their sub-economies perform in the international division of labour. Core states are now the industrial heartlands which monopolize skills, technology and capital, peripheral states in contrast tend to be labour-intensive raw material producers, and semi-peripheral states have sufficiently complex economic processes and strong state structures to situate them between the core and the periphery.[45] When this division of labour was first set in place in sixteenth-century Europe, an alliance between capitalist landowners and merchants led to the creation of strong state mechanisms in core countries, while the conflicting interests of these groups in peripheral countries produced weak state structures. These differences in state strength, Wallerstein contends, in turn generated an entrenched system of ' "unequal exchange" which is enforced by strong states on weak ones, by core states on peripheral

---

43 Wallerstein, *The modern world system*, p. 348.
44 Immanuel Wallerstein, *Geopolitics and geoculture: essays on the changing world-system*, Cambridge University Press, Cambridge, 1991, p. 141.
45 Wallerstein is at pains to stress that the semi-periphery is not 'a residual category': 'The semiperiphery is a necessary structural element in a world-economy ... These middle areas ... partially deflect the political pressures which groups primarily located in peripheral areas might otherwise direct against core states and the groups which operate within and through their state machineries.' ibid. pp. 349-50.

areas'.[46] Core states use their power to create an international climate conducive to the free movement of capital, and peripheral states willingly or reluctantly accept their allotted role in the world economy and adopt domestic social policies appropriate to the needs of international capital. Hegemonic core states play a particularly important role in structuring the capitalist world economy. For instance, Wallerstein stresses the importance of American power in the creation of the post-1945 international economic order, arguing that the Marshall Plan, US policy in Latin America, and Washington's support of decolonization were all attempts to free American capital through the creation of an open trading structure.[47] The rise and decline of hegemons is thus one of the crucial 'variables' in determining the 'relative tightness or looseness of the world system'.[48]

In the preceding section on realism, I argued that structural theories which emphasize systemic influences on the nature and behaviour of states necessarily lead to a conception of the state as a unitary, purposive actor, a coherent agent capable of interpreting and responding to environmental imperatives. This is true not only of realist theory but also of world systems theory. Because realists define the international system as a field of forces governing relations *between* territorially distinct units, they draw a sharp distinction between the domestic and the international. To sustain the image of the state as a unitary actor, therefore, they must either argue that states have the power and authority to command unity within their borders (the classical realist move) or claim that the assumption of state unity is valid theoretically if not empirically (the neorealist move). Solutions such as these, however, are not suited to world systems theory because the structures and processes of the capitalist world economy transcend the domestic and the international. To constitute a unitary actor responding to global systemic pressures the state must instead be defined as a coherent, clearly identifiable administrative agency situated at the apex of national political power. Hence Wallerstein's view that states are 'centralized apparatuses for the domination of labor in the service of capitalist production'.[49]

---

46 Wallerstein, *Capitalist world economy*, p. 18.
47 ibid. p. 31.
48 ibid. p. 25.
49 Wallerstein, *Geopolitics and geoculture*, p. 140.

As such, state interests closely align with those of national economic elites, although Wallerstein is at pains to stress the 'relative autonomy' enjoyed by 'state managers'.[50] World systems theorists thus adopt a structural Marxist, not an instrumental, Marxist view of the state, defining the state's interests in terms of its role in the protection and reproduction of capitalist social relations rather than the direct expression of particular bourgeois interests.[51]

In short, world systems theory portrays the state as a functional institution within the capitalist world economy. It claims that the nature of the state—its strength or weakness—is determined by the position it occupies within the system, and it assumes that primary state interests are dictated by the local managerial requirements of the capitalist system. It follows from these propositions that foreign policy is once again defined as an externally oriented strategic action. Despite the fact that the capitalist world economy straddles the domestic and international realms, and although its all-encompassing processes and structures generate a distinctive conception of the unitary state, world systems theorists nevertheless retain a sense of the internal and the external, thus preserving the conventional idea of foreign policy. While domestic policy involves those actions states take to fulfil their managerial role within their jurisdictional boundaries, foreign policy consists of those strategies that states employ to extend their influence beyond such boundaries. Not surprisingly, world systems theorists consider the structural imperatives of the capitalist world economy to be the primary determinant of a state's foreign policy. The foreign policies of core states thus share a species similarity, as do the policies of peripheral and in turn semi-peripheral states. This is not to say that world systems theorists ignore the influence of military and political competition on foreign policy, rather they see such competition as a consequence of underlying economic structures and processes.[52] As we shall see,

---

50 Wallerstein, *Capitalist world economy*, p. 20.
51 For an excellent comparison of instrumental and structural Marxist approaches to the state, see Clyde W. Barrow, *Critical theories of the state: Marxist, neo-Marxist, post-Marxist*, University of Wisconsin Press, Madison, 1993.
52 Wallerstein argues that 'the logic of the system's development has been to reproduce parallel hierarchies of core and periphery within both the world economy and the interstate system'. *Geopolitics and geoculture*, p. 140.

accounts of Australian foreign policy that draw on world systems theory see military-political relations between states as nested within the larger framework of the capitalist world economy.

World systems theory has been widely criticized for attributing the emergence, the nature and the behaviour of states to the logic of the capitalist world economy.[53] Two lines of argument stand out. Charles Tilly claims that world systems theory cannot account for the organizational structures developed by the early Absolutist states, a failure he attributes to the theory's neglect of the role warfare played in the process of state formation. The emergence of territorial states, he contends, and the various organisational forms they assumed, resulted from the dialectical interplay between capital and coercion, between mutually reinforcing Procrustean and mercantile interests.[54] Developing a second, but related, line of criticism, John Meyer argues that world systems theory fails to explain the gradual convergence of state forms. Contrary to Wallerstein's argument, core and peripheral states have not developed distinctive political institutions that reflect their class position within the capitalist world economy. In fact, state-forms in both sectors have shown a remarkable degree of convergence: 'Both rich and poor societies evolve similar institutional arrangements, in important respects. Education expands everywhere. So does urbanization. So do all sorts of state services and communications systems.'[55] We can explain this convergence, Meyer contends, only by acknowledging the existence of a powerful world polity, a world-wide institutional structure which defines what constitutes a legitimate state and justifiable

---

[53] See especially, Aristide R. Zolberg, 'Origins of the modern world system: a missing link,' *World politics*, vol. 33, no. 2, January 1981, pp. 253-81; and Theda Skocpol, 'Wallerstein's world capitalist system: a theoretical and historical critique,' *American journal of sociology*, vol. 82, no. 5, 1977, pp. 1075-90.

[54] Charles Tilly, *Coercion, capital, and European states, AD 990-1990*, Blackwell, Oxford, 1990, p. 11. Some world systems theorists have responded by denying that they emphasize economic over military determinants. Christopher Chase-Dunn, for instance, argues that economic and geopolitical competition 'constitute a single integrated logic in the modern world-system'. See his *Global formation: structure of the world economy*, Blackwell, Oxford, 1989, p. 108.

[55] John W. Meyer, 'The world polity and authority of the nation-state', in *Institutional structure: constituting state, society, and the individual*, eds George Thomas et al, Sage, London, 1989, pp. 115.

state action, a system of social rules that are integral to modernity but independent of the capitalist world economy.

In spite of these explanatory weaknesses, world systems theory, and its attendant assumptions about states and their foreign policies, has provided the basic conceptual and analytical apparatus for a second, noteworthy perspective on Australian foreign policy, namely that associated with the work of Joseph Camilleri. The extraordinarily prolific and wide-ranging nature of Camilleri's scholarship—which includes major studies of Chinese foreign policy, sovereignty, the state and nuclear power, and Australia's relations with the United States—makes it difficult to characterize without risking oversimplification.[56] This having been said, certain recurring explanatory themes are apparent in his work, themes explicitly indebted to world systems theory.

Following Wallerstein, Camilleri believes that human social activity now forms a single, encompassing world system organized around the structures and processes of the capitalist world-economy. 'The systemic model developed by Wallerstein,' Camilleri contends, 'is theoretically instructive in that it synthesizes three interacting relationships: that between the state and the expansion of capital, that between the international division of labour and the world market and that between states and varying configurations of power.'[57] Within this unified system, the logic of the capitalist world-economy holds sway, providing—among other things—the initial impetus for the rise of sovereign states. Again echoing Wallerstein, Camilleri claims that territorial states emerged as functional institutions serving the needs of local capitalism: 'The functions of the state did not derive so much from the logic of sovereignty or the will of sovereigns as from the needs of national economic expansion, the main beneficiaries of which were the emerging

---

[56] See Joseph A. Camilleri, *Civilization in crisis: human prospects in a changing world*, Cambridge University Press, Cambridge, 1976; *An introduction to Australian foreign policy*, Jacaranda, Milton, 1979; *The web of dependence: Australian-American relations*, Macmillan, Melbourne, 1980; *Chinese foreign policy: the Maoist era and its aftermath*, Robertson, Oxford, 1980; *The state and nuclear power: conflict and control in the western world*, Wheatsheaf, Brighton, 1984; *ANZUS: Australia's predicament in the nuclear age*, Macmillan, Melbourne, 1987; Camilleri and Jim Falk, *The end of sovereignty?: the politics of a shrinking and fragmenting world*, Edward Elgar, London, 1992.

[57] Joe Camilleri, 'Reflections on the state in transition,' in *Critical politics: from the personal to the global*, ed. Paul James, Arena Publications, Melbourne, p. 145.

capitalist classes.'[58] Camilleri, like other world systems theorists, is adamant that despite this functional role, the state, and the system of states, has evolved 'a degree of political autonomy even though the manner and context in which it is exercised will vary greatly from state to state, issue to issue, and one period to the next'.[59] Individual state interests and policies are not direct expressions of ruling class-interests, and the anarchical interstate system itself generates independent geopolitical pressures on the nature and behaviour of states. Nevertheless, this recognition of state autonomy simply leads Camilleri, like Wallerstein, to adopt a structural Marxist, not an instrumental Marxist, conception of the state. Without necessarily acting as 'the executive committee of the bourgeoisie', the 'modern industrial state', he argues, 'has played a leading role in protecting and expanding the international capitalist relations of production'.[60]

On the surface, Camilleri's analysis of Australian foreign policy bears a striking resemblance to that of leading realists. Like Bell, his interpretation emphasizes the geopolitical determinants of national policy. 'After 1945', begins his best-selling *Introduction to Australian foreign policy*, 'Australian governments were increasingly compelled to respond to the rapidly changing balance of power in Asia.'[61] As a small, insecure state, Australia responded to this threat environment by forging an alliance with the United States, the dominant regional and global power. Camilleri interprets subsequent developments in Australian foreign policy as a series of responses to the perceived imperatives of the changing international balance of power, particularly the military and political position and objectives of the United States. Adopting a similar position to Bell, he argues that the decline of regional threats and the progressive shift to a multipolar balance of power has enabled Australia to develop a more independent foreign policy, even if it remains far more constrained than he would wish.[62] Given this emphasis on

---

58 Camilleri and Falk, *The end of sovereignty?*, p. 26.
59 ibid. p. 82.
60 ibid. p. 83.
61 Camilleri, *Introduction to Australian foreign policy*, p. 1.
62 In 1980 he wrote that the 'net effect of the trend towards multipolarity has been to enhance Australia's room for diplomatic manoeuvre and provide it with a limited sphere of influence ... But the transition from *virtual subservience* to *associate dependence* is tentative and clearly circumscribed by the continued asymmetry of the Australian-American relationship.'

the systemic determinants of the geopolitical order, it is not surprising that throughout Camilleri's various accounts, domestic influences on foreign policy appear primarily as intervening variables.[63] This is not to down play the significance he attaches to such factors, it is merely to observe that his work reflects Waltz's analytical dictum that consideration of systemic forces should provide the first cut in any explanation of foreign policy, with domestic factors being introduced subsequently to account for specific policy decisions and variations.[64]

Important as they are, these realist-like interpretive moves do not represent the deep theoretical foundations of Camilleri's analytical framework. As we have seen, world systems theorists nest the geopolitical balance of power within the larger structures of the capitalist world economy. This is clearly apparent in Camilleri's discussion of American hegemony, an account which stresses the structural/functional role that American power performed in the extension of global capitalism after the Second World War. Washington's containment policy, he contends, 'was aimed at the Soviet state precisely because its policies threatened the free play of market forces and in particular the continued growth of the world capitalist system'.[65] Given this economic interpretation of American hegemony, it is not surprising that Camilleri also highlights the underlying economic functions of the Australian-American alliance. He writes that the 'alliance is part of a wider strategic and political framework the express purpose of which is to facilitate the free flow of transnational capital in general and American capital in particular'.[66] Because he ultimately grounds the ANZUS alliance in the structures and processes of the capitalist world economy, his assessment of this long-time centrepiece of Australian foreign policy ranges beyond the conventional military-security implications weighed by Bell and others. 'One of the most serious drawbacks of the existing alliance relationship', he argues, 'is the stifling effect it has had on Australian diplomacy and the independent initiatives it could take,

---

The web of dependence, p. 137.
[63] This approach characterizes all three of his major works on Australian foreign policy. See his *Introduction to Australian foreign policy*; *The web of dependence*; and *ANZUS*.
[64] Waltz, *Man, the state, and war*, Columbia University Press, New York, 1959, ch. 7.
[65] Camilleri, *ANZUS*, p. 48.
[66] ibid. pp. 50-1.

regionally and internationally, in support of policies and institutions that can advance prospects for a more humane, egalitarian, peaceful and sustainable world order.'[67] Yet in spite of Camilleri's broader understanding of the systemic pressures bearing on Australia's external affairs and its influence on the judgments he reaches, his perspective nevertheless retains the narrow conception of foreign policy as a strategic action, a set of responses to structural imperatives and constraints.

The interrelated assumptions that there is a single world system organized around the structures and processes of the capitalist world-economy, that territorial states arose as a response to the functional requirements of that system, and that foreign policy is a strategic action driven by systemic imperatives, have together provided the basic framework for Camilleri's recent writings on globalization.[68] To begin with, his preoccupation with the causal power of the capitalist world-economy leads to an overly economistic conception of globalization. Irrespective of the complexities introduced in his various writings, Camilleri basically defines globalization as the increasingly fast and extensive internationalization of economic activity, a development he interprets as the latest stage in the evolution of the capitalist world-economy.[69] He argues that these changes in the nature of the capitalist world-economy have affected states in two ways. At the most fundamental level, they have made redundant or eroded some of the sovereign state's most fundamental powers, powers which capitalism first demanded. '[W]hereas in the early stages of capitalist development national economies and nation-states were decisive in the internationalization of economic activity, in the contemporary period systemic interaction on a global scale appears to have acquired a dynamic of its own.'[70] At a more immediate level, globalization has produced new centres of economic power, increased intercapitalist rivalry between states, and decreased America's capacity to co-ordinate international economic

---

67 ibid. p. 46.
68 These include *The end of sovereignty?*, as well as several articles, notably 'Reflections on the state in transition' and 'Music of the sphere', *Arena magazine*, no. 13, November 1994, pp. 33-7.
69 For instance, in 'Music of the sphere' his introductory remarks on globalization are solely concerned with economic processes and developments (p. 36).
70 Camilleri, *The end of sovereignty?*, p. 78.

activity.[71] These aspects of globalization, Camilleri contends, represent the main systemic imperatives driving Australian foreign policy. Focusing on the Hawke and Keating governments' emphasis on Asia, he argues that it 'is difficult to make sense of Australian policies and actions towards Asia without placing them in the context of the internationalization of economic activity, which has steadily gathered pace in the last twenty years'.[72] He goes on to attribute Australia's increasingly independent foreign policy to the impact of globalized economic activity on American power. 'One of the ironies of globalization', he writes, 'was the gradual demotion of the United States in the overall architecture of Australia's economic and foreign policy.'[73]

Camilleri's world systems perspective on Australian foreign policy has two principal virtues: it highlights the impact of economic structures and processes on the nature and behaviour of states, and it focuses attention on the economic, as well as the geopolitical, determinants of foreign policy. Although this represents a significant improvement on realism's crude geopolitical structuralism, it nevertheless provides an inadequate framework for understanding the relationship between globalization and state behaviour. First, as argued in the introduction, globalization involves more than the internationalization of economic activity, even if this constitutes one of its key dimensions. Moreover, other important aspects of globalization—such as international institutionalization—are irreducible to economic determinants. Secondly, as we have already observed, the state's role in constructing global structures, as well as its role in reconstructing its own identity and realm of legitimate action, are obscured by narrow structuralist theories, and world systems theory is no exception. It is not surprising, therefore, that Camilleri tends to ignore these dimensions of Australian foreign policy, only raising them as possible corrections to what he presents as the overly reactive nature of Australia's current external posture.[74] Overall, world systems theory may well expand the menu of systemic pressures bearing on the state, particularly the Australian state, but its understanding of structure remains too confined to accommodate

---

71 Camilleri, 'Music of the sphere', p. 34.
72 ibid.
73 ibid. p. 36.
74 ibid. p. 37.

the multidimensional structures and processes of globalization. And its structural determinism obscures the mutually constitutive relationship between emerging global structures and the state.

Constructivism

In recent years constructivist scholars have launched a sustained attack on structuralist theories of international relations. As we have seen, both realist and world systems theories deduce the nature and behaviour of states from the structural properties of the systems in which they are embedded. To overcome the limitations of these theories, constructivists adopt a structurationist perspective, that is one which emphasizes the mutually constitutive relationship between social agents and social structures. Drawing heavily on the work of social theorists such as Anthony Giddens, they advance two linked propositions. The first contends that social structures define what constitutes a legitimate actor as well as an actor's realm of justifiable action. This emphasis on legitimacy points to an important difference between the constructivist conception of structure and those offered by realists and Marxists. In contrast to the materialist predilections of the latter two theories, constructivists argue that the international system has a crucial institutional dimension, a system of powerfully constitutive social rules. As Giddens observes, social structures consist of 'rules and resources recursively implicated in social reproduction'.[75] These 'institutionalized cultural rules', constructivists argue, 'define the meaning and identity of the individual [actor] and the patterns of appropriate economic, political, and cultural activity engaged in by those individuals'.[76] This brings us to the second key constructivist proposition. In spite of the considerable constitutive power they attribute to social structures, constructivists insist that such structures do not exist independently of state practices. Social structures, they contend, are nothing more than routinized discursive and physical practices which persist over an extended temporal and spatial domain. 'It is through reciprocal

---

75 Anthony Giddens, *The constitution of society*, University of California Press, Berkeley, 1984, p. xxxi.
76 John Boli, John W. Meyer and George Thomas, 'Ontology and rationalization in the Western cultural account,' in *Institutional structure*, eds Thomas et al., p. 12.

interaction', Wendt argues, 'that we create and instantiate the relatively enduring social structures in terms of which we define our identities and interests.'[77] Together, these two propositions attempt to capture what Giddens calls the duality of social structures, the way in which 'the structural properties of social systems are both the medium and the outcome of the practices they recursively organize'.[78] By emphasizing this interactive relationship, constructivists lay claim to a richer understanding of state agency and a more dynamic conception of international systemic structures.

Constructivist international relations scholarship has assumed two principal forms. Modifying Waltz's classic typology, I call these variants *third image constructivism* and *fourth image constructivism*.[79] The former accepts the neorealist penchant for system-level theorizing (Waltz's third image), while the latter adopts a more encompassing perspective that incorporates domestic and international phenomena (Waltz's second and third images combined).

Third image constructivism is exemplified by Wendt's path-breaking theoretical work. In an effort to engage mainstream scholars, Wendt is committed to both systemic theory and the image of the state as a unitary actor. Like other constructivists, he believes that the identity of the state informs its interests and in turn its actions. He distinguishes, however, between a state's corporate identity (its internal human material, and ideological characteristics) and its social identity ('the meaning an actor attributes to itself while taking the perspective of others').[80] Because of his commitment to system-level theory, Wendt is forced to bracket the corporate sources of state identity, focusing entirely on the constitutive role of international social interaction. For all intents and purposes therefore, he follows conventional theorists in treating the state as a unitary actor, a move he fully admits. Third image constructivism thus adopts a relatively narrow conception of the structuration process, simply contending that institutional structures

---

77 Alexander Wendt, 'Anarchy is what states make of it: the social construction of power politics,' *International organization*, vol. 46, no. 2, Spring 1992, p. 406.
78 Giddens, *The constitution of society*, p. xxxi.
79 Waltz, *Man, the state, and war*.
80 Alexander Wendt, 'Collective identity formation and the international state,' *American political science review*, vol. 88, no. 2, June 1994, p. 385.

constitute states as legitimate international actors and state practices in turn reproduce such structures. This concentration on systemic processes is adequate so long as we are not trying to explain fundamental changes in state identity or social structures. Social interaction undeniably replicates hegemonic definitions of state identity, but how do these forms change? Without introducing non-systemic sources of state identity—such as domestic political culture—at some point in the structuration process, third image constructivism offers an overly static conception of the state and the international system, providing no clue as to how agents or structures are transformed.

Fourth image constructivism, in contrast, is more concrete and historical, and explicitly shuns Wendtian system-level theorizing. Its principal concern is to understand the nature and dynamics of international change, both change within a given system and change from one system to another. Because of this emphasis on international transformation, fourth image constructivism exhibits two distinctive characteristics.

First, its leading proponents—notably John Ruggie and Friedrich Kratochwil—treat domestic and international structures and processes as two faces of a single, global social order, and then consider the mutually constitutive relationship between this order and the state. This does not mean that they deny the existence of domestic and international realms, instead they see this partitioning of human social activity as a unique historical construct, the chief consequence and characteristic of a distinctly modern political order built around territorial, sovereign states. To recognize the historical nature of this territorial order, they contend, is to recognize that its rise, persistence and transformation can only be explained through reference to generalized political, economic, ideological and military processes. These processes generated and have helped sustain what we now categorize as domestic and international phenomena, and thus take conceptual and analytical priority.

Secondly, Ruggie and others define the sovereign state not as a unitary actor but as a distinctive system of rule. This definition rests on a clear distinction between the state (the structure of governance) and government (the agent of governance). States provide the institutional framework for government action, and government action in turn reproduces the institutional apparatus of government. In Peter Katzenstein's words:

The state is a structure of governance and rule that defines, institutionally and legally, political authority in society. States do not act—governments do. This relation between states as structures and governments as agents is complex. States shape both the interests and the powers of governments. But states exist only insofar as their existence finds expression in government practices and the norms that sustain them. Government practices are conditioned (but not determined) by the state and social structures of which they are a part.[81]

Territorial sovereign states have been the dominant systems of rule for the best part of four centuries, but fourth image constructivists insist that radically different structures of governance preceded—and are likely to follow—the present sovereign order. Such structures, they contend, need not be territorial at all, they may not be territorially fixed, or they may be based on non-exclusionary forms of territoriality.[82] Whatever form they take, as systems of rule change, new agents are endowed with political authority, and, more importantly, the nature and jurisdictional scope of that authority varies.

These paired assumptions about the generalized, global nature of social structures and processes and about the state as a system of rule have informed two distinctive, yet complementary, analyses of international change, one focusing on grand shifts between international systems, the other on recent changes within the modern system. Ruggie's ambitious work exemplifies the former concern with epochal transformations. Fundamental change, he argues, occurs when there is a redefinition of the principle on which political units are separated—the 'mode of differentiation'. The shift from the medieval order to the modern represented just such a transformation, with the principle of sovereignty supplanting the old heteronomous mode of differentiation.[83] Changes in material environments, strategic behaviour and

---

81 Peter J. Katzenstein, 'International relations theory and the analysis of change,' in *Global changes and theoretical challenges: approaches to world politics for the 1990s*, eds Ernst-Otto Czempiel and James N. Rosenau, Lexington Books, Lexington, 1989, p. 297.
82 John Gerard Ruggie, 'Territoriality and beyond: problematizing modernity in international relations,' *International organization*, vol. 47, no. 1, Winter 1993, p. 149.
83 John Gerard Ruggie, 'Continuity and transformation in the world polity: toward a neorealist synthesis,' *World politics*, vol. 35, no. 2, 1992, p. 279.

social epistemes spurred this revolution, Ruggie argues.[84] And further changes in these parameters, he contends, represent the appropriate indicators of another fundamental shift in the mode of differentiation and, in turn, the nature of the international system. Although guarded in his predictions, Ruggie identifies such changes in the European Community's construction of 'multiperspectival institutional forms' and in the rise of a new social episteme around global environmental protection.[85] Both entail the 'unbundling of territoriality', perhaps marking the decline of sovereignty as the dominant system of rule and the dawn of a postmodern form of international politics.

In contrast to Ruggie's world-historical preoccupations, Kratochwil's recent work confronts the more limited, if equally perplexing and contentious, question of why the Cold War stand-off between the superpowers came to such an abrupt conclusion, sparking, among other things, the collapse of the Soviet Union itself.[86] Although Kratochwil uses the same language of fundamental change in world politics, unlike Ruggie he is primarily concerned with changes within the modern system of sovereign states, changes from one international order to another, specifically the rise and decline of the post-1945 order based on two mutually antagonistic blocs.

International orders, Kratochwil argues, vary according to their constitutive rules and practices which dictate particular and contrasting modes of interstate interaction. As a fourth image constructivist, he believes that domestic and international social phenomena interact to condition the rules that structure international orders, a view which shapes his explanation of the origin and demise of the Cold War.[87] He and Rey Koslowski attribute the instigation of the Cold War order

---

84 Ruggie, 'Territoriality and beyond', p. 168.
85 ibid. pp. 168-74. For more on territoriality and the environment, see Robyn Eckersley's chapter in this volume.
86 See Friedrich Kratochwil, 'The embarrassment of changes: neo-realism as the science of *realpolitik* without politics,' *Review of international studies*, vol. 19, no. 1, January 1993, pp. 63-80; and Rey Koslowski and Friedrich Kratochwil, 'Understanding change in international politics: the Soviet empire's demise and the international system,' *International organization*, vol. 48, no. 2, Spring 1994, pp. 215-48.
87 '[I]nternational change is a multilevel phenomenon in which precedence cannot be accorded *a priori* to either domestic or international structures.' Koslowski and Kratochwil, 'Understanding change', p. 224.

to Stalin's determination that occupying Soviet forces would dictate the nature of subject countries' social systems. This move, they argue, violated the established norms of the European state system and prompted a hostile response from Western states. The resulting stand-off, which left Europe partitioned for four decades, was cemented and reproduced by the rival Brezhnev and Truman doctrines. Over time, Koslowski and Kratochwil contend, a system of rules governing international conduct emerged which enshrined the superpowers' respective spheres of influence, rules clearly reflected in the Helsinki Accords which recognized the permanent division of Europe into Eastern and Western blocs.[88] This order remained robust until there was a sea change in Soviet domestic politics, characterized by Gorbachev's rise to power, the advent of 'new thinking', and the jettisoning of the Brezhnev doctrine. By the end of the 1980s these internal transformations had fractured the normative foundations of the Cold War order and begun to spawn an entirely different, if embryonic, set of international behavioural norms.[89] This rapid shift from one international order to another, Koslowski and Kratochwil argue, cannot be explained by changes in the material balance of power—which remained stable throughout the late 1980s—nor through reference to purely systemic forces. Normative principles of international conduct structured and sustained the Cold War order, and domestic factors were crucial in both the construction and dissolution of that order.[90]

At the beginning of this chapter I suggested that the most interesting feature of contemporary change is the three-dimensional mutually constitutive relationship between states and emerging global structures and processes. In the preceding two sections I have argued that structuralist theories of international relations capture only one dimension of this relationship—the way in which international structures determine the nature and behaviour of states. Furthermore, such structural determinism reduces foreign policy to a strategic action conducted by

---

88 ibid. pp. 228-33.
89 ibid. pp.233-47.
90 'Fundamental change of the international system occurs when actors, through their practices, change the rules and norms constitutive of international interaction. Moreover, reproduction of the practice of international actors (i.e., states) depends on the reproduction of practices of domestic actors (i.e., individuals and groups).' ibid. p. 216.

unitary states, thus obscuring its important constitutive dimension. In contrast, constructivist theory, especially fourth image constructivism, is attuned to all three dimensions of contemporary change. As the above discussion indicates, it not only expands the conception of international structure to include institutional rules, norms and principles, it also recognizes how state practices construct and reproduce those structures. Moreover, constructivism acknowledges the way in which government foreign policy—through the construction of international standards of conduct—can act to redefine the identity of state itself, feeding back into the domestic arena and restructuring a particular system of rule.

Constructivism thus provides a more useful framework for the analysis of Australian foreign policy than that offered by structuralist theories. In the first instance, it facilitates a deeper reading of the principles underlying the current Labor government's policy. The military, economic and institutional dimensions of globalization highlighted by Evans and Grant are more comfortably accommodated within constructivism's expanded conception of structure, a conception that acknowledges both the autonomy and interconnection of such structures. The activism of the government's 'new internationalist' foreign policy also becomes more intelligible from a constructivist standpoint, one which recognizes both its constitutive as well as its strategic dimensions. And finally, constructivist theory comprehends the way in which foreign policy reproduces and reconstitutes the nation-state itself, thus making sense of Evans' and Grant's previously quoted claim that 'Australia's foreign policy is presently acting as an important catalyst in building a new Australian identity'.[91]

In the second instance, a constructivist perspective sheds greater light on the practice of Australian foreign policy and its full implications for the Australian state. The example of human rights serves to illustrate this point, especially since it goes right to the heart of the Keating government's policy of 'good international citizenship'. In 1991 Australia signed the First Optional Protocol of the International Covenant on Civil and Political Rights, thus recognizing the power of the United Nations Human Rights Committee to rule on complaints by individuals and groups about human rights violations by their home states. Signing

---

91 Evans and Grant, *Australia's foreign relations*, p. 322.

this protocol, Kathryn Sikkink argues, represents one of two crucial elements in a comprehensive human rights policy; the other is the linkage of human rights concerns to other foreign policy objectives.[92] This is not only because such actions strengthen international human rights institutions, but also because they establish a powerful legal-moral nexus between these institutions and subnational actors which has the power to transform the structure of the state itself. The salience of this nexus is clearly apparent in recent actions by Tasmanian gay and lesbian groups to overturn the state's anti-homosexual laws. Exploiting the Federal government's accession to the Protocol, these groups appealed directly to the UN Human Rights Committee, arguing that Tasmania's laws placed Australia in violation of its international human rights obligations. The Committee ruled in their favour and called for the Australian government to overturn the offending laws. The Tasmanian government's refusal to comply with the decision forced the Federal government to intervene, using its external affairs powers to override state law. The net result was a restructuring of the balance of power within the Australian federal state, a move which state premiers attacked as a violation of their sovereignty. Malcolm Fraser, the former Prime Minister, attacked the emerging nexus between UN institutions and domestic interest groups as a fundamental threat to Australian national sovereignty.[93]

Structuralist perspectives on international relations, the state and foreign policy obscure the more interesting and salient features of the above case. From such perspectives, international human rights norms are not seen as important structural elements of the international system; at best they are considered secondary to the 'real' material incentives and constraints bearing on state behaviour. In turn, national economic and strategic policies are emphasized, with human rights concerns treated as soft elements of foreign policy that are inevitably sacrificed when choices get tough. Human rights norms and policies are only considered salient, therefore, when states are prepared to transcend material interests

---

92 Kathryn Sikkink, 'The power of principled ideas: human rights policies in the United States and Western Europe,' in *Ideas and foreign policy: beliefs, institutions, and political change*, eds Judith Goldstein and Robert O. Keohane, Cornell University Press, Ithaca, 1993, pp. 142-43.
93 *Australian*, 17 August 1994, p. 13.

to force other states to cease oppressing their populations. A constructivist perspective on international human rights does not deny the importance of economic and military structures and processes, nor does it ignore the way in which human rights concerns are frequently subordinated to material objectives, or the failure of the international community to compel offending states. We can see this very clearly in the case of Indonesia's invasion of East Timor. What constructivism does is treat international human rights norms—along with other norms, rules and principles—as important structural elements of the global system. Moreover, it sees these institutions as products of state practices, such as the accession by Australia and roughly 75 other states to the First Optional Protocol. Finally, it assesses the salience of these institutions not only in terms of the international community's willingness to coerce violators—which constructivists nevertheless consider crucial—but also in terms of how the international human rights practices of individual states feed back on their internal political structures, as in the Australian case.

Conclusion

This chapter has examined how competing theories of international relations have conceptualized the state. I argued that leading theoretical perspectives fail to capture important dimensions of the mutually constitutive relationship between states and emerging global structures and processes. Their structural determinism and their image of the state as a unitary, strategic actor obscure the way in which state practices reproduce and reshape global structures and in turn transform the state itself. Recent developments in constructivist theory provide a more adequate conceptual and analytical framework for understanding this relationship, capturing the key constitutive dimensions of state action. These observations have important implications for how we study Australian foreign policy in an increasingly globalized world. The preceding discussion did not offer a comprehensive survey of Australian foreign policy analysis, my purpose being simply to show how structural realist and Marxist theories have informed two of the most prominent interpretations. Handicapped by blinkered theoretical frameworks, these perspectives have yielded particularly thin readings of Australian foreign policy. A constructivist standpoint promises a more sophisticated interpretation, one based on a multidimensional conception of global structures and processes and a richer understanding of state action that embraces both its constitutive and strategic aspects.

The application of constructivist insights to the interpretation of Australian foreign policy may help to reinvigorate Australian scholarship's contribution to key theoretical debates within the discipline of international relations. With the exception of the important interventions made by Australian postmodernists and critical theorists, in recent years Australian international relations scholars have tended to be theoretical consumers, not producers. Furthermore, there has been a general trend toward theoretically unreflective empirical analysis, in which foundational assumptions are left undisclosed and undeveloped and theoretical implications buried. While this criticism should not be overstated, a conscious engagement with current developments in constructivist theory may well help counter these tendencies. Constructivist theory is still in its infancy, and although the theoretical foundations have been laid, further progress will depend on the redesign and strengthening of these foundations through concrete historical and contemporary analysis. As we have seen, work currently focuses on epochal transformations and shifts from one international order to another. Little if any effort has been made to apply constructivist insights to foreign policy analysis, and here Australia represents an ideal and timely case study. Global structures and processes are indeed transforming the Australian state, but the relationship is reciprocal, with state practices helping to constitute the international order while redefining the Australian system of rule itself.

8

The state of postmodernity: beyond cultural nostalgia or pessimism

John Hinkson

'More than ever before', says Ralph Miliband, we 'now live in the shadow of the state'.[1] The modern state, especially the state-form familiar to the twentieth century, has powers which set it apart from the state in any other era. Yet the observer of contemporary politics would also be struck by arguments and practices which seem to contradict this truism: which deny that this continues to be a social structural necessity.

Practical politics during the 1980s became pre-occupied with forms of economic rationality which rejected the interventionist state and sought deregulatory policies supportive of a minimal state. At the same time, some social theorists proclaimed the rise of 'local narratives', dismissing any synthetic or comprehensive tendencies in narrative or interpretation as promoting processes which are inseparable from the 'totalizing' modern state.

The question addressed in this chapter is what meanings these perspectives carry for theories of the state as well as for practical forms of the state. Do these developments, in their own right or as signs of more basic changes, justify the reconceptualization of the modern state? Are we seeing a mere swing of the pendulum, as many economic rationalists would have it, or do these challenges point to processes beyond such a familiar ebb and flow? And last but not least, can these transformations be seen through the prism of the Australian state?

---

1 Ralph Miliband, *The state in capitalist society*, Weidenfeld and Nicolson, London, 1969, p. 1.

THE STATE OF POSTMODERNITY

This chapter will criticize views which, by implication, dismiss the need to re-theorize the state. It will proceed by arguing for the need to rethink state theory in terms of the concept of the postmodern state[2]. Any such attempt will necessarily be exploratory and partial. Moreover, it will unavoidably be over-generalized. Only further work can achieve the balance of general and specific analyses proper to an account of significant change.

In the pursuit of this question the argument will take seriously the proposition which sees any theory of the state as simultaneously a theory of society. This approach to the state, as David Held reminds us,[3] is actually the legacy of Marx. It is Marx who places the state firmly within socio-economic settings and related interests. This is certainly to say that state and society are inter-related; it is also to argue that those inter-relations are crucial for any account of the nature of the state, although care must always be taken not to reduce one to the other. Thus, any argument about a postmodern state must also be about a society which has taken on qualities able to be called postmodern.

While the argument of this chapter will work within this method it will become clear that no familiar Marxian socio-economic account will be adequate to clarify the nature of such a postmodern state or society. Social accounts of modernity, including its class and market relations, can give little insight into those qualities which lead one to refer to the postmodern state. Nor does the modification 'advanced capitalism', as one finds in many writers such as Miliband and Habermas, sufficiently recognize the significance of the change.

The postmodern state: interpretive issues

Accounts of postmodernity provide a number of comparative reference

---

[2] The term 'postmodern' is not crucial here. Any notion which is sufficiently suggestive of epochal change would be adequate. Nevertheless the choice of 'postmodern' is not arbitrary. For postmodern theorists engage processes, including new notions of space and time, which are central to issues related to a rethinking of the theory of the state. We must learn to separate this or that 'postmodern view' from the underlying orientations of postmodern theory. For if the former may be characterized as tending towards the superficial, the deeper orientations engage matters of long-term significance.

[3] David Held, 'Central perspectives on the modern state', in *States and societies*, Martin Robertson, Oxford, 1983, p. 25.

points which allow a contrast between contemporary settings and those of recent modernity.[4] One common theme is the difference between a modern unified self and a postmodern decentred self.[5] Another is the heightened emphasis on space in social thought in the context of real processes of internationalization and symbolized by notions such as the global village. Yet another reference point is the information revolution—that development in scientific practice which gives us, amongst other things, the communications revolution and high-tech production.[6]

All of these postmodern themes suggest significant transformations of society. Even the notion of the postmodern self allows us to ask about the nature of social change such that the self becomes an issue of practical politics as seen through such notions as 'the personal is political'. Yet, none of these themes, so important to arguments about postmodernity, raise the question of the postmodern state. This is not an omission engineered by the selection of biased examples. For the most part, postmodern theory has an attitude towards the state which paradoxically throws new (if obsessive) light on the nature of the modern state while being blind towards the state in our time. A dualism between modern 'totalizing' forms, which correspond to grand narratives, and postmodern specificity and decentredness apparently leaves little conceptual space for a postmodern state.[7] The argument of this chapter

---

4   This interest in comparative social forms is not found in the work of most postmodern theorists. For them a comparative account continues the theme of periodization within a grand narrative of progress. Postmodernity, it is said, escapes all such narratives and de-legitimates them. This chapter, to the contrary, is interested in developing a material account of the circumstances of change.
5   Not all contrasts between nineteenth century and twentieth century versions of the self take this form of unified/decentred. Habermas, who will give no place to the postmodern, engages similar distinctions when he speaks of the intuitive 'philosophy of consciousness' view of the subject and his own theory which grounds the subject in a theory of intersubjectivity.
6   There are a number of writers who take up postmodernity in this way, perhaps the best-known of whom is Jean-Francois Lyotard. See his *The postmodern condition*, Manchester University Press, Manchester, 1984.
7   I will not take up in this article the question of 'governmentality' which has emerged under the influence of Foucault. Here I will merely mention that this too is a version of the demise of the state in a somewhat paradoxical form. For governmentality is a gloss on Foucault's dictum that 'power is everywhere' and as such can be argued to represent the state as everywhere or, in effect, nowhere. Many of the themes of this scholarship are discussed in Rob Watts, 'Government and modernity: an essay in thinking governmentality', *Arena*

will be that this has been an overly excited and superficial reaction to profound changes in the social order, one which needs radical revision. The source of such a revision will partly lie in an examination of the state-society relation. It cannot be sufficiently emphasized, however, that this will only be helpful if the new ways in which power is experienced are able to be related to changes in the social order and then explored with more care and conceptual clarity than one typically finds in postmodern accounts of postmodernity.

All of the above examples are strongly grounded in changes in practical reality. Yet, as indications of practical changes in society, the examples stand merely as empirical generalizations. Like many of the themes of postmodern theory, they reflect an intuitive feel for a changed setting, but give little interpretative insight into the nature of that change or its significance. The writer who *does* wish to interpret those changes by drawing upon contemporary theories of the state is in no better situation. In this case it is because of the nature of interpretation supported by those theories. Contemporary theories of the state and theories of society are largely modified theories drawn from the practical settings of modernity. Thus when changes in social setting occur they may be given empirical recognition, but when it comes to a judgment of their significance they slip between the categories of social theory.

Thus the technological change implicit in a reference to the information revolution or to internationalization is interpreted by the state theorist, at best, as a change where all institutions and persons now have available to them radical technological forms which reorient their behaviour. With the state, for example, we now have powerful surveillance technologies available to it with some major implications for the power and the practical workings of the state. But it is not, they say, a change which requires any more basic rethinking. That is, the state theorist has no interpretive frame able to engage the empirical generalization about the implications of the new technologies.[8]

---

journal, no. 2, 1994, pp. 103-58.
8 In many ways this is more of a problem than with the postmodern theorist. For if the best of the latter writers rely on intuitive feel, those who work within theoretical frameworks drawn from other circumstances are disposed to generate predictable responses to emergent events and processes, responses dictated by their frame of interpretation. At this point one

It is important to be clear here about what difference this makes. In a recent short article on the contemporary state David Held[9] has outlined what he regards as a major re-orientation in state theory given the processes of globalization. These processes cut across the familiar context of the state, in particular breaking up those territorial boundaries to which we have become accustomed in modernity. His reflections engage some of the themes within postmodern social theory such as de-territorialization and a meta-narrative of democracy, major questions which certainly deserve our concern. Nevertheless it is my argument that these questions are described both by Held and various postmodern theorists in terms which are far too empirical. An emphasis on globalization and internationalization without significant attendance to the underlying processes at work, as well as to perspectives appropriate to their understanding, will quickly lead towards what he in fact proposes: an argument about organizational forms which work beyond the boundaries of the nation-states. This is an argument abstracted from any inquiry and response to changes in self and cultural process, let alone any sense of a shift in the nature of the contradictions influencing social and cultural conflict around the state and civil society.

This is certainly not to suggest that empirical generalizations are of no interest. They are crucial reference points for a reworking of state theory; but by themselves they do not give sufficient insight into the nature of the new situation. And arguments about world government may well need to be made, but there are many questions which need our attention before that proposal can be given a rounded consideration.

The problem with attempts which adjust theories of the state by simply focusing on the technological revolution is that they lack a sufficiently social account of the change. They rely on an approach to technology which is especially modern; either it treats technology as a tool, or, as in the case of Marx, as a given for a definite period—as one finds with modes of production. We need to ask whether this technology, that of the communications and information revolution, is strictly comparable with past technological forms; and to pursue this question requires an investigation of the social processes which support

---

can speak of theoretical dogmatism.

9   'A vote of confidence in democracy', *The Australian*, 10 March 1993, pp. 20-1.

the innovation.

How then can the communications or the information revolution be thought of sensibly as a social relation? It requires that these technologies be seen as elements which lie at the heart of how certain relations between self and other are formed. This is to speak of social relations in a new way, one which is distinctive in the degree to which it is able to conceive of social relations as working through technological mediation.[10]

Much work has been done indirectly on technologically mediated relations through investigations of the economic market and how it works via the mediation of money. Through money we can have an extended relation to the other and, as Marx emphasized, exchange commodities. But the commodity market is not the only example of social relations which are extended in this way. For example, much more neglected than the market are those relations which are facilitated by the printed word. It is the relations of the intellectual culture which are the main carriers of this type of technologically mediated interchange. The intellectual culture reaches across what it regards as parochial settings and does so via the extension provided by the printed word. These technologically mediated relations are especially important for understanding the information revolution because the latter is precisely their product. That is, emergent technical means which facilitate new forms of social extension were generated in those settings which were already characterized by these historic carriers of social extension.

The ways in which social practices of this kind have a very special quality of extension through time and place because of technological mediation must lie at the core of any understanding of how our settings today can be described as postmodern. Obviously this cannot be because of the technological mediation carried by the printed word, a form of relation closely tied to modernity. But the communications revolution, which is the technological product of the practices of academic institutions and related research institutes, also launches academia into a new phase of extended practice. In our times, the new forms of

---

10   Readers of *Arena* are in a position to realize the degree to which this way of speaking about social relations is drawn from the work of Geoff Sharp. See his 'Constitutive abstraction and social practice', *Arena*, no. 70, 1985, pp. 48-82.

technological mediation—that is, structures associated with information on the one hand and technologized image on the other—are themselves projected materially across all the institutions of society. One expression of this revolution is the high-tech renovation of the work process; another expression with even more profound implications is the making over of the social relations of everyday life, via the new mediums of communication. It is these conceptual and practical reference points which must be our concern if we are to take hold of the processes of change which lead to the use of notions like postmodern society or postmodern state.

The postmodern state: some structural issues

Whether one speaks of a modern or a postmodern state, it is an error to seek a formulation which is rigid in the particular shape it takes. The varied characteristics of the modern state, which have included major changes in its representative constituencies, in the character of its political parties and in its programmes, did not invalidate the usefulness of the concept over against other forms such as the medieval state. The minimalist state, the interventionist state and the socialist state were all modern. Nor is there one narrowly defined form which can be identified as the postmodern state. Any such concept must be able to hold together universality at one level with variety at another.

In other words, any concept of the postmodern state must take into account the crucial structural forces which lead us to speak of a postmodern society while bearing in mind that any particular shape for a postmodern state (or society) will be significantly open to history and politics. However, the distinctive quality of the postmodern state relates to those developments which have been described in terms of the revolution of information on the one hand and the revolution of image on the other. For these underlying processes, with different structural potentials, are tied to an intellectual revolution which, for better or worse, is the postmodern condition. They generate new processes which require the state to respond in unfamiliar ways.

In Australia, resonating with similar developments around the world, the most obvious expression of this shift in the nature of the state is associated with economic rationality and related processes of deregulation. Attempts to familiarize this shift, to deny its profound novelty, come from all quarters. For example, the economic rationalists invoke Adam Smith and neo-classical political economy as though here we have a mere swing of the pendulum away from a phase of Keynesian political-economy.

While John Howard has some good reasons to see political-economy in this way it must be remembered that the Labor party pursues an economic-rationalist agenda of its own. In other words, in line with labour movement parties around the world, the socialist elements of its practical policies have been displaced by deregulatory policies which favour the market. This certainly relates to the deregulation of financial markets; it also relates to the pruning back of welfare provisions which indicates the end of the post World War II concept of the welfare state together with a shift in the role of the state in the pursuit of economic development: the state now largely restricts itself to a facilitating role rather than the possible supplier of capital.

To simply formulate this strategy as a new focus on the market will generate little insight into the new situation. There are two aspects to why this simple view needs a different line of insight; both affect the practice of the contemporary state. Firstly, it is important to see the way in which this market is not what is usually meant by a market. And secondly, the major impetus towards a restructuring of the relations of state and market lie outside of what has been theorized as state or market-based: the practices of the intellectually trained. These two aspects taken together can be shown to give a unified practice—unified, that is, in the form of the communications revolution—which justifies the concept of the postmodern state.

It is striking how our politicians, their advisers and also their broad publics take the nature of contemporary markets for granted. When Paul Keating announced his deregulation of finance markets and reversed 'socialist' policies it certainly caused a flurry, but it did not direct attention towards the nature of the market which had just emerged victorious from many decades of state constraint. When in the late 1980s Laurie Carmichael led a group of unionists and government advisers on a tour of northern and central Europe and prepared the document *Australia reconstructed*[11], laying the basis for a broad developmental strategy

---

11 'The report by the Commission to Western Europe to the ACTU and TDC', Australian

which put aside almost one hundred years of union activity in Australia, comments were made about the specific recommendations but not the shift in general conditions which made the recommendations possible. Outlining a new co-operation between worker and boss around an export-led recovery and a new role for education in the reconstitution of productivity as well as the production process proper, it proposed a revolutionary change in political behaviour which should have been seen to be a challenge to all prior forms of political economy.

I am going to argue that in both these examples one can see at work the driving force of an institution of a new type: that of the postmodern market. The characteristics of this market are not equivalent to the classic market of writers such as Adam Smith or more recently Karl Marx. Nor does it support the political ideologies of liberalism and socialism within which possible forms of the state have been pursued. Along with the transformation of market forms one can find significant transformations of political ideologies.

The postmodern market no doubt contains the kernel of the familiar experience of the market but it also needs to be seen as taking a new shape propelled by a new force, that of the communications revolution.[12] At least three characteristics of this postmodern market will be identified before asking what such a change means if one interprets it as arising out of a radical enhancement of technologically mediated social relations.

Speed, breadth and depth: these are the elements in which a reconsideration of the doctrines of an Adam Smith or a Karl Marx need to be pursued. Speed and breadth are quite familiar ways of grasping the medium in which globalization proceeds. Communications in the information mode allows us to approach the speed of light and be in the midst of the Chicago Futures market, the Los Angeles riots, or the haemorrhaging in the Balkans. Breadth is able to be illustrated through similar examples but now with an emphasis on the global reach of the system of communications and its ability to achieve more

---

Government Publishing Service, Canberra, 1987.

[12] This vague association is, however, not sufficient; it will not be able to go beyond the intuitions of many postmodern writers about our changed setting; while the argument of this paper values these intuitions, left in that form they will lend support to the often unsustainable over-generalizations which characterize many accounts of postmodernity.

successfully what had always been an orientation within modernity—in that case through sea transport, the telegraph and the printed word.

Depth. Here we encounter greater difficulty in assessing the nature of the postmodern market because it requires that we step beyond relatively clear technological effects and recognize the meaning of speed and breadth in the context of personal formation.

Jurgen Habermas has gone to some length in his work to argue that Marx assumed certain modes of working-class cultural formation in his analysis of state and market. That is, the classic market always stood in relation to a sphere of personal solidaristic formation which was essentialized and therefore left untheorized. This is the setting of what Habermas terms the philosophy of consciousness, where the subject was simply grasped intuitively as a ground for philosophy prior to the twentieth century. As he has emphasized, this ground can no longer be handled in this way for it is those settings which have been thrown into upheaval by contemporary processes.

An argument about depth in the postmodern market takes these observations of Habermas as given, but seeks to interpret them in ways which raise radical concerns well outside of his frame of reference. For here depth refers to a market more powerful in its ability to assimilate spheres which have always been within the realm of non-market relations. That is, the mass media should not be merely grasped as various contents circulated globally at high speed which affect, positively or negatively, our cognitive knowledge. Nor should it be merely be characterized as a process of instrumentalization which colonizes the life-world. For the mass media remake our cultural relations through the drawing of self-formative processes into a market calculus. What is crucial here in the postmodern market is the way in which identity and the cultural lifestyle are interwoven with technologically mediated relations with a distinctive logic,[13] one which significantly displaces cultural relations grounded more strongly in history and place.

It is this market, the postmodern market, which has emerged with such force in the 1980s. It is this market which is the carrier of globalization and deregulation. The state controls of an earlier era stand helpless and unresponsive before such an unfamiliar force. In Australia,

---

13 See Geoff Sharp, 'Extended forms of the social', *Arena journal*, no. 1, 1993, pp. 221-37.

the purely economic sway of the state in affairs such as the management of the currency or of the economy more generally shifts towards this market. Here indeed lies one major plank of the forces which call into being a postmodern state but, as we will see, this is a narrow example of a much broader field of phenomena which carry such an effect.

A step towards a more balanced account can be taken by addressing more directly the role of intellectual technique and the social stratum which is the carrier of that technique, the intellectually trained. Here we have had much discussion of post-Fordism and flexible skilling, the need for a 'brain-based' recovery, the emergence of a new vocationalism within education which makes claims to be the simultaneous carrier of general education, and the drawing of the higher education sector into closer relations with industry.

In all of these developments within the social structure it is possible to outline a major shift in the character of social strata as long as one makes the prior step of rearticulating the technological revolution in social terms. Whether one speaks of a postmodern market or postmodern forms of production and life-ways, it is the way in which the social structure is now framed by the intellectual culture which begins to come into the foreground. This allows one to give significance to the change in the character of the stated-based tertiary institution as it approaches the economy with its own novel technique as well as all of those radical shifts in government educational strategy associated with 'Dawkinsism'. And if one turns to the social structure itself, it is the intellectually trained who can be seen to be taking up positions of privilege relative to modern social strata. This is not of course to deny the power of capital or the significance of property, but it is to claim that both of these are now modified by a new force which comes to be a constituency in its own right.

Whether one speaks of the shifts in the occupational structure which give a place of prominence to certain groupings of the intellectually trained while the bottom falls out of other middle-range occupations and many are forced to the margins of society; or whether one speaks of the pathologies of the emergent modes of personal formation which call into being intellectually trained forms of counselling and other advice: these are the strata which are privileged by the emergence of a society which is distinctively postmodern.

Abstraction, de-territorialization and cultural identity

An underlying and enduring theme of theories of the state revolves around the degree to which the state is necessarily differentiated from its public or its civil society. One expression of this, a focus of periodic radical ferment, is raised in the question of participatory democracy. The democratic impulse is taken to the point where it is proposed that only those state forms consistent with the direct involvement of all of its constituent members will be defended. The model of this form of participation is that of the small-scale oral speech community. This is of course an extreme account, one which bypasses those many moderate accounts of democratic participation which are available to us; but in its extreme form it illustrates a certain alienation of state from civil society which is implicit, if not so obvious, in the more moderate participatory accounts. This is often enough referred to as the romantic Rousseauian version of the democratic state.

Behind this debate stands the question of social abstraction. For such a debate only bites in circumstances where the state stands in relative abstraction to its various publics. While proto-models of the state in an undeveloped form can be found, by and large, there is no state without the commodity market and there is no state without the technology of writing. The whole debate on participatory democracy stands against a background where the state as an institution emerges in settings where social relations are technologically mediated in some way. It is this mediation which simultaneously calls into existence the more systematic efforts of intellectuals to provide the means of social integration and the emergence of a centralized state-form which addresses the radically extended society and establishes power within definite boundaries.

Thus if we are to gain insight into the nature of the postmodern state it is important to bear in mind that any state is abstractly situated relative to its citizenry, abstracted by the force of technological mediation. Even those effervescent moments where the state and its citizens seem to come together in the fervour surrounding some particular event or process is arguably an illusory (and dangerous) overcoming of structured abstraction.

The abstraction of the postmodern state is of a different order again; it is set within the emergent technologies of the postmodern era—and this is to lay abstraction on abstraction. It is to multiply the forms of technological mediation within society while enhancing the capacity of the state to work through technological mediation.

There are many aspects to how this form of social abstraction, of postmodern technological mediation, affects the contemporary state. Let me introduce them by reflecting on some changes to social institutions and how these affect the institution of the state.

Within modernity the system of wage labour and the system of education (as well as the work of intellectuals more generally) were important institutions for the social integration of citizens. In this period the state played a central role in social integration and, as Althusser pointed out, education most strikingly represented the state in the promotion of such social arrangements. In this respect the institution of the school influenced the self-formation of young people by introducing them to the wider and more complex world of society at large: those social settings which worked on different, more abstract, principles to the more parochial localities of which they had first-hand knowledge.

These social arrangements which saw the school closely tied to the interests of the state represented a phase of the intellectual culture and the intellectually trained which also predominantly tied the latter to the state. This too is the era of the relatively stable and inclusive ideology or what is now often enough described as the grand narrative.

In postmodernity this integrative emphasis in education is of less importance for the simple reason that new social integrative mechanisms have emerged. To some significant degree education in this integrative role is overshadowed by the age of the mass media.[14] Here one can say that it is increasingly the media which now introduce the child to the wider world.[15] Television in particular carries a definite form of knowledge. Unlike education which is burdened with the technologies of print—which can only significantly shape us if we have been educated for many years—the electronic media take hold of the everyday with enormous power. Thus, in the most basic form of social integration,

---

14 This aspect of social integration has been discussed at greater length in my *Postmodernity: state and education*, Deakin University, Geelong, 1991.
15 It is important to note that this is an observation of structured processes rather than a judgment about which is better or worse.

THE STATE OF POSTMODERNITY

we are increasingly constituted as a self through these emergent processes tied to more powerful forms of technological mediation: a self which takes the culture of consumption for granted and in turn gives us a general orientation in a world itself reconstituted by information and technologized image.

That these forms of social integration move outside any substantial formal relation to the state and are largely located within the postmodern market would seem to be of great significance. For a start one can see why, with the postmodern state, the issue of whether education should be privatized becomes a more relaxed, less ideological question. It is certainly not the threat to the social order and to state legitimation it once seemed.

But here one can also see another shift of historic proportions. For within modernity, up to quite recent times, the intellectually trained have found a setting largely within the institutions of the state. This is of course not likely to cease entirely, but the emergence of the postmodern market and postmodern logics of production generate transformed settings which, as never before, give an alternative place to the intellectually trained. Crucial here is how the intelligentsia are less tied to public forms associated with the state and significant numbers of that stratum begin to criticize such public forms. These are certainly matters which remain unresolved and will have a long history, but the postmodern state will never resemble the modern state in this regard. The era of the intellectually trained who become a constituency in their own right is the era of the postmodern which seeks a different balance between state and market.

These developments which demonstrate the emergence of new institutions, in turn transforming the functions of the modern state, need to be balanced against the changed expectations placed upon educational institutions—expectations facilitated by the postmodern market and in part demanded by the state. If education finds its role of social integration of the citizen somewhat diminished in postmodern circumstances, this is offset to a degree by the new ways in which intellectual technique finds a practice in the renovation of the economy.

This is by far too complicated a matter to go into in any detailed way in this chapter. Suffice to say that educational institutions have expectations put upon them—within Australia the recent examples are associated with John Dawkins as Minister for Employment, Education and Training—which draw them into closer associations with the economy: partly to engage directly with technological innovation, partly to facilitate new forms of training for work. The latter have gone through various developments in the course of a set of sequential government reports: firstly the Finn report, then the Mayer report and culminating in the report by Laurie Carmichael, *The Australian vocational certificate training system*.[16] These reports manage to combine such notions as 'flexible skilling' and 'generic competencies' but most commentators have not realized the degree to which these notions gain their general qualities from the emergent powers of intellectual technique.[17]

From the standpoint of the postmodern state the point is that while the state may be active in facilitating this transformation of state-related institutions, there is no long-term reason, contrary to modernity, why the close relation between state and educational institutions need be the rule. This is to say that the new force at work in these general rearrangements of function and the relation of institutions to the state, the post-modern market, is a stronger carrier of the imperatives of social order than previously. This is probably the reason why postmodern perspectives often imply the demise of the state. Indeed, as will be argued in the next section, the forms of *dis*-order which are inseparable from the order of the postmodern market may yet call a powerful and quite unattractive form of the postmodern state into being.

However that may be, this increased differentiation between social institutions, where the integration between institutions which made up the state comes apart in some significant respects, is one strong illustration of the effects of a new level of social abstraction within the social order. Social abstraction affects a differentiation of social power and in the process the tangibility of 'the state', never a simple matter, becomes even more elusive.

Another way in which this practical realignment can be illustrated

---

16 National Board of Employment, Education and Training, Canberra, 1992.
17 Generic competencies are a general form of skill. They cannot be reduced to any particular skill. They have the same form as that general ability learnt within the context of intellectual training to take a particular practice apart and put it back together again. Intellectual technique is not the skill associated with the 'dedicated machine'. Rather it is the technique appropriate to the universal machine, the clearest example of which is the computer. There is no better entry into the *general* skills needed for working with computers than formal philosophy.

is by the rather unprecedented relation of the postmodern state to territory or place. As the reader is no doubt well aware, the state is typically defined as an institution or set of institutions which hold power in one way or another over a given territory. Every state has many organizations within its boundaries, but the state differs from those other organizations in its sovereign control, via legal or other means, of a definite place with borders. Within those borders, individuals and corporations may own property and control various processes, but they do so within the framing terms of the state's power.

One of the ways in which postmodern theory implicitly challenges the modern state is by its emphasis on what is called de-territorialization, a theme others refer to as globalization. What such writers have in mind here is what this chapter has chosen to call the postmodern market, and how this facilitates flows of trade, persons and organizations across state borders. Indeed this process has taken on such proportions that the state has had to relinquish much of its control over its borders in order to participate in the emerging international order. Real difficulties for effective policy have emerged, especially in the control of economies, because extra-national bodies stand outside any particular state and, from that position, pressure them to comply with their interests.

In some respects this is not a new phenomenon, but its scale has no historical comparison. Some are tempted to see this as an end and a new beginning: the end of the territorial state and the beginning of the era of the regime of the eternally flexible super-organization, one which is tied to no particular place. While one could hardly deny the empirical realities which support this vision, it is important to note that it is based on an extrapolation of developments which assume, rather than theorize, the postmodern market. Whatever history and politics may make of this development, the postmodern state will have to cope with pressures of this type to a degree never faced by the modern state.

The question of state and territory interweaves with another which is even more pressing today, that of cultural identity. The familiar solution to cultural identity, which we associate with the modern nation-state, entails the creation of citizens who gain their identity as a nation related to the territory of the state. Here we find a state-controlled commodity-market—admittedly with some significant, though not dominant, flows across state boundaries—and a print-based intelligentsia with an allegiance in large part to a given territory.[18] Thus, for this state-form, one can speak of what many postmodernists have complained: the development of grand narratives which privileged a social order oriented to the nation at the expense of cultures or gender divisions. These were the conditions in which one could speak of a state with relatively clear boundaries.

The postmodern market which cuts across this order calls out cultural identities which have no such strong associations and could be reasonably described as appropriate to 'citizens of the world'. In the forefront of this development, promoting and taking for granted a globalized self, are the intellectually trained. This more flexible and abstract/extended mode of cultural formation has a rather unclear status within postmodern writing. For while there is a strong sense in which cultural identities of this kind shape quite fundamentally the themes, sensibilities and preoccupations of the postmodernist[19], they nevertheless focus their surface concerns elsewhere, in particular on questions of cultural difference. As implied above, it is the local and the regional cultural forms which have their explicit sympathy, hence their critique of the marginalization of cultures by the modern state.

Both these emphases upon cultural formation—the more extended and the regional/ethnic—cut across the typical nationalist identity of the modern state. But in postmodern writing there is a certain blindness to how the implicit commitments to an extended cultural formation undermine, and in that way call out in a militant, seemingly defensive form, commitments to regional cultures. And, as might be expected in such circumstances, there is a matching blindness towards a critical interpretation of the extended cultural modes which are manifestly so important to postmodern themes.

There can be no doubt that these are not mere theoretical questions

---

18 I say in 'large part' because this allegiance was always ambiguous in the sense that the technological mediation afforded by the printed word need not have been constrained by national borders. However, in modernity the intellectual culture and the intellectually trained lacked the power and sense of social independence they have since gained to give full expression to the logic of their cultural formation.
19 For example, these sensibilities are situated within a collapsed sense of space and a 'self' inseparable from multiple selves. See my 'Post-Lyotard: a critique of the information society', *Arena*, no. 80, pp. 123-55, for an account of how this works in one major figure in contemporary social theory.

given the rise of various cultural fundamentalisms and the great range of ethnic revivals and conflicts which typify world politics at this time. Are these conflicts the last sighs of cultures which have no future? Or is there here a crucial development which will typify the preoccupations of the postmodern state for as long as it exists?

Cultural identity, in the view being developed here, has as one of its aspects the more open forms of self-formation which are supported by the postmodern market. This radical cultural formation threatens modes of formation which rely on history and place, generational bonds as well as ethnic association, for their affectivity. It is this relationship—between two contradictory, yet complementary, cultural orientations—which generates such a powerful response from ethnic cultures. To see it this way poses very new dilemmas for any practice of the postmodern state. There is no sense in which it can be simply portrayed as struggling with resurgent regional cultures from the past. For while these cultures can be seen to be reviving a more culturally informed notion of territoriality, they are typically also wishing to enter the 'modernizing' processes still associated with postmodern culture. This positive aspect of resurgent forms of cultural consciousness leaves the postmodern state caught between two potentially explosive tendencies, both of which make their demands on the state-form in ways quite novel relative to modernity.

Cultural politics and cultural contradiction

The previous section attempted to outline some of the key issues which will characterize the strains and forms of restructuring associated with the postmodern state. They are a selection from a variety of processes which will take a distinctive form in the postmodern era. In that discussion some attempt was made to discuss the structural changes in a way consistent with a great variety of postmodern state-forms. That is, the emphasis was on some relatively universalistic changes which will have general effects on the postmodern state whatever particular shape it might take.

In this section a different approach will be adopted, one with more emphasis on dynamics and cultural political choice. The aim of the section will be to generate a stronger sense of the possible diversity of state forms *within* the general category of the postmodern state. As with the previous section there will be a focus on possible responses to distinctive postmodern processes, but here the emphasis will be on a diversity of responses that affect this or that structure of the postmodern state rather than those relatively diffuse qualities that mark off the postmodern from the modern state.

In the articulation of the themes of abstraction, de-territorialization and cultural identity, it became clear that all of these processes carry definite strains for any version of the postmodern state. Given the processes of abstraction, the emergent state must find a solution to its greater differentiation from its publics. This gains further definition if cultural identity is the focus because the state is caught between processes of cultural formation which draw citizens towards an international setting and forms of cultural formation which seek a stronger emphasis on regionalism. The state structures must find a way through this dilemma, bearing in mind that the two directions are related, not separate, developments.

Thus those very processes which help delineate the postmodern state also can help to generate a sense of its political possibilities. This is because they are carriers of contradiction. That this is so is not surprising; the same could be said of the modern state. The method used by Marx to outline the shape and possibilities of the modern state always proceeded by a focus on social contradictions, in particular those of labour and capital. But in postmodern settings we encounter new forms of contradiction, those which grow from the emergence of the intellectually trained into the foreground of postmodern social structures. These can be described as cultural contradictions, limitations which relate to a mode of cultural formation grounded in technological mediation.[20] It does not follow that the contradictions of labour and capital, which we associate with modernity, go away. But they are now drawn into and reshaped by a new setting which has other concerns in dominance.

These are indeed complex matters beyond the more specific concerns of this chapter. The argument will therefore be simplified by the use of two illustrations, the first reworking the materials already discussed

---

20   This notion I have drawn from the work of Geoff Sharp. See 'Constitutive abstraction and social practice'.

around cultural identity and the second addressing issues of postmodern economy. It will become clear that the two illustrations are analytically rather than empirically separate, and in this sense are mutually supportive in their consequences for the postmodern state.

If one were to pursue the question of a postmodern state simply by reliance on the themes found in postmodern writing it would be hard to avoid drawing the conclusion that market-forms, albeit ones elaborated by the communications revolution, will overwhelm all other modes of cultural formation. Let me take this as one possible tendency of the postmodern era and explore what this might mean for the postmodern state.

It goes without saying that a social formation of this type would be radically internationalized; it would also be characterized by social strata thoroughly dominated by the intellectually trained, the main carriers of the techniques which accompany technologically mediated social relations. From the standpoint of cultural identity there would be only a fleeting attachment to place, as the other of this cultural formation would be substantially a construction of the image industries.

It has already been argued that this is a mobile and rather unstable form of identity formation, one which leaves the self constantly searching for ways of stabilizing its points of reference. No doubt there are more or less sophisticated ways of leading such a search and constructing a lifestyle but, putting this aspect aside, this is a general process which follows the logic of technologically mediated relations and produces a radically individuated self. It is not that this version of a postmodern self is asocial, but rather that the other in such sociality is so mediated by the extended relation that no tangible other is a substantial reality for the self beyond a fleeting presence.

This is one reason why it makes sense when Fredric Jameson takes up the theme of schizophrenia as the disease of postmodernity.[21] Lacking any stable reference points the self enters a logic which can only give it a fleeting ground.[22] Multiple realities are no longer aspects of a larger reality, in principle able to be integrated by the self. They

---

21 'Postmodernism, or the cultural logic of late capitalism', *New left review*, no. 146, July 1984, pp. 53-92.
22 One does not have to argue for an essentialist ground to make a distinction between relatively stable grounds and those which move as does the fleeting other.

constantly threaten to fly apart and stand on their own terms.

In this sense alone one can see how a society of this type will produce massive welfare strains on the postmodern state. I am not speaking here of asylums which would have to be financed by the state, so much as of the heavy toll such a society would have to cope with because of distorted forms of self-development. Whether the postmodern state will be able to respond in a supportive mode is a matter of some considerable doubt. [See Rob White's chapter in the present volume.] This is especially so if the orientation towards the postmodern market continues to legitimate economic rationalist policies which squeeze the finances of the state. But perhaps of more interest in this illustration is the way the postmodern state has new means at its disposal to handle a 'disruptive' citizenry by virtue of the new technologies, and how these facilitate and demonstrate a heightened form of abstraction in the relation of state and citizen.

This is to speak of the surveillance state in a more developed form than was ever available for study by Michel Foucault. And this proceeds because of the new means produced by the intellectual culture and managed by the intellectually trained. But contrary to most accounts of the surveillance state, this situation can be seen to be a consequence of the new technologies and associated strata on the one hand, and desired modes of self-formation on the other. In such a situation, science fiction images of a repressive state holding at bay significant groupings of ungovernable citizens—perhaps organized around this or that fundamentalism—gain a definite credibility, and offset visions of good living long associated with what has been regarded as the best of 'development'.

Recent debates around the issue of changed sentencing laws in Victoria may serve to illustrate the questions I have in mind here. The state has sought to respond to community fears and concerns about violent crime, especially crimes of passion and unbridled violence against women, by increasing the terms of imprisonment quite radically. One commentator, Robert Manne, who writes with a strong sense of humanity from a conservative position, captures much of the concern widespread in the community. With a feeling for the reality of the situation and for the victims, both present and future, he justifies the laws. Many of these criminals, he asserts, are on all the evidence not open to rehabilitation, and we must therefore put aside the (modern) liberal model which has informed legal and penal practice for over a century. He draws these conclusions with regret but observes, in a commonsense mode: 'This is, unhappily, the way we live now.'[23]

One would not wish to deny the strength of moral concern which informs these judgments, yet it is important to clarify how conclusions left in this form are counterproductive. For while we have indeed entered a phase of social living which lends support to such conclusions, this is only so if we pursue a politics which is simply empirically informed. For the argument which Manne develops is one which assumes an extrapolation of the present forms of postmodern society and a state forced more and more into a repressive mould—the only defensible reaction to the disorder of that society apparently available. There is a logic here which will call out new modes of 'realistic' response with an all too predictable spiral as the outcome. No better justification for an escalation of surveillance could be found.

It does not follow that tough sentencing laws are inappropriate. They may be quite necessary for the medium term, but they need to be seen as secondary relative to a practice of cultural and political transformation concerned to reverse the deteriorating conditions of postmodern social life. This would be inseparable from a renewal of a comprehensive perspective able to enthuse and give ethical direction through various possible postmodern pathways. A repressive postmodern state is one possibility amongst others.

The era of postmodernity certainly has more positive potentials than those found in the view just outlined. If, on the contrary, the underlying tendencies within postmodernity are not simply taken for granted, but are brought into relationship with the search for renewal of regional cultures, the postmodern state could have quite a different form. Any exploration of such possibilities would entail largely putting aside the instrumental surveillance possibilities of the state, and the taking up of interpretative potentials uncovered by the more extended modes of social relation. And this would mean that regional cultures cannot simply retrace their former steps. Any renewal would need to be reflexively made—that is, made with greater recognition of how cultures make life choices and that one cannot assume that one is simply

---

23 'Sanity and scales of justice', *The age*, 27 May 1993, p. 17.

born into choices which are made for you.

In such a circumstance a positive postmodern state would have little similarity to either the modern state or the repressive forms discussed above. It would be a state which no longer rode over the cultures of its region and would facilitate the holding together of these relations with a sector of social activity oriented to the international setting. Here one would have a case of deep diversity within the bounds of the postmodern state joined with the looser associations and possibilities of technologically mediated relations. The citizen of such a state would be drawn in their allegiance between regional associations, commitments to the state and broad international associations. If this seems too unstable a mix, one needs only to keep in mind the repressive possibilities of a state not so constrained by regional cultures.

The recent attempts of the Australian state to give substantial recognition to profound cultural difference within its own territory, that of Aboriginal cultures through the Mabo legislation, might be viewed as potentially a culturally co-operative act of a positive postmodern state. In other words, the postmodern state can go beyond its all too familiar modern grand-narrative form by simply privileging globalized cultural forms, but there is a choice. And one of the questions this would raise is whether any significant place is to be given to indigenous cultures apart from being treated as a fleeting flavour of the moment.

Let me now turn to that other concern of this section, the postmodern economy, and explore its possible impacts on the postmodern state. As far as economy is concerned the critical question is the degree to which postmodern settings are to be remade by the leading force in economic production today, the information revolution. To the extent that the postmodern economy simply goes down that road of high-tech production the negative prospects are relatively clear.

The logic of promoting the dominance of technologically mediated relations entails the removal of all constraints upon the postmodern market such that the internationalist logic of extended relations would take precedence over all other modes of exchange and social relation. The mode of production adopted in such a setting would leave no choice but to give precedence to high technology over all other possible ways of producing commodities, and if it gained momentum the logic of automated production must become a reality in all spheres of the economy.

The dominance of the globalized postmodern market and postmodern modes of production would generate settings which in turn call out a certain form for the postmodern state. For a start, one need only think of an economy so internationalized that the state would have little control over its budget and would be largely in the hands of transnational organizations able to use one state against the other. Such a state would have to take a defensive form towards its environment, and more generally take on a siege mentality.

But whatever is said here about these possibilities needs to be deepened by a consideration of social strata within such a social setting. For what this version of postmodern society and postmodern state holds open to us is a radical elaboration of the information revolution. And we already have some knowledge of what this means given the developments of the last decade. The point is that postmodern forms of production are distinctive in their assumption that productivity is simply a function of minimizing the labour of the hand. Thus one finds already in our society a logic which leaves growing numbers of people excluded from any meaningful place in economic production. This has not only happened to working-class occupations. There is now considerable evidence that the 1980s produced shifts in occupational structures that have eliminated many middle-range occupations and marginalized their occupants.

Some writers (Barry Jones comes to mind[24]) take this up and seek to defend it positively as a new era of potential 'creative leisure'. What this view leaves unaddressed is how such a society can convey that sense of inter-dependence which accompanies co-operative work and which has always been central to the work-process. The experience of the other as a flesh-and-blood reality, engaged in mutually necessary endeavour, is lost. Thus this society loses a crucial form of social integration and identity formation. To suggest then, that the social product of such a society can be equally distributed is surely an overly intellectual response. The glaring reality is one of an increasing 'dependency' amongst citizens one which places at threat the very notion of the citizen. Given the abstraction between state and citizen, and the

---

24 *Sleepers wake! technology and the future of work*, Oxford University Press, Melbourne, 1982.

growing difficulty of developing empathy between citizen and citizen in the circumstances of the new modes of personal formation, one could anticipate an ossification of relations between social strata and a hardening of relations between the state and excluded social strata.

It is not an exaggeration then to say that many citizens will find their place within society radically marginalized. Nor is it overly dramatic to see South-Central Los Angeles or Harlem as models of the processes of exclusion which accompany this negative version of postmodern development. New contradictions will generate radical class divisions, divisions which occur both within the developed world and between the developed and 'undeveloped' world.

What response is possible here for the postmodern state other than a version of what has been described as a repressive one? This conclusion, which supports one stream of my earlier reflections on cultural identity, arises out of the strains generated by what could be called over-development: strains which have as a consequence that large and growing numbers of people cannot be satisfied by the settings and associations offered them by either state or society.

If this is the logic of a development which is excessively global, what alternative could one see for a postmodern economy? This question certainly takes us into unmapped territory, for arguments in the field of economic development have always been situated within assumptions which allow an unconstrained development of technology. This is one aspect of the grand narrative which lives on in the present form of postmodernity, and which informs the practices of the intellectually trained who seem, for the moment, to have no interest in challenging its hold. In this account, postmodern writings which emphasizes regionalism and local narratives are insufficiently informed about the grand narratives which continue to make their mark. One could reasonably say that the tendency to see only local narratives may be a well-intentioned attempt to hold at bay the logic of technocratic totalities—as for example in the work of Lyotard—but it does so too schematically and proceeds too strongly by denial of the overbracing forces and structures at work.

If however one were to hold together a perspective which faced the reality of postmodern grand narratives (and how they now work to undermine regionalism in both economy and culture) with a determination to make regionalism a living reality within the more

THE STATE OF POSTMODERNITY

general frames of postmodern culture, a different approach with a practical policy might well emerge. From the standpoint of economy this would seem to require a recognition that the postmodern market and postmodern productive modes will not go away, nor will their attendant internationalist inclinations. It would involve assigning these orientations and occupations to a sector of postmodern life rather than allowing them to overwhelm all aspects of that life. This would be to envisage an economy which has a strong globally oriented commodity-sector in one of its aspects, but with other sectors which do not enter into the postmodern market at all. These non-market sectors would be organized on a non-commodity basis and would enjoy a rejuvenation of non-commodity relations and forms of production. This is of course a controversial matter because it points in part to forms of 'household' economy which have been rightly criticized in their known historical forms as exploitative and sexist. But exploitation and patriarchy are by no means necessary outcomes of face-to-face economies, especially if any such rejuvenated institutions were informed by the interpretative insights which are the cultural gains of postmodern development.

Thus in this version of postmodernity there would be a major role for the state in holding together and facilitating at least two diverse forms of economy. One would be oriented in its major aspect to mental labour and international economy; the other would be imbued with an appreciation of the best of human cultures, practices able to hold together both mental and bodily forms of endeavour. The genius of the mind needs to be informed by the 'genius of the hand'. Rather than the simple dominance of an internationalized economy with social divisions made all the more transparent by large numbers of socially redundant people, these two aspects of economy would have to entail rights for all citizens to be employed. Everyone would necessarily have a right to some place in both economies and this would obviously mean part-time work in the high-tech sector as well as some crucial decisions about what aspects of the economy overall are to be open to high-tech forms of production.

The role outlined here for the state is, in effect, one which pursues postmodern forms of co-operation, as opposed to the modern version of the socialist state which sought co-operation through state control of the market. Certainly there can be no sense in which postmodern co-operation can be achieved by a state endlessly accruing power. With the new powers of the intellectually trained we can easily see how that strategy is one which has no progressive future.

The role for the postmodern state would need to be more circumscribed. A state structure of some kind is certainly needed to facilitate the relations between the various cultural orientations and economies, but to do this it must give more social space to regional cultural groupings than the state ever could in modernity. They will be the primary focus of an ethic of co-operation, where regionalized cultural identities reinforce regionalized non-commodity production.

Conclusion

The reader may quite justifiably feel that these reflections on the postmodern state are both insufficiently fleshed out and radically selective. All I can do here is appeal to their sympathies and point out that the whole question of postmodernity and the postmodern state is one of great generality which is only beginning to take a recognizable institutional shape. We live in the midst of a major transformation and however well we attempt to delineate its form at this time, we can be sure that such a task will be much easier fifty years from now.

Yet there are important reasons at this time for us to attempt to grasp the nature of these changes and explore their meanings for social life. Practical politics already take these processes for granted and, given the apparent significance of the emergent social powers of a social strata which are constituted in technologically mediated social relations, there would seem to be every reason to begin a process of analysis and interpretation which can then be built upon.

While we must acknowledge the difficulty of grappling with these changes, we now have sufficient experience of their effects to see the overgeneralized and overstated character of many of the early enthusiastic reactions to postmodern phenomena. There is no better example of this than the announcement by many postmodern theorists that we have now entered the Age of Democracy. For it is possible to now see that what was regarded as democracy, especially important in the sudden demise of the East European states, is more accurately viewed as the emergence of a radical form of self-formation which allows the self to be experienced as radically autonomous and, as such, hostile to bureaucratic forms which cannot give such a self a social place.

THE STATE OF POSTMODERNITY

The argument of this chapter has been that this fleeting form of the self is inseparable from extended modes of social relation which carry their own form of power. If unconstrained, this form of power will produce social divisions and settings that will turn the whole tradition of democracy into a poisonous heritage. The issue of democracy in the postmodern state is itself inseparable from a form of politics which will pursue democracy in ways clearly differentiated from the modern versions of the democratic state. In particular, a democratic postmodern state will need to be one which can give a significant place to cultural groupings largely denied by modern forms of representation. These questions are interwoven with the degree to which the postmodern state can make its contribution to overcoming the most radical forms of social division generated since the demise of slavery.

9

As nation and state: a postmodern republic takes shape

Paul James

> ... whatever shape the federal republic of Australia takes, there will be something unstructured, if not deconstructed about it. I imagine it as aleatory, impressionistic, figurative, eclectic bebop. I'm only just game enough to say it: it might be the first postmodern republic, and I mean that in the nicest possible way.
>
> Don Watson, 1993

Across the globe in recent years we have seen wars, skirmishes, riots, demonstrations and street-murders, all conducted in the name of the modern 'blood and soil' nation. Nevertheless, during those same years, particularly in regions such as North America, Japan and Western Europe, it has become increasingly apparent that the modern nation-state has been fundamentally changing. Some commentators now question the continuing centrality of the nation-state in contemporary international relations. While it is clear that we are not witnessing the death of nationalism nor a movement towards a world of so-called post-nations, it seems equally clear that all is not as it was. In this context, the subject of the present chapter is the transformations and continuities of the Australian nation-state. Australia is not unique in the general contours of its history, but neither does it simply replicate transformations elsewhere. The task is to keep both the particular and the general in perspective.

Australia was born into a world of ambiguously consolidating nation-states and still-vigorous but soon-to-die empires. This was a world experiencing both the modernizing upheaval of traditional certainties and the formation of new, apparently natural, categories of meaning. Despite prevalent ideologies which conceived national formation as the rediscovery of primordial continuities, it was a world where for the first time two hitherto separate categories of polity and community, state and nation, were being drawn systematically into that high-modern hyphenated synthesis we call the nation-state. Late nineteenth-century Australia was framed by this context of modernity even as it developed its own peculiarities.

It is the argument of this chapter that although Australia may have been one of the last Western capitalist countries to become in the classical sense a 'modern nation-state', it was (to rephrase Marx) changing before it could comfortably ossify. It was never able to take the classification of modern nation-state for granted. In the late twentieth century, Australia has emerged as among the first wave of countries for which it makes increasing sense to use the term 'postmodern nation state'. (The hyphen is left out intentionally to signal the partial undermining of the older taken-for-granted relationship between nation and state.) Despite obvious continuities from the past, and notwithstanding contradictory pressures in the present, the contemporary nation state is fundamentally different from the polity-community which federated at the beginning of the century. Amongst other transformations, there has been a change in the way in which the connection between state and nation is lived. Always an uneasy, though ideologically naturalized, amalgam under conditions of modernity, the polity-community nexus has come under new strains. In particular the boundaries of the territory of Australia have become increasingly permeable, deregulated and 'deterritorialized'. Expressed more accurately, they have become increasingly transversed by materially abstracted processes, including the exchange of electronic capital and the circulation of communications culture against which the old kinds of regulation are less and less effective. With this abstraction of territory and sovereignty has also come a transformation of the structures and images of the Australian community. The hegemonic image of Australia as a homogenous culture of Anglomorphy into which new arrivals and the original 'nomads' would as a matter of course integrate, has been largely overtaken by ideologies of multiculturalism, liberal pluralism, and postmodern republicanism.

Sustaining this argument is open to all kinds of misinterpretations. It appears to be susceptible to criticisms rightly levelled at those theories which set up one-dimensional schemes describing the epochal supersession of the age of modernity by a condition of postmodernity. It appears to parallel theories which either over-homogenize the present or turn it into a structureless melange of fragments and settings of micro-politics. Using the adjective postmodern is also risky. One might be either misaligned with the methodologies and politics of post-structuralism or accused of the trendy appropriation of a concept that is now too easily applied to almost every aspect of contemporary life. In some ways it is not crucial whether or not the adjective postmodern is employed. However, it is the very currency of the term which makes it more politically useful than a neologism. At the very least it allows us to engage critically with a range of debates from the high theoretical to the popular cultural—from discussions of 'the cultural logic of late capitalism' to renditions by speech-writers and poets of the importance of being a postmodern republic. Using the descriptive terms postmodern and postmodernity does not necessarily make one a postmodern*ist*, someone taking political pleasure in fragmentation, indeterminacy, multiplicity, or what David Goodman more critically calls 'empty, undiscriminating openness'.[1] In this sense I remain unconvinced by the comment made by Don Watson cited at the head of the present chapter. Before filling this out, there are some questions of method to be clarified. Although the main lines of the chapter's political argument are explicable without the reader working painstakingly through the next couple of pages of theoretical exposition, the section is necessary for elaborating the argument's analytical base.

---

1 David Goodman, 'Postscript 1991—Explicating openness' in *Celebrating the nation*, eds Tony Bennett et al., Allen & Unwin, Sydney, 1992, p. 198; also Gerry Gill, 'The enchantment of openness', *Arena*, 89, 1989, pp. 5-14. For one of the earliest Australian examples of a postmodernist who criticizes late-modern nationalism for its oppressive closure see Andrew Lohrey, 'Australian nationalism as myth', *Arena*, 68, 1984, pp. 107-23.

A note on methodological abstraction[2]

How is it possible for the present approach, which continues to work out of the tradition of historical materialism, to subsume some of the language and insights of other traditions, including post-structuralism, without being reduced to contradictory eclecticism? As a first step, the primacy of the category 'mode of production' is displaced, taking it out of its orthodox location in an economically reductionist base-superstructure framework. This is done not by rejecting the category itself, but by extending Marx's analysis of the mode (the forces and relations) of production to an understanding of other *modes of practice*, in particular, exchange, communication, organization and enquiry. The approach parallels, but has significant divergences from, Jurgen Habermas's move to recognize the analytical and political advantages of separating out communication (interaction) and production (work).[3] It also has some overlapping concerns with Mark Poster's discussion of the importance of what he chooses to call the 'mode of information'. However, it rejects any implicit suggestion in his work and that of others such as Gianni Vattimo that in the contemporary period a new mode of information is assuming an emergent pre-eminence over the mode of production.[4] Rather, it argues that to understand the transition from industrial capitalism to information capitalism

---

[2] The approach derives from that developed over the last decade or so in the pages of the journal *Arena*. The article which was most influential in my early reading was Geoff Sharp's 'Constitutive abstraction and social practice', *Arena*, 70, 1985, pp. 48-82. In writing the present chapter I would like to thank Tony Bennett, Joe Camilleri, Peter Chritoff, Robyn Eckersley, Hugh Emy, Boris Frankel, Alan Roberts and Stephanie Trigg for their helpful comments

[3] John Keane, 'Work and interaction in Habermas', *Arena*, 38, 1975, pp. 51-68.

[4] Gianni Vattimo, *The transparent society*, Polity Press, Cambridge, 1992; Mark Poster, *The mode of information*, Polity Press, Cambridge, 1990. See particularly pp. 64ff. where Poster critically confronts the *Arena* critique of post-structuralism: here I think he misunderstands Gerry Gill's argument. As a side-point it is worth noting why I use the term 'mode of communication' rather than Poster's term, 'mode of information'. Firstly, as a concept denoting a social relational practice (communicating through all its various means and techniques), 'mode of communication' is much broader than 'mode of information', a concept denoting an *outcome* of an epistemological practice. Secondly, I take information to be only one possible register in a broad epistemological range: 'wisdom', knowledge, information, data.

as the dominant but not exclusive *formation of practice* we have to study each of the changing modes of practice and the uneven conjunctures between them. Our examination of the changing nature of the nation and state proceeds by the same method to explore how community and polity have been reconstituted by changes in the modes of production, exchange, communication, organization and enquiry. This has the side-effect of facilitating a manageable approach to a question which has never been adequately addressed in the literature: what is the relationship between capitalism and the nation-state? This question becomes relevant here as background to the argument that with the change in the form of capitalism (understood as a social formation structured as intersecting modes of practice) the form of the nation-state has also been changing.

The second step is more complicated. It entails seeing this kind of social formational analysis as one level, set within a broader theory of levels of methodological abstraction. Except in the case of the most positivistic empiricism, most theories implicitly acknowledge two levels: a first-order abstraction of empirical description based on observation, experience, recording or experiment, abstracting evidence from that which exists or occurs in the world; and a second-order abstraction, a method of some kind or other for ordering and making sense of that empirical material. The present approach works across four such levels of theoretical abstraction: from the self-explanatory first-order abstraction (1) *empirical generalization* drawing out general descriptions from the details of history and place; through (2) *social formational analysis* (already discussed above) examining the conjunctures of modes of practice in a particular social formation; to (3) *social integration analysis*, examining the intersecting modes of social integration (and differentiation)—expressed here as (i) relations of face-to-face integration, (ii) relations where agents and institutions of agency such as the state mediate and extend social integration, viz. agency extension, and (iii) relations where disembodying media, technologies and techniques such as mass communications come to mediate and extend social integration, viz. disembodied extension. Finally, the most abstract level of analysis to be employed here is

A POSTMODERN REPUBLIC

(4) what might be called *categorical analysis*. At this level, based upon an exploration of the ontological categories of a social formation—categories of social being such as time, space, the body—generalizations can be made about the dominant categorical frame(s) of that social formation or its fields of practice and discourse. It is only at this level that it makes sense to generalize across modes of being and to talk of ontological formations, societies formed in the (uneven) dominance of, for example, tribalism, traditionalism, modernism or postmodernism: hence the possibility of discussing the transformations of the nation-state under conditions of an emergent postmodern capitalism. The present chapter thus works in the same direction, while not going as far, as John Hinkson's chapter to suggest firstly that postmodernity is an emergent (dominant) layer of practices and meanings rather than an epochal shift transforming all before it. Secondly, it suggests that what we are calling postmodernity is to be understood as an emerging set of structures (instantiated patterns of practice) rather than a dissolution of structure into fragments.

By moving back and forth across the four levels of methodological abstraction it is intended that the chapter will both empirically and analytically illustrate its core argument about the emergence of a postmodern nation state. Most generally, I argue that the contemporary nation state is increasingly held together at the level of disembodied extension and structured by the emergence of increasingly globalized and abstracted modes of practice. It is these very processes of integration and structuration which ironically are giving rise to the sense that the nation-state as we have known it faces an impending crisis. There is obviously still much to be filled out in the method, but for present purposes I draw attention to the summary appended below. Returning to expound the detail of the substantive argument, the first task is to describe the *modern* nation-state so as to provide a point of comparison for later discussion.

The modern Australian nation-state

In Benedict Anderson's oft-quoted definition the nation is an imagined political community, 'imagined as both inherently limited and sovereign'.⁵ What the definition picks up on, however, are peculiarly modern sensibilities, ideologies-in-general framed by and constitutive of a mode of communication-production that he calls print-capitalism. These are sensibilities which in the contemporary period are being called into question, or at least given new meaning. By making explicit how new meanings are being added over the top of old terms we can clarify the historical specificity of the modern nation-state, highlight how the supposedly coherent grand narratives of our modern imaginings were partial and contradictory, and then assess to what extent they are now being challenged. A number of grand (though always contested) narratives are relevant to the modern nation-state: the notions of boundedness and sovereignty; assumptions about the virtues of both 'high-cultural' homogeneity and genealogical integrity; and claims to the civilizing value of 'assimilating' backward ways of life, and to the progressive necessity of a comprehensive internal regulation of the civic culture and the national economy.

Described at the level of the categorical, the modern nation was imagined as being bound in time and space and embodiment, that is, within a particular territory, history and ethnicity. These are the stuff of the ideologies of 'blood and soil'⁶ now treated with ambivalent scepticism, embarrassment, even horror, by the intellectually trained citizen. At the same time, contradictorily, they are the stuff of postmodern nostalgia. The shift is significant without being absolute, for these ideologies of the concrete still play a more than residual role on occasions such as Paul Keating's kissing the ground at Kokoda during his 1992 trip to Papua New Guinea. The modern past is therefore not entirely a foreign country: it is reproduced in the present—in Keating's case it is self-consciously drawn upon for dramatic effect—even as it is challenged. In general the modern nation-state was imagined as

---

5 Benedict Anderson, *Imagined communities*, 2nd edn, Verso, London, 1991, p. 6.
6 The ideologies of 'blood and soil' range from the 'search for roots' to *Blut und Boden* fascism. The former can be criticized for their nostalgia and superficiality but they cannot be damned simply by showing they are on a continuum with the latter.

having a territorially delimited space demarcated by (abstract) lines on a map. The lines represented,[7] were lived, as the unabashedly real boundaries of the homeland,[8] boundaries which in principle could be surveyed and systematically controlled at all levels of interchange.[9] It was imagined as being a historically bounded community in the sense of having a collectively lived and continuous linear history which was clearly separable from the past and future of other nations. And it was imagined as a genealogically bounded community in which membership rested primarily upon the 'natural rights' of natal embodiment (and only secondarily upon the 'artificial' rites of legal passage). These ontologies of space, time and embodiment were, ironically, lifted out of the attachments to place and kin integral to more traditional societies, and transformed just as those societies were being destroyed or marginalized. In the nineteenth century the 'protection' of these transformed ways of life was seen as best carried out by the modern state, itself consolidating around a relatively new mode of organization: technical-rational bureaucracy. From there it was only a short step to the synthesis of nation and state and to the modern definition of nation-state sovereignty. As Joe Camilleri and Jim Falk write:

> sovereignty, as both idea and institution, lies at the heart of the modern and therefore Western experience of space and time. It is integral to the structure of Western thought with its stress on 'dichotomies and polarities', and to a geopolitical discourse in which territory is sharply demarcated and exclusively controlled.[10]

---

7 It will be argued that the meaning of 'representation' has become increasingly complicated. I take Fredric Jameson seriously when he suggests that 'simulation' is overtaking 'representation' (*Postmodernism or, the cultural logic of late capitalism*, Verso, London, 1991, ch. 1) but treat it as an overlay in tension with rather than simply replacing prior meanings.
8 The concept of the 'real' is not placed in inverted commas here because except in the hands of a few *avant-garde* intellectuals it was not then lived with the suspicious self-consciousness we are beginning to feel in the present.
9 They could also be extended, but it was only legitimate to do so across residual frontier zones into 'empty' areas. See Anthony Giddens (*Nation-state and violence*, Polity, Cambridge, 1985, ch. 4) on the difference between the traditional frontier and the modern border.
10 Joseph A. Camilleri and Jim Falk, *The end of sovereignty? the politics of a*

This was the context for the shaping of Australia, but it was never straightforward.

Australia was eventually to become a self-assumed nation-state but never one with unambiguous and unqualified conviction. At the beginning of the twentieth century when declarations were being made internationally about the coming of age of a world of nations, Australia was still a state-structure without an indigenous sense of a historical, let alone an ethnic nationality. Henry Parkes' famous 'crimson thread of kinship' for example, was not so much a reference to national community as an advocacy of empire ethnicity. Notwithstanding the emergence of indigenous nationalisms, Australia was more defined by its landscape than by an imagined community of its people.[11] It was conceived as an ancient continent drifting in empty time; as an empty space occupied according to the then legally dominant doctrine of *terra nullius*.[12] Australia was an isolated great island upon which a fragment of the Mother Country might eventually grow up, forged in the cultural struggle to tame Nature's Cruel Laws. Through the nineteenth century, geographers, cartographers and meteorologists, both amateur and professional, had audited the landscape: 'Australia exhibited some remarkable landscape authorship: in that regard it was entirely representative of what is usually described as a promiscuously assertive century ...'[13] However, the inventories,

---

shrinking and fragmenting world, Edward Elgar, Aldershot, 1992.

11   Benedict Anderson's term 'imagined community' has entered the academic lexicon as the most common (theoretically loaded) synonym we now have for the nation-state. Explicitly footnoting the term to its original source is thus almost unnecessary except that it has been so widely misunderstood as pertaining predominantly to the world of ideas, of imagination and signification. Hence, I disagree with Anne-Marie Willis (*Illusions of identity: the art of nation*, Hale and Iremonger, Sydney, 1993) at least when she says 'the "physical reality" of Australia turns out to be no more than a series of shifting signs' (p. 15). Despite such comments her discussion of the privileging of landscape as the central signifier of Australianness is subtle and relevant to the present argument (ch. 3). I have the same ambivalent response to Richard White's *Inventing Australia*, Allen & Unwin, Sydney, 1981.

12   Interestingly, Henry Reynolds argues that the doctrine may have come to be dominant and uncontested but it was not the straightforward inheritance of British law it is so often been assumed to be: ('*Terra nullius*? never, never', *Australian*, 3 July 1993).

13   J.M. Powell, *An historical geography of modern Australia*, Cambridge University

accounts and statistical mappings did as much to reinforce the diversity of the continent and to set up global comparisons as to underpin the attempt to see Australia as a whole. Similarly, it is clear from Graeme Davison's work that in 'time-management, as in many other things, Australia was "born modern" '.[14] Here again the tension is already between the local, the national and the imperial (global). Forging a national or standard sense of time (this finally occurred in 1895) ironically involved replacing localized regimes of already-modern time by an imperial (global) reference point, Greenwich Mean Time. Nonetheless, nation-statehood, a much less demanding object than the immanent telos of nationality, was for the interlocutors of the 'people of Australia' the imminent outcome of political action. Though it could not simply be signed into being in 1901, nationhood could be forged in practice and over time.[15]

On 26 January 1888 the centennial of British settlement had been celebrated. As Tony Bennett so elegantly puts it, 'Neither marking, nor marked by, time's passage, Australia was consequently exiled from the centre of the discourses in which ostensibly, it was celebrated'.[16] If it is right to say that the 1888 commemoration occurred in colonial, imperial and racial time rather than national time, then by 1901 things were changing. A new layer of meaning and practice had been tentatively instituted, symbolized in the act of federation and centring on the state of

---

Press, Cambridge, 1988, p. 11. See also Geoffrey Blainey (*The tyranny of distance*, Sun, Melbourne, 1966) on spatial *extension*; and Paul Carter (*The road to Botany Bay: an essay in spatial history*, Faber and Faber, London, 1987) on spatial *ontology*.

14 Graeme Davison, 'Punctuality and progress: the foundations of Australian standard time', *Australian historical studies*, 99, October 1992, p. 187. See also his 'Time in our time', *Arena magazine*, 6, 1993, pp. 44-7.

15 John Eddy and Deryck Schreuder, eds, *The rise of colonial nationalism*, Allen & Unwin, Sydney, 1988, ch. 5; and Noel McLachlan, *Waiting for the revolutions: a history of Australian nationalism*, Ringwood, Penguin, 1989, ch. 6. The sentence is written as an implicit critique of the tone of Jacques Derrida's claim (in 'Declarations of independence', *New political science*, 1986, pp. 7-15) that it is the signing that 'invents the signer' as 'they invent (for) themselves a signing identity'.

16 Tony Bennett, 'Introduction: national times' in *Celebrating the nation*, eds Bennett, et al., p. xiv.

Australia. *Modern* nation-statehood was now a possibility, but strangely it was never to become a stable reality. The ontologies of modern time, space and embodiment eventually predominated, but never in an uncontradictory way. The ignominy of having such a recent beginning, one marked either by federation or by convict settlement rather than one ambiguously emerging out of the mists of traditional time, could not easily be resolved with the ideologies of modernism. Neither could the problem of being unable to comprehensively settle the land: long after federation 'empty spaces remained, like obscene accusations' of national failure.[17] We had to populate or perish. By the same process, the drive for genealogical integrity was doomed. White Australia could not provide more than an antipodean semblance of national homogeneity. Even as late as the second coming of Robert Menzies, and with the stable background of the long capitalist boom, themes of traditional empire loyalty overlaid the local sense of nationhood.[18] By the time of the 1988 Bicentenary, empire loyalty had become a residual or at least confused orthodoxy. And, ironically, by then the classical conception of a homogenous and sovereign nation-state was also passing into history.[19]

The state of the postmodern nation

There is much more that could, and should, be said about the form of the modern nation-state and about Australia's birth within an already globalizing system of modern sovereign states. However, the notes above serve as a sufficient sketch for drawing a comparative outline of transformation of the contemporary Australian state and nation. It should already be obvious that the argument is not as crude as to posit a new Great Divide. Once upon a time, so that

---

17 Powell, *An historical geography*, p. 66.
18 Stephen Alomes, *A nation at last?*, Sydney, Angus and Robertson, 1988, ch. 5; John Arnold, Peter Spearritt and David Walker, eds, *Out of empire*, Melbourne, Mandarin, 1993.
19 For an elaboration of the way in which the architects of the Bicentenary accommodated the change see Peter Cochrane and David Goodman, 'The great Australian journey: cultural logic and nationalism in the postmodern era', in *Celebrating the nation,* eds Bennet et al.

A POSTMODERN REPUBLIC

story goes, we had a bounded territory, a homogeneity of culture, and a hierarchy of increasingly centralized state power: now we have deterritorialization (deregulation), a heterogeneity of cultures (multiculturalism), and a rolling back of the state (a proliferation of contending political pressures and a decentralization and dispersal of state structures). Put in that dichotomous and uncritical way it is no wonder that the sceptics are up in arms.[20] It is not that the description is out and out wrong, but there are intense political battles to be fought over such partial representations. The problem with the sceptics' critique however is that they have gone in the opposite direction to posit an overriding continuity of capitalism. They are spurred on by personal experiences such as finding that their struggle to find books in the Coburg library is hindered rather than helped by that harbinger of the postmodern information society, the computer.[21] The present argument accepts many of their points about structural continuities going back to the nineteenth century. Moreover, I agree with the criticism that postmodern*ist* descriptions of transformation 'from the "armed" psyche of modern nationalism ... to a "feel good", postmodern nationalism' tend to succumb to an all-too-familiar tendency to project this 'flow', as Meaghan Morris puts it, onto a 'binary grid opposing fragment to structure, fluid to solid, blur to line, dispersiveness to decisiveness ...'.[22] Nevertheless, my argument is that enough has changed in the structures of state and nation and the subjectivities of citizenship and nationalism to warrant some cautious generalizations about a postmodern reframing of existing institutions, practices and sensibilities. Rather than the end of sovereignty (Camilleri and Falk), the end of geography (O'Brien), the end of organized capitalism (Lash and Urry), and the beginning of a borderless world (Ohmae), we are experiencing a

---

20 See for example Alex Callinicos, *Against postmodernism*, Polity Press, Cambridge, 1989.

21 Rob Watts, 'Postmodernism and its discontents', *Arena magazine*, no. 6, 1993, pp. 39-42. See also his chapter in the present volume for a more nuanced version of this argument.

22 Meaghan Morris, *Ecstasy and economics*, Empress Publishing, Sydney, 1992, p. 42.

reconstitution of sovereignty, space, the nature of borders, capitalism, and of social life in general.

We can begin our discussion of the postmodern nation state in the realms of subjectivities, making use of contemporary popular-cultural and academic descriptions; not using the descriptions as direct support for our thesis but more as evidence in spite of themselves. Surely something is happening when a right-conservative American journal heads its cover-page with the question 'Is America still a nation?' and publishes an article entitled 'The postmodern state'[23] (no question mark or interpretative insecurity here); when a left-wing Australian speech-writer and prime-ministerial adviser gives a speech at one of Melbourne's ruling-class restaurants advocating that Australia become the first postmodern republic;[24] and when an Indonesian poet writes the following half-defensible, half-risible sentiments:

> I began to imagine Australia being the first country in the world to separate the idea of a 'nation state' from the desire to have one centre, one logos, one myth. Perhaps this is a post-modernist concept of nationhood. Maybe this is something feasible in a lucky country, where people can jump easily from one place to another, whose self-perception is not threatened by the 'Other', and whose horizon moves among buildings, cars, holidays and consumables.[25]

Something is happening, but not necessarily in accordance with the descriptions put forward by the proponents of postmodern republicanism. The first thing to note is a kind of postmodern, even (post)national, 'exceptionalism'.[26] In the past, national

---

[23] James Kurth, 'The post-modern state', *The national interest*, 28, 1992, pp. 26-35. The article is full of historical distortions and methodological *faux pas*. (With thanks to Andy Butfoy for this reference.)

[24] First reported in the *Age*, 26 March 1993, and later reproduced in full as Don Watson, 'Birth of a post-modern nation', *Australian*, 24 July 1993. Presumably the editors of the *Australian* did not think their readers would be totally bemused by such a banner headline. (With thanks to Troy Riley for the latter reference.)

[25] Goenawan Mohamad, 'Australia by name, postmodernist by nature', *Sunday Age*, 12 July 1992.

[26] For a further example of this see Jacques Derrida's discussion of how France assigns for herself the '*exemplary*' task and 'avant-garde position' in advancing the

intellectuals working within the frame of modernism tended to claim exceptional status for their own nation as a nation—even if this lay paradoxically in seeing that nation as further than others down the evolutionary pathway to true cosmopolitanism. In the new setting the temptation to see one's own nation as exceptional continues but it is opened to the possibility of eulogizing other nations, and of seeing the exceptional nation as passing beyond nationhood. Here an American academic is calling Germany and Japan the 'perfect nation-states' but still claiming a (*post*-national) exceptionalism for the United States as the 'prototypical postmodern society, ... no longer a nation-state'.[27] An Indonesian poet is extolling the virtues of the exceptional confusions of identity in Australia. And an Australian speech-writer (who incidentally used to work as a satirist writing scripts for a comic impersonator of Australian prime-ministers) is both advocating a 'new inclusive nation' and projecting the possibility of Australia becoming an exceptional postmodern republic. (See the quote at the head of this chapter.[28])

The second point is that such post-national evocation requires an intellectual distancing, a position of emotional and political safety. It tends to be expressed through four main modes of operation: a critical, though not usually self-critical, separation of the author from what is being described; a pragmatic, and sometimes crudely instrumental, calculation of possible benefits; a tendency towards the vision being content free; and an ironical self-protective use of wit and pastiche. Don Watson's speech combines all four. It is critically heartfelt while shying away from the often all-consuming passion of modern nationalism. It is unashamedly instrumental, espousing a national interest in becoming a post-nation: how better to ride with the tide of global capitalism and enhance 'our competitiveness ... our posture and status abroad, especially in Asia'.[29] It is lacking much content. And it has the safe distance

---

subsumption of the European nations within the post-national setting of 'Europe' (*The other heading*, Indiana University Press, Bloomington, 1992, pp. 49-54).
27   Kurth, 'The post-modern state', p. 33.
28   Watson, 'Birth of a post-modern nation'.
29   ibid.; also the *Age*, 26 March 1993.

of hyperbole. The speech begins with an address to the poultry in his backyard (keep in mind that the novelty of this address derives in part from the influential backroom-status of its author):

> I say to them—and imagine the tears running down their beaks like perspiration on the nose of a Baptist when he's telling a fib—I say to them after all this, when you have seen the age of the fence posts, the ruins of farms which are after all as much ruins as the ruins of ancient Greece, and the human cost the same, surely this country has been through, seen enough ... surely, I say to them, Australia can be a republic.[30]

The third point to emphasize, at least as important as the preceding points, is that although postmodern nationalism is an ideology with generalizing pretensions[31] it is still only an emergent sensibility, actively lived only by the intellectually trained, and actively espoused only by certain individuals of that class. Even amongst most of those persons who give affirmative answers to opinion polls on republicanism (going as high as 66 per cent of those polled in February-March 1992, and 63 per cent in February 1994) there is no clear or overriding proclamation of postmodern-nationalism-as-such. It is an ideology whose name is still to enter the common lexicon.

How then has it so rapidly emerged to become a leading voice in the current debates over the future shape of Australia? How can it be so easily linked to what has been called minimalist republicanism? Apart from the obvious reason, that is, the influence of the proponents of the postmodern republic, a crucial source of this prominence is the undemanding openness and minimal of content of postmodern nationalism. It is presented as 'a recollection of an absence that can appeal to anyone'.[32] More precisely, postmodern

---

30   ibid.
31   It is therefore a more apparently useful concept than that of 'post-nationalism'. See Chilla Bulbeck's sceptical piece 'Republicanism and post-nationalism' in *The republicanism debate*, eds Wayne Hudson and David Carter, New South Wales University Press, Kensington, 1993.
32   Doug White, 'The minimalist nation', *Arena magazine*, 5, June 1993, p. 5; and for a very different end, also cited in Alan Atkinson, *The muddle-headed republic*,

nationalism recollects an absence that appeals particularly to people formed within the apparently open structures of globalizing capitalism. It incorporates some of the traces of classical or modern nationalism such as a ritualistic sense of embodied solidarity—evidenced in the return of the Unknown Soldier[33] —without any of the demands of ultimate sacrifice and unquestioning loyalty implicit in the older, more comprehensive identity conferred by the modern nation-state. If the modern nation-state was experienced as both publicly and intimately structuring one's life-world then the postmodern nation (even when it is not named as such) is increasingly *experienced* as an unstructured, and at times even optional, background choice.[34] At the same time under conditions of postmodernity the state is most often viewed either as a baleful institution to be minimized and deregulated or as a necessary, if intrusive, organ of public administration, as a provider of essential services for the vulnerable. There are not many state-utopians left in the world.

To say that under conditions of postmodernity the nation state is experienced as becoming less structured is not to suggest that our subjective sense of the present provides us with an accurate

---

Oxford University Press, Melbourne, 1993, p. 117, in a chapter entitled 'Postmodern patriotism'. For an indication of the shallowness of 'minimalist republicanism' it is worth having a browse through the two volumes of *An Australian republic: the report of the republic advisory committee*, AGPS, Canberra, 1993, and John Hirst's reply to Atkinson's monarchism, *A republican manifesto*, Oxford University Press, Melbourne, 1994.

33   The exercise was full of contradictory cross-currents. A group such as the Victorian executive of the RSL which in an earlier period would have most probably been in full support was its most vocal critic (*Age*, 11 November, 1993), while the ALP received more kudos from a military celebration than it had on any occasion since Remembrance Day, 1945. The designer of the tomb, Janet Laurence, talked explicitly of the desire to appeal to all: 'its abstract nature could speak about other losses and absences to future generations who would not have an immediate link with World War I' (*Australian*, 4 November 1993).

34   The process, it must be stressed, is uneven. Despite the changes brought about by the 1993 Citizenship Amendment Bill, Australia is now the only country amongst the old Commonwealth states which cancels the citizenship (nationality) of citizens who become naturalized elsewhere. Contemporary commentators are now arguing that this act, instituted by the classical nation-state in the nineteenth century, is a breach of the Declaration of Human Rights (*Age*, 18 November 1993).

picture. The image of the nation-state as an aging leviathan, more comfortable lumbering amidst the inglorious structures of the past, is belied by the alacrity with which 'it'[35] has recently taken up various administrative techniques such as electronic information storage and other forms of disembodied surveillance. Rather than collapsing into disorganized, decentred micro-practices, the structures (the dominant *modes of practice*) are changing. Life at the face-to-face level may be becoming more fragmented in the sense that personal relations have less certainty, but social life is being restructured and reintegrated at a more abstract level. This restructuring offers new, and potentially dangerous, possibilities for political practice. The restructuring can be briefly sketched by drawing upon the methodology set up earlier in the chapter.

The changing modes of practice: production, exchange, communication and organization

It is no accident that I choose to begin with the practices of production: despite the avowals of the poststructuralists and the radical Weberians it is still a relevant category of analysis. Based upon their subjective sense of the 'disorganization' of the present, too many commentators make the classical categorical error of confusing a change in the form of a mode of practice for the declining salience of a category of theory. Take the following example from a recent book called *Postmodernization*:

> If the focus of this book had been processes of modernization then this chapter would probably been placed somewhere towards the beginning rather than towards the end. Production is the key axial process of modern societies—the way it is organized might be held to determine, or at least to have serious consequences for, political, cultural and

---

35 It almost goes without saying that 'it' is shorthand for the patterns of practices and discourses of the many persons (intellectually trained agents) who work in the many apparatuses which we call the 'state'. Using the shorthand references is not necessarily to imply that 'the state' operates as a single homogenous entity, nor to reify 'it' as a hypostatized object acting organically or anthropomorphically. Contrary to some of the more pedantic postmodernists, such designations as 'state' and 'society' continue to be useful.

other developments ... Postmodernization precisely involves a reversal of determinacy so that the fragments of a hyperdifferentiating culture impact upon, disrupt and deconstruct arenas of social structure which might previously have been thought impervious to change.[36]

What the authors of *Postmodernization* are arguing is that under conditions of modernity, production ruled the determinative waves: now under conditions of postmodernity, a 'hyperdifferentiating culture' is the determinant process, albeit a disruptive one. The argument of the present chapter is that rather than involving a 'reversal of determinacy' (a claim which, incidentally, also overemphasizes the centrality of production under conditions of modernity) postmodern capitalism involves a number of interconnected developments across the various modes of practice which have, in the heightening of long-term processes, lead to enormous change.[37]

The most important of these in the area of production and relevant to the changing nature of the nation-state is the increasing globalization of production. The new economic jargon of the 1990s—'world's best practice', 're-engineering', 'deregulation', 'world-wide consistency' and 'globalization'—all express a reorientation of production in a period when the local, the national and the global are more integrated than ever before.[38]

Some examples from the motor industry should suffice: Hella

---

36 Stephen Crook, Jan Pakulski and Malcolm Waters, *Postmodernization: change in advanced society*, Sage, London, 1992, p.167. The first sentence of my paragraph above is an intentional rewriting of a sentence of theirs, also from page 167.

37 A number of theorists list the kind of changes to which I am referring, though mentioning those authors here does not necessarily suggest an agreement with either all the changes they list or the way in which they set about prioritizing such a list: Scott Lash and John Urry, *The end of organized capitalism*, Polity Press, Cambridge, 1987; David Harvey, *The condition of postmodernity*, Basil Blackwell, Oxford 1989; and Barry Smart, *Modern conditions, postmodern controversies*, Routledge, London, 1992. The fact that I emphasize a dialectic of continuity and discontinuity rather than an epochal discontinuity makes me sympathetic to critiques of the above authors for their occasional tendency to overstate the 'break' between modernity and postmodernity.

38 See for example Christopher Chase-Dunn, *Global formation: structures of world economy*, Basil Blackwell, Cambridge, 1989; Anthony McGrew and Paul Lewis et al., *Global politics*, Polity Press, Cambridge 1992. On the implications for Australia see particularly Hugh Emy, *Remaking Australia*, Allen & Unwin, Sydney, 1993, ch.7.

Australia sells one of its New Zealand-built components to GM's German Opel subsidiary for incorporation into the Spanish-built Barina, a car which is marketed in Australia. Apollos (from American-owned GMH) and Camrys (Japanese-owned Toyota) are the same car, as are Toyota Lexcen and Holden Commodore. The Camry, manufactured at Toyota's Altona plant which officially opened in April 1995, is to be exported to more than a dozen countries; for example, a deal has been recently signed to send components in kit form to South Africa for assembly. The Altona plant itself was made possible at a cost of $420 million because Toyota needed to export domestic capital from Japan to counterbalance the high value of the yen. Another non-Australian company, the transnational Mitsubishi, is currently Australia's largest exporter of motor vehicles, and as a recent advertisement proudly testifies, they 'had to compete internationally for the right to design and build the Magna Wagon here in Australia'.[39] In the words of their managing director, the company manufactures 'in Australia as an integrated member of a global vehicle-producing network'. From GMH to Mitsubishi the techniques and technologies of production, and increasingly, as the Keating government deregulates the labour market and falls back to International Labor Organization [ILO] minimum standards, their industrial relations practices are determined by the structures of global competition.

The global is no longer conducted as a series of lines of connection as it was under conditions of classical modernity, but has come to be an overbracing layer of integration. Similarly, the mode of exchange is being revolutionized. It is not simply that the empirical volume of traffic in traded commodities has increased, for though we can cite supporting figures (such as 70 per cent of grocery items sold in Australian supermarkets come from or are controlled by international sources), the movement of material commodities no longer continues to climb exponentially—it is reaching the limits of environmental and commercial sustainability. Of course, trade continues to be important

---

[39] *Age*, 15 January 1994. And in a crude cultural twist on the post-Holden connection between cars and national identity, one of Mitsubishi's other ads is headlined 'Ninety per cent of Australians don't know where they live'. The four-wheel drive Pajero will help you find out with 'all the comfort and features of a luxury European sedan'.

—witness the intensity of the current trade and tariff liberalization debates.[40] However, overlaying that form of exchange there has been a qualitative development in the area of what we might call *disembodied exchange*, exchange at an increasingly abstract level. On-line trading systems such as GEMMnet (the Global Electronic Marketing and Merchandising Network) are being set up by companies including Woolworths to manage the world-wide purchasing of goods. More impressively, the extraordinary volume of capital exchange in its various forms through the now electronic stockmarkets, and the commodification of exchangeable information as intellectual capital, give us a foretaste of the nature of the developments.

The immediacy and impact of change are signalled by events in the last decade: most prominently business folklore refers back to the computerized minutes of the 1987 stock-market crash, and the frenzied day in which the Australian dollar fell by three US cents after Paul Keating spoke to John Laws on Sydney radio and used the expression 'banana republic'. The information revolution has contributed to a new kind of market, a postmodern market (John Hinkson) which electronically traverses the continuing borders of modernity. And Australia is part of that market as one of the central nodes in the global exchange network:

> The daily transactions on the Australian foreign exchange markets in Australian dollars now amount to around $20 billion. In Sydney, the ratio of daily foreign exchange transactions in Australian currency against daily trade commonly ranges between 20 or 30 to 1. This compares with figures ... of perhaps 25 to 1 internationally and 10 to 1 on United States daily trade. Such intensity of activity is probably less significant than that foreign exchange markets are now asset markets as well as reflecting normal trade transactions. This poses some problems [for the state] in managing monetary and exchange rate policy ... [41]

Australia now has a $500 billion-a-year foreign exchange market,

---

[40] Ironically, despite the assumptions built into the current debate, this is an area where it is still possible to regulate exchange within the (modern) terms of a demarcated, state-administered territoriality.

[41] Stuart Harris, 'The international economy and domestic politics' in *Governing in the 1990s*, ed. Ian Marsh, Longman Cheshire, Melbourne, 1993. (With thanks to Hugh Emy for this reference.)

part of the world's $1400 billion-a-day currency market (and that's not counting other forms of capital exchange such as swaps, futures, forwards and options). In 1994 the federal treasurer, Ralph Willis, ruled out as uncompetitive a proposal by John Langmore to impose a transaction tax of 0.5 per on currency movement. Since then we have not heard a word at the federal level about micro-taxing the flow of global capital.

Any discussion of exchange obviously leads into the issue of the changing dominant forms of communication. Here as before the argument is not that the more embodied forms of communication are being replaced, but rather that touch and voice, writing and print are being increasingly overlaid and framed by more abstract modalities of communication: digitally encoded and electronically transmitted either by means of terrestrial and relay networks or by the wireless world of the satellite. Early in 1993 Telecom announced that Australia was about to be connected to the global optical fibre network via a system called PacRimEast running under the Pacific Ocean. While this development may seem to be a simple upgrade on the under-sea system that first linked us to the Mother Country in the 1870s, the difference is twofold: (1) the exponential growth in, and normalization of, the use of such technologies (the cables carry up to 100 000 telephone calls simultaneously); and (2) the interconnection and increasing intermeshing of these mediating technologies, particularly through the mass media. The more recent announcement by President Clinton of the United States' national data superhighway (SH) project[42] to develop 'universal' networks of optic fibre and coaxial cable is only the latest venture in a whole series of *converging* developments which have been connecting the local, national and global. They impact directly upon Australia.

Over the last couple of decades there has been a generalizing spread, unprecedented in human history, of the technical apparatuses for overcoming the temporal and spatial limits of embodied communication. For example, the computer-connected global system, Internet, which in the mid-1980s had a few thousand sub-

---

42   *Australian*, 8 March 1994.

scribers, including Australia's universities, now services ten million users. The number of Internet-connected networks has doubled every year since 1990; software programmes, such as Mosaic introduced in 1993, make it possible to navigate around this global 'cyberspace', including all of its Bulletin Board Systems, data-bases and electronic catalogues. Of the nearly 200 countries connected to Internet, Australia is the second heaviest user. (Do you remember the early 1990s when the term Email conjured up the name of a whitegoods manufacturer?)

Stranger than fiction, it can be anecdotally noted that Howard Rheingold's book, *The virtual community: homesteading on the electronic frontier* was nominated by *Business week* as one of the best business books of 1993.[43] The broader point is that as part of burgeoning level of mass and person-to-person communications, computer-mediated networking contributes to the globalizing and electronic abstraction of national and local cultures.[44]

All of this bears heavily upon the mode of organization and by extension upon the two dominant organizational forms of the late twentieth century—the transnational corporation and the state. In the context of the present chapter the key question becomes 'to what extent are we thus seeing the transformation of the Australian state?' I want to conclude by challenging the suggestion made by some postmodernists that under present conditions we are seeing a devolution and disorganization of the powers and responsibilities of the state. The sophisticated but flawed analysis of a book already discussed above, *Postmodernization*, can be used to exemplify this new version of the 'withering away of the state' thesis.

---

[43] Maximilian Walsh, 'Will colonization by big business be good for cyber-space?', *Age*, 11 January 1994. Howard Rheingold's book was released in Australia as, *The virtual community: finding connection in a computerized world*, Secker and Warburg, London, 1994.

[44] See Mike Featherstone, ed., *Global culture: nationalism, globalization and modernity*, Sage, London, 1990; Anthony King, ed., *Culture, globalization and the world-system*, Macmillan, London, 1991; Brian Murphy, *The world wired up*, Comedia, London, 1983; David Lyon, *The information society*, Polity, Cambridge, 1991, ch. 6; Vincent Mosco and Janet Wasko, eds, *The political economy of information*, University of Wisconsin Press, Madison, 1988; and Jon Bird, et al., eds, *Mapping the futures: local cultures, global change*, Routledge, London, 1993.

In a chapter entitled 'The shrinking state' its authors write:

> The economic, political, and cultural aspects of this devolution converge on a single, postmodern 'disorganization complex'. The convergence of such trends, combined with a tidal wave of anti-etatist sentiments among elites and such strategically important social categories as the young, the educated and the urban, heralds more than a temporary retreat. The process appears to be a major reversal, part of a historical shift which closes the twentieth century and marks the end of its distinctive etatist project.[45]

Proclaiming the death of something is always risky, but especially so when it is coupled with a claim about the reversal of dominant historical developments. The book rightly argues that the state of modernity involved processes of increasing centralization, bureaucratic rationalization and economic regulation. However, by setting up an overly dichotomous contrast, the state of postmodernity is mischaracterized as in effect reversing these trends. The reality in Australia, as elsewhere, is far more contradictory—a dialectic of continuity and discontinuity working across various levels.

The authors of *Postmodernity* are breaking new ground in attempting to specify how the state is changing. Nevertheless, they do not have the conceptual tools to make their case. The state is not shrinking. It is not withdrawing *carte blanche* from either the lifeworld or the economic sphere. There is no one-way movement of vertical decentralization involving 'the redistribution of power and responsibility downwards to the lower territorial levels, localities and self-governing bodies'.[46] Rather, we are seeing a simultaneous movement towards the centralization of decision-making and a greater pressure to take account of the minority groups and local factors. We are seeing overt deregulation in some areas, particularly as already mentioned in monetary policy, while the mechanisms of regulation continue to be more and more finely calibrated. Michael Warby provides us with some telling

---

45   Crook et al., *Postmodernization*, p. 80.
46   ibid., p. 98.

statistics.[47] Despite some ups and downs, both the percentage of total government outlay as a proportion of GDP and the detail of government legislation have been increasing over the past two decades. In the period 1960–69 a total of 1181 Commonwealth Acts were passed comprising 7544 pages of legislation; in 1980–89, 1691 Acts comprised 29 299 pages. In the year 1991, 216 Acts were passed with almost as many pages of legislation as were processed in the whole of the 1960s. Deregulation, it seems, entails a greater detail of legislation than ever before. But more than that, there have been qualitative changes. The state is embroiled in a new level of regulation, surveillance and cross-correlation of information made possible by the computer in conjunction with the heightened intellectual training of its agents. It has more techniques and technologies than ever before allowing for the abstraction of power across time and space, even as the constraints on the efficacy of these mechanisms of power has increased. We therefore find ourselves with a state which has recognizable continuities with the past, but one that is being *re*structured to cope with a changing domestic and global order:

> an infinitely more complex state than ever before, one not simply intervening more or getting weightier, but one also drawn into the structures of everyday life by the changes and gaps and tensions within everyday life itself—while the private and personal have expanded (and contracted) too, in complex ways. To 'get government off our backs' as President Reagan wished to do, often paradoxically requires more intervention, not less.[48]

Conclusion

No one doubts that over the past few decades the country we call Australia has been changing. The lines of debate diverge over the extent, nature and political implications of the changes. This chapter contends that the changes are now sufficiently far-reaching to warrant

---

47 Michael Warby, 'Myth of the shrinking state', *Age*, 25 February 1993.
48 P. G. Cerny cited in Rob Watts, 'Government and modernity: an essay in thinking governmentality', *Arena journal*, 2, 1994, p. 144.

describing Australia as one of the first postmodern nation states. Importantly, the process of change has been one of restructuring and reconstitution, not simply one of disorganization and fracturing. It has been a process which is continuous with the past but can be marked off as involving qualitative (discontinuous) and patterned outcomes. While at the level of face-to-face relations, life is more fragmented and transitory than it was even within the transitory world of modernity, at a more abstract level the modes of practice of late capitalism structure newly dominant forms of integration. These have come to overlay rather than replace the previously dominant ontological formations of tribalism (prior to White displacement) and traditionalism/modernity thereafter.

When Don Watson says that whatever institutional shape the republic of Australia takes, 'there will be something unstructured, if not deconstructed about it ... aleatory, impressionistic, figurative, eclectic bebop ...' he is giving expression to a central ideology of the coming period, one that masks the nature of the emerging structures and subjectivities of integration (and power). His hopes can be described as a postmodern nostalgia for the future, a belief in the goodness of fragmentation as if the oppressions of modernity will be overcome in the breakdown and replacement of its institutions by more open ones. To the extent that the proponents of republicanism call for the end to the patrilineal and tradition-based power of a person born on the other side of the world, they have a strong case. However, as yet, most republicans fluctuate between two extremes: a minimalist (modernist) position which in proposing a few constitutional amendments utterly fails to come to terms with the political implications of being a nation state in a globalizing world; and a postmodernist position which rhetorically celebrates a culture of openness while instrumentally giving over to the economic imperative of going with flow of global capitalism. There are other choices.

By recognizing that the nation state will continue to be a relevant structural level of polity-community, albeit one caught between localism and globalism, we can begin to avoid the potentially dangerous pulls of each. We can begin to *re*-construct the nation state as a culturally based institution which qualifies the ravages of globalism while it works across and beyond the limitations of parochial localism. It seems ironical now, as the nation state falls from grace as the dominant centre of social relations, that it should offer the possibility of positively mediating the local and the global. But then we live in different times. The openings are there for a new kind of Australian nation: for example, a polity which on the one hand writes into its constitution a concrete obligation to financially and socially support the needs of strangers across the globe, and, on the other hand, sets up the legal and social conditions for local regions and local communities, including Aboriginal peoples, to take over more of the responsibility for managing their own futures. In this kind of future the intermeshing layers of locality, nationality and globality could work to qualify and enhance each other, rather than be subsumed under the latest wave of capitalist development as the prophets of globalism would have it.

Appendix **LEVELS OF THEORETICAL ABSTRACTION**

The overall argument is that a comprehensive theory of social relations and subjectivities has to work across a manifold of levels of theoretical abstraction. Below is set out one possible way of conceiving such a manifold.

I. *Empirical Generalization*

(a) In particular:
- Biographies of particular persons.
- Histories of particular polities such as 'post-settlement' Australia.
- Descriptions of particular institutions, fields of activity of discourses.

(b) In general:
Drawing on particular accounts and studies, analysis at this level attempts to be more comparative and to survey the longer term, for example:
- Histories of the practices of 'personhood', gender relations, class-based life-worlds.
- Comparative histories of a political form such as 'the nation-state'.
- Descriptions of an institution-in-general such as 'bureaucracy', fields such as 'the law', or discourses such as 'social democracy'.

At this level, analysis which emphasizes the particular, and does not reach for more abstract ways of understanding, runs the risk—however detailed its description—of superficiality or empiricism. Nevertheless, empirical generalization remains a basic level of analysis necessary to any approach in order to avoid abstract theoreticism.

II *Social Formational Analysis*

(a) In particular:
Analysis at this level of theoretical abstraction proceeds by resolution of particular *modes of practice*. The present approach complicates 'classical historical materialism' by analytically distinguishing five primary modes:
1. modes of production,
2. modes of exchange,
3. modes of communication,
4. modes of organization,
5. modes of enquiry.

In practice, no *mode of practice* exists as a separate, autonomous form. The rationale for this five-fold classification is that it avoids some of the reductionism of a classical 'mode of production' approach without becoming too unwieldy.

(b) In general:
Drawing on analyses of particular modes of practice, analysis at this level attempts to describe conjunctures between such modes. Generalizations are made about the structural connections between dominant modes of practice, thus allowing for the short-hand designation of actually existing formations of practice, for example:
  (reciprocal) tribalism,
  (absolutist) feudalism,
  (industrial) capitalism,
  (information) capitalism,
These designations, like all classifying schemes, can only be used as working descriptions, not reified entities. When formations are defined in terms of the dominant *formation of practice*, this is not to rule out subordinate formations.

III. Social Integration Analysis

(a) In particular:
Analysis proceeds by resolution of *levels* of social integration (and differentiation). While in theory one could distinguish any number of levels of integration, the present approach sets out three such levels:
1. face-to-face integration,
2. agency-extended integration,
3. disembodied integration.

In practice, no *level of integration* exists as a separate, autonomous form.

(b) In general:
Drawing on analyses of levels of integration, generalizations can be made, firstly, about the *intersections* between these (ontological) levels—for example, charting the emergence of ontological contradictions—and, secondly, about the complexities of social life as summarized at less and more abstract (epistemological) *levels* of theoretical abstraction. Following the second path, generalizations can be made which further enrich and contextualize our understanding of particular life histories, fields and discourses (Level I), modes and formations of practice (II), and the ontological categories and formations of social life (IV), for example:
- agency-extended (industrial) capitalism,
- disembodied (information) capitalism,
- modern (patriarchal) capitalism.

IV. Categorical Analysis

At this level, analysis works by reflexively 'deconstructing' categories of social ontology. It attempts to take nothing for granted, including the epistemological and ontological assumptions of its own approach (especially the tendency of some deconstructive projects to give priority to the so-argued 'liberatory' potentialities of practices of deconstruction).

(a) In particular:
Structural genealogies (as distinct from 'classical' histories or descriptions—see I(a) above) of particular categories of existence such as:
time and space, culture and nature, gender, embodiment, knowledge, language, theory, and the unconscious.

(b) In general:
Drawing on discussions of particular ontological categories, generalizations can be made about different forms of ontological formation (and different epistemes), for example:
traditionalism, modernity, postmodernity, phallocentrism.

As with all other concepts in the present approach to 'levels of theoretical abstraction' they remain provisional concepts, provisional as tested against the criterion 'Are they useful for understanding the complexities of social life?' At this level, analysis which is not tied back into more concrete political-ethical considerations is in danger of abstracted irrelevance, utopianism without a subject, or empty spiritualism.

Index

Aboriginal land rights, 4, 145, 158
  -*terra nullius* doctrine, 232
Aboriginal people, 124, 156, 158-60, 218, 249
Absolutism, 18, 161-2, 180
Abstraction,
  -abstract rights, 153
  -as lived, 32, 49
  -between state and citizen, 219-20
  -material or social abstraction, 31, 53, 207-10, 212, 214, 225, 240, 243, 244, 245, 247
  -of the state, 207-8, 210, 216, 225, 229, 247
  -theoretical or methodological abstraction, 21, 29-32, 33, 167, 227-9, 250-1
Accord, the 60, 61-3, 65, 71, 98, 143
Action-centred networks, 105
Affirmative action, 144, 152
Africa, 11
Albinski, Henry, 173
Allen, Judith, 29
Almond, Gabriel, 17, 26
Althusser, Louis, 208
America, *see* United States
American Political Science Association, 25, 36
Anderson, Benedict, 229, 232n.
Andorra, 10
Anglomorphy, 225
Anti-homosexual laws, 193
Anti-Vietnam-war movement, 139, 141
ANZUS, 183
Arbitration Commission, 142
Ashley, Richard, 168
Asia, 145, 182, 185, 237
Australia, *passim*
Australia card, 3
Australian Conservation Foundation (ACF), 98, 105
Australian Council of Trade Unions (ACTU), 60
Australian dollar, 4, 243

Australian Labor Party (ALP), 2, 4, 38-73 *passim*, 140-2, 156, 174, 192, 203
  (*see also*: the Curtin, Chifley, Whitlam, Hawke, and Keating governments)
Australian Mining Industry Council, 95
Australian women and the political system, 147
Australia reconstructed, 203-4

Backlash, 143
Bahro, Rudolf, 81
Baldock, Cora, 147, 149
Balkans, 204
Barrett, Michele, 146
Barrow, Clyde, 30
Battin, Tim, 39
Beazley, Kim, 126
Beck, Ulrich, 75, 80
Behaviouralism, 14, 26
Beilharz, Peter, 47-8
Bell, Coral, 173-4, 182, 183
Bicentenary, the, 234
Bjelke-Peterson, Joh, 94
'Blood and soil', ideologies of, 224, 230
Blueprint for a green economy, 80
Brazil, 90
Brezhnev doctrine, 191
Bringing the state back in, 25n., 36
Britain, 10, 25, 61, 138, 145, 146, 150, 154, 155, 224
  (*see also*: England)
Broom, Dorothy, 147
Brundtland report, 97, 100
Bookchin, Murray, 81
Bulbeck, Chilla, 159
Bulletin, 131
Burchall, David, 43
Bureaucracy, 28, 60, 77, 99, 102-6, 107, 120, 127, 138, 151, 152, 170, 173, 222, 250
Bureaucratic-industrial complex, 104
Bureaucrats, technocrats, femocrats, 148, 152

INDEX

Bureau of Statistics, 125
Business and finance, 38, 65, 68, 70, 71, 114, 143, 203, 241-5
Business week, 245

Cairns, Jim, 59
Calhoun, Craig, 47
Camilleri, Joe, 162, 181-5, 231, 235
Capitalism, (*see also*: Modes of practice, production) 3, 12, 32-33, 40, 46, 48, 53, 58, 72, 74, 78, 80, 89, 102, 109-10, 112, 120, 146, 176-84, 197, 225, 226, 234, 235-6, 237, 248-9
-information capitalism, 227, 250, 251
-postmodern capitalism, 229
(*see also*: Market, postmodern)
-print capitalism, 230
Carlie, M., 86n., 105
Carmichael, Laurie, 203
Carr, E. H., 167-8, 169-70
Carroll, John, 58
Cass, Bettina, 147, 149
Castles, Francis, 47
Catley, Bob, 45
Cerny, Phil, 69, 72
Chifley, Ben, 52
Chifley government, 58, 71
Child care, 115, 119, 140, 142, 144, 145, 149, 151, 152
Childe, Gordon, 43
China, 181
Christie, I., 86n., 105
Christoff, Peter, 91
Citizens, citizenship, 16, 47, 50, 59, 86, 91, 110, 120, 105, 207, 208, 216, 218, 221, 230, 235, *also*:
-Citizenship Amendment Bill, 239n.
-'dependency' of, 219-20
-non-citizens, 76, 84
Civil society, 154, 200, 207
Class, 36, 49, 56, 121, 124, 136, 140, 146-7, 152, 153, 175, 197, 205, 220, 223, 250, *also*:
-middle class, 39, 147, 152, 159
-ruling class, 45, 146, 176, 182, 236
-underclass, 67, 109-137 *passim*
-working class, 39-43, 46, 49, 51, 54, 57, 61, 63, 71, 129, 133, 135, 137, 219

Clinton, Bill, 244
Coercion, 110-11, 128, 169-70, 180
Cold War, 162, 174, 190-1
Colonialism, 139, 157-60
Common good, 6, 83
Commonwealth Employment Service (CES), 118
Communications revolution, *see* Information revolution
Communism, 12, 74, 171
Communitarianism, 170
Community, 13, 14, 15, 76, 81, 82, 84, 97-8, 106, 122, 126, 136, 141, 169, 176, 216, 225, 230, 231, 249, *also*:
-face-to-face community, 207, 240, 248
Connell, Bob, 45, 46, 148, 152, 153
Conservatism, 9, 25, 216, 236
Constitutional change, 3, 28, 145, 158-9, 248-9
Constructivism, 165-6, 186-95
Contradiction,
-cultural contradiction, 200, 201, 213-22 *passim*
-ontological contradiction, 234, 251
(*see also*: State, contradictions of)
Co-operation, an ethic of, 218, 219, 221-2, 249
Core states, 177-8, 179, 180
Corporatism, 62, 71, 74, 99, 134
Corporatization, 4, 35, 64
Court, Charles, 94
Court, Di, 148, 152, 153
Cox, Eva, 138, 147
Crean, Simon, 62
Crick, Bernard, 23
Criminology, 28
Crook, Stephen, 34-5, 246
Crowe, Annie, 131-2
CSIRO, 105
Cultural anthropology, 26
Curthoys, Ann, viii, 6, 30
Curtin government, 56, 58, 71

Daedalus, 25
Daly, Herman, 83
Davison, Graeme, 233
Dawkins, John, 62, 209
'Dawkinsism', 206
Decentralization, 82, 86

De-industrialization, 67
Deleuze, Gilles, 32-3
Democracy, 23, 48, 76, 79, 82, 83-5, 107, 108, 135, 136, 139, 153-7, 161, 200, 207, *also*:
-'age of democracy', 222-3
Department of Employment, Education and Training (DEET), 209-10
Department of Prime Minister and Cabinet (PMC), 141, 144
Department of Social Security (DSS), 119, 134
Depression, 1930s, 55-6, 59
Deregulation, 4, 35, 39, 60, 64, 68, 70, 111, 145, 196, 202, 203, 205, 225, 235, 239, 241, 246-7
Deterritorialization, 29, 33, 200, 207-13 *passim*, 214, 225, 235
Disembodiment, 53, 244-5, 251
Domestic violence, 141, 145, 151, 216
Dowse, Sarah, 138, 141, 148
Dryzek, John, 103
Dyson, Kenneth, 24

Earth Summit (1992), 75, 94
Easton, David, 17, 19, 24, 26
East Timor, 194
Eckersley, Robyn, viii, 6, 11
Ecological modernization, 100-1
Ecologically Sustainable Development (ESD), 97-101, 104
(*see also*: Sustainable development)
Economic development, 90, 99, 184, 203, 216, 220
Economic growth, 66, 67, 68, 72, 74, 114
Economic rationalism, 18, 34, 39, 42, 60-1, 63, 73, 113, 120, 144, 196, 202
Economics, theory and policy, 15, 56, 61, 73, 175-6, 185, 194, 209, 230, 241-7, *also*:
-face-to-face economies, 221
-green economics, 81-85
-micro-economic reform, 37, 69, 246-7
-neo-classical economics, 57-8, 60, 77, 78-80, 83, 203
-steady-state economics, 83
(*see also*: Capitalism; Keynesianism; *and* the Market)

Ecopolitics, 40, 74-108
Education, 59, 65, 82, 110, 114, 117, 128, 149, 151, 180, 204, 209, *also*:
-as socially integrating, 208-9
-new vocationalism, 206
-training programmes, 115, 117, 118, 120, 129, 151
Eisenstein, Hester, 148, 150
Electoralism, 42, 51-2, 59, 62
Emancipation, 154, 175
Empires, imperialism, 224, 232, 233
(*see also*: Colonialism)
Empirical generalization, 199, 200, 228, 250
(*see also*: Abstraction, theoretical)
Emy, Hugh, vii, 6, 7
England, 17, 18, 45, 150
(*see also*: Britain)
Enlightenment ideals, 153, 155, 157
Enterprise bargaining, 63, 114
Environment, 2, 6, 10, 75-108 *passim*, 162, 175, 219, 242
-ecological crisis, 74, 77, 89-90, 102, 107
-implications for the state, 75-108, 178, 190
-movement, 40, 75, 81-2, 98
Environmental impact assessment (EIA), 97
Equal opportunity, 4, 142-3, 145, 152
Ethnic conflict, 11, 24, 131, 213, 224
Ethnicity, 124, 152, 157, 212-13, 230, 232
Europe, 9-11, 23, 24, 25, 100, 107, 161, 176, 177, 191, 203, 222, 224, *also*:
-European Union, 86, 107, 190
Evans, Gareth, 164, 192
Exclusion, 219-20
(*see also*: Marginalization)
Fabianism, 43, 49
Fascism, 110
Falk, Jim, 162, 231, 235
Faludi, Susan, 143
Family, 57, 110, 117, 124, 146, 170
-family allowances, 115
Federalism, 85-9, 90, 93, 96, 114
Federal-state conflict, 85-97 *passim*, 193
Federation, 54, 233-4
Feminism, 6, 30, 40, 138-160

-femocratism, 141-5, 147-52, 155, 160
-radical feminism, 157-8
(see also: Liberal feminism)
Figgis, J. N., 18
Finn report, 210
Fordist society, 56
-post-Fordism, 206
Foreign policy, 161-195 passim
-idealism, 169
Foucault, Michel, 29, 33-4, 216
Framework Conventions on Climate Change, 94, 99
France, 10, 23, 45, 145
Frankel, Boris, 24n., 58
Franklin River, 87-8
Franzway, Suzanne, 148, 152, 153
Fraser, Malcolm, 193
Fraser government, 68, 142
Fraser Island, 87-8
Free trade, 10, 114, 178
(see also: Trade)
French Revolution, 161-2
Full employment, 50, 56, 63, 66, 67, 68, 114

Gallup poll, 123
Game, Ann, 147, 154
Gelber, Harry, 173
Gender relations, 47, 50-1, 57, 66, 115-16, 122-3, 142, 146, 149, 153-5, 157, 158, 250
Gender shock, 148, 150
German state tradition, 21
Germany, 23, 90, 237
Giddens, Anthony, 25, **186-7**
Global Electronic Marketing and Merchandising Network (GEMMnet), 243
Globalism, 6, 71, 162-3, 174, 191, 194, also:
-global capitalism, 4, 32, 134, 214, 237, 239, 247, 248
(see also: Capitalism)
-global commons, 83
-global co-operation, 75, 107, 164, 172, 218
-global communications, 204, 205, 244-5
-global economy, 8, 12, 58, 64, 106, 107, 145, 162, 164, 174, 176, 183, 219, 220, 221, 242-4
(see also: Market, global)
-global exchange, 4, 242-3
-global production, 124, 241-2
Globalization, 8, 10, 11, 33, 35, 54, 57, 67, 162-4, 176, 184-6, 200, 204, 205, 211-12, 229, 234, 241-5
'Global village', 198
Goodman, David, 226
Goodnow, Jacqueline, 147
Gorbachev, Mikhail, 191
Goss Labor government, 143
Gough, Ian 112
Governance, 29, 31, 38, 70, 106, 188-9
Governmentality, 33-4, 198n.
Gramsci, Antonio, 45
Grant, Bruce, 164, 192
Gray, John, 13
Gray, Robin, 94
Graycar, Adam, 112
Green parties, 74, 82, 100
Gregory, Bob, 123
Guattari, Félix, 32-3
Guild socialism, 18
(see also: Socialism)

Habermas, Jürgen, 25, 84, 101, 197, 198n., 205, 227
Hagan, Jim, 46
Hall, Stuart, 26
Hancock, Eleanor, 148
Hardin, Garrett, 78-9
Hawke, Bob, 36, 38, 40, 54, 58, 59, 60, 62, 72, 96, 98, 144
Hawke government, 38-42, 61-65, 68, 70-1, 96, 143-4, 164, 185
Hayden, Bill, 60, 62, 63
Held, David, 197, 200
Helsinki Accords, 191
Herz, John, 168
Hilmer report, 6n.
Hinkson, John, viii, 4n., 6, 12, 32, 229, 243
Holland, Stuart, 65
Howard, John, 203
Howe, Brian, 62
Human rights, 136, 157, 162, 175, 192-4, 239n.

Identity, cultural, 211, 212-13, 214, 215, 219, 220
(see also: National identity; the Self)
Image industries, 215
Image revolution, 202, 209
Immigration, 11, 55, 115
(see also: migrants)
Indonesia, 194, 236, 237
Industrial revolution, 161
Industrial society, 75
Industries Assistance Commission, 59
Information revolution, 8, 162, 198, 199, 200-2, 204, 209, 215, 218-19, 235, 243-5
Intellectual culture, the concept of, 206, 208, 216
Intellectually trained, the, 53-4, 55, 203, 206, 208, 212-16 *passim*, 220, 221, 230, 247, *also*:
-era of, 209
-intellectual technique, 206, 210, 215, 247
Intergovernmental Agreement on the Environment, 94-6
International Covenant on Civil and Political Rights, 192-3, 194
International Labor Organisation (ILO), 242
International relations, 145, 161-195, 218
-anarchical structure of, 166-7, 168, 172, 175-6, 182
Irving, Helen, 156, 160
Irving, Terry, 44-5, 46
James, Paul, ix, 7, 32, 36
Jameson, Fredric, 215, 231n.
Jamrozik, Adam, 112, 119, 121,
Janicke, Martin, 76, 104
Japan, 10, 224, 237, 242
Jessop, Bob, 25, 30
Jobs Compact, 115
Job Search, 115
Johnson, Carol, 142
Jones, Barry, 219

Kakadu National Park, 87-8
Katzenstein, Peter, 188-9
Keating, Paul, 40, 58, 59, 62, 68, 70, 98, 144, 145, 203, 230, 243
Keating government, 6n., 38-42, 62-64, 70-1, 145, 164, 185, 192, 242
Kelly, Paul, 46
Kelty, Bill, 62
Kennett, Jeff, 6n.
Keohane, Robert, 171-2
Keynesianism, 42, 55-6, 57, 58, 60-3, 66, 69, 203
King, Rodney, 130
Krasner, Stephen, 35
Kratochwil, Friedrich, 188, 190-1
Kurds, 11

Laborism, 38-73
Labour market programmes,
(see Education, training)
Labour movement, 41-43, 45-46, 49, 51-2, 61, 62, 66, 203
(see also: Laborism)
Lake, Marilyn, 156-7
Landcare initiative, 88, 105
Langmore, John, 244
Lash, Scott, 235
Late-modernity, 4, 6, 54
Latin America, 178
Law, 18, 82, 85, 154, 231, 250, *also*:
-internationalization of, 8
-legal powers and procedures, 31, 91-2, 96, 189, 216-217
-legal order, 19, 55, 75-6, 129, 133, 135, 170, 232
-legal reform, 142-4, 193, 248-9
-legal rationality, 34
Laws, John, 243
Left, the, 38, 44, 62, 63, 139
(see also: New Left)
Legitimation, 3n., 69, 101, 110, 120, 134, 161, 163
Liberal democracy, 13, 84, 110, 171
(see also: State, liberal democratic)

Liberal feminism, 150, 153-5, 157
Liberal pluralism, 17-24, 36, 225
Liberalism, 12, 15, 17ff., 42, 55-56, 78, 139, 153-5, 204, 216-17, *also*:
-as anti-state, 18, 70
-contract liberalism, 153, 155
-economic liberalism, 111, 113
-liberals, 10, 13
-libertarians, 79, 80

INDEX

-neo-classical, 19, 77-80
-neo-liberal institutionalism, 171-2
-social liberalism, 42, 57, 58, 59-60, 111, 113, 120, 155
Life-world, the concept of, 49, 53, 205, 239
Lombard, M., 122
Los Angeles and the riots, 130-1, 135, 204, 220
Lynch, Lesley, 147
Lyotard, Jean-Francois, 198n., 220

Mabo decision, 158, 218
McEachern, Doug, 99
McIntosh, Mary, 146
Macintyre, Stuart, 45
MacIver, Robert, 19
Mackay, Hugh, 5
McQueen, Humphrey, 45
Maddox, Graham, 38-9
Managerialism, 64, 103, 120, 134-5
Mann, Michael, 25
Manne, Robert, 58, 216-17
Marginalization, social 117-18, 121, 129, 133-5, 206, 212, 219
Market, (*see also*: Capitalism) 9-16 *passim*, 36, 38, 57, 58, 60, 62-4, 68, 78-80, 82, 108, 113, 117, 128, 134, 144, 155, 176, 181, 197, 203-6, 207, 215, 221, *also*:
-foreign-exchange market, 243-4
-free market, 12, 56, 59, 61, 66, 71, 79, 111, 144
-futures market, 204, 244
-global market, 10, 70, 219, 242-4
-postmodern market, 4n., 204-6, 209, 210, 213, 216, 218, 219, 221, 243
Markey, R., 46-7
Marshal Plan, 178
Marx, Karl, 197, 200, 204, 214, 225
Marxism, 13, 25, 26, 27, 29, 80, 101, 140, 146, 153, 154, 164-6, 175-86, 194, 197, *also*:
-base-superstructure framework, 227
-historical materialism, 227
Mayer report, 210
Media, 2, 132n., 140, 205, 225, 244, *also*:
-as socially integrative, 208-9, 228

(*see also*: Television)
Menzies, Robert, 70, 234
Methodological individualism, 18, 21
Meyer, John, 180
Migrants, 51, 125
(*see also*: Immigration)
Miliband, Ralph, 196, 197
Military, 145, 173, 174, 177, 180n., 182, 183, 188, 192
Modes of practice, 227-9, 240-7, 248, 250, *also*:
-modes of communication, 202, 204-5, 227-8, 230, 244-5, 250
-modes of enquiry, 227-8, 250
-modes of exchange, 218, 227-8, 242-4, 250
-'mode of information', 227
-modes of organization, 34, 227-8, 242-4, 250
-modes of production, 177, 198, 200, 209, 218-19, 221, 227-8, 230, 240-2, 250
Modernity, 33, 34, 39, 65, 189, 197, 198, 199, 200, 208, 209, 210, 213, 214, 224, 226, 241, 242, 243, 248, 251, *also*:
-and the ALP 52-73
Modernization, 52, 58, 65, 67, 68, 213, 224, 240
Muetzelfeldt, Michael, 63
Multiculturalism, 145, 225, 235
Multinational corporations,
(*see* Transnational corporations)
Murray-Darling initiative, 88, 105-6

National Association of Forest Industries, 95
National Farmers Federation, 105
National identity, 145, 159-60, 164, 192, 212, 224-49 *passim*
National interest, 169, 170, 171, 237
Nationality, 157, 233
National integration, 20, 169
Nationalism, 11, 55, 232, 235, 237, 239 *also*:
-death of, 224
-postmodern nationalism, 235, 236-9
Nation-building, 23, 24, 76
Nation-state, 11, 63, 65-6, 68, 69, 70,

75-76, 159, 176, 184, 200, 224-49 *passim*, 250
-modern nation-state, 224, 225, 229-34
-postmodern nation state, 225, 229, 234-40, 248
-'post-nations', 224, 237
Neo-classical economics, 13, 16
(*see also*: Liberalism, neo classical)
New internationalism, 165, 174, 192
New Left, 44-5, 57, 140
New Right, 57-8
Newstart, 115, 118, 129, 134
New World Order, 75

Offe, Claus, 25, 101
Office of the Status of Women, 144
Ohmae, Kenichi, 235
One Nation, 6n., 70, 71, 101
Ontological formations, 229, 248, 251
Orchard, Lionel, 13
OECD, 67, 68, 80

Palestinians, 11
Pakulski, Jan, 34-5, 246
Papua New Guinea, 230
Parkes, Henry, 232
Parliament, 28, 41, 46, 49, 135, 139, 140, 143, 156
Parsons, Talcott, 19
Pateman, Carol, 147, 153-5, 159
Pearce, David, 83
Peripheral states, 177-8, 179, 180, 220
Phillips, Anne, 156, 160
Playing the state, 148, 150, 153
Pluralism, 14, 17-20, 29
Poggi, Gianfranco, 31
Poiner, Gretchen, 148
Police; police powers, 33, 114, 128, 129, 133, 135
Political identity, 36
Political science, 14-27, 35-6, 147
-American, 10, 14, 17
Politics among nations, 168
Poster, Mark, 227
Post-industrialism, 4
Post-structuralism, 13, 29, 35, 159, 220, 226, 227, 240
Postmodern economy, 39, 218
(*see also*: Market, postmodern)

Postmodern era, 162, 207, 213, 215
Postmodern self, 198, 206, 212, 215
-and schizophrenia, 215-16
Postmodern society, 6, 34-5, 39, 197, 201, 202, 206, 217, 219, 237
(*see also*: Republicanism, postmodern; State, postmodern)
Postmodernism, 16, 29-30, 32, 36, 38, 64, 139, 157-60, 190, 195, 196-223 *passim*, 226, 229, 230, 235, 245, 248
Postmodernity, 4, 72, 197, 198n., 199, 208, 217, 226, 229, 239, 241, 251
Postmodernization, 9, 29, 241
Postmodernization, 34-35, 240-1, 245-6
Post-war reconstruction, 23, 58
Poulantzas, Nicos, 25, 29n., 135, 146, 154
Poverty, 66, 109, 111, 117, 120-7, 130, 135, 137, *also*:
-poverty line, 119, 122, 123
Power, 32-4, 36, 118, 135, 153, 167, 168-70, 171, 172, 177, 178, 191, 193, 199, 221, *and passim*
-abstraction of, 247-8
Pringle, Rosemary, 147, 148, 153, 154, 159
Print, 208, 244, *also*:
-relation to modernity, 201, 205
Prisons, 33, 216
Privatization, 4, 35, 39, 64, 71, 79, 86, 209
Private sector, 64, 69, 148
Protectionism, 114
Public interest, 83, 104
Public order, 22
Public sector, 15, 58, 64, 68, 70, 142
Public service, *see* Bureaucracy
Public sphere, 62, 64, 153, 207, 209
Pusey, Michael, 42, 60

Quebecois, 11

Race, 152, 157, 158
Racism, 49, 55, 135, 158
Rational choice, 14, 78
Rationality, bureaucratic, technical, etc., 53, 55-6, 63, 64, 77, 85, 102-5, 144, 231
Reagan, Ronald, 72, 143, 247

INDEX

Realism, the theory of, 164-75, 178, 182, 186, 194
-classical realism, 166-75
-neo-realism, 166-72, 187
Recession, 69, 88, 113, 142
Refractory girl, 141, 147
Regionalism, *see* Territory, regionalism
Reid, Elizabeth, 141
Religion, 11, 52
Republicanism, 5, 28, 49, 139, 145, 157-60, 164, 165, 225, 234, 248-9, *also*:
-postmodern republic, 5, 224-49 *passim*
Resource Assessment Commission, 101
Resource security, 95-7
Reus-Smit, Chris, ix, 5, 36
Rheingold, Howard, 245
Right, the, 38, 44, 130
Risk assessment, 84, 100
Risk society, 74, 80,
Robinson, M. 58
Rowley, Kelvin, 45
Ruggie, John, 188-90
Rwanda, 11
Ryan, Lyndall, 141, 150

Sabine, George, 19
Sale, Kirkpatrick, 81
Sawer, Marion, 141, 144, 147, 148, 151, 155, 159
Scandinavia, 156
Scott, Andrew, 40
Security, 33, 166, 168, 173-4, 183
Self, Peter, 13
Self, the, 200, 209, 212, 215 *also*:
-and other, 201, 215n., 236
-modern self, 198
-self-formative processes, 205, 208, 213, 216, 222-3
(*see also*: Postmodern self)
Sexual contract, 153-4
Sikkink, Kathryn, 193
Simms, Marian, 147
Sisters in suits, 148, 151
Skocpol, Theda, 25, 27, 31
Smith, Adam, 203, 204
Social contract, 154
Social control, 28, 33, 34, 109, 110, 121, 126-7, 216-17
Social democracy, 4, 10, 43, 44, 50, 81, 111, 120, 141, 144, 250
Social extension, 201-2, 207, 212, 215, 217, 218, 223, 228, 229, 244-5
Social integration, 208-9, 219, 228, 242, 248, 250
Socialism, 25, 26, 43-46, 49, 51, 120, 139, 141, 150, 203, 204, 221
Social movements, 39-41, 42, 51-2, 61, 62, 66, 72, 162
(*see also*: Anti-Vietnam-war movement; Environment movement; Labour movement; *and the* Women's liberation movement
Social redundancy, 221
(*see also*: Unemployment, long-term)
Social security, 2, 56, 66, 134, 152
Sociology, 28, 147, *also*:
-historical sociology, 26-7
Sovereignty, 8-10, 18, 19, 20, 35, 75, 77, 107, 158, 181, 189-90, 193, 211, 230, 231, 235, *also*:
-national sovereignty, 4, 66, 230, 234, 235
-loss of, 10, 162
Soviet Union, 11, 183, 190, 191
Space and spatiality, 53-4, 76, 85, 100, 136, 186, 198, 201, 230, 231-6, 244-5, 247, 251, *also*:
-place, 201, 205, 211, 215
(*see also*: social extension)
Speed, 204-5
Staking a claim, 148, 152, 153
State, *passim*
-Absolutist states, 161-2
(*see also*: Absolutism)
-accountability, 76
-anti-state sentiments, 3, 246
-as unitary actor, 166, 169-73, 176, 178, 187, 192, 194
-boundaries, 6n., 8, 31, 76, 82, 169, 178, 200, 207, 210, 212, 225, 230, 231, 235, 242-5
-capitalist state, 141
-centralized form of, 207, 246
-contradictions of, 1, 5, 33, 48, 102, 106, 112-13, 141, 146, 246-7
(*see also*: Contradictions)
-death of, 16-17, 24, 72, 109, 162, 210, 246

-decentralizing the, 18, 34, 235, 246
-deconstructing the, 16, 245-6, 248
-definitions of, 9n., 20, 211, 240n.
-deregulation, 28, 205, 239, 246-7
(*see also*: Deregulation)
-'good' state, 82, 83
-intervention, 47, 56, 59, 63, 68, 70, 71, 72, 78, 96, 111, 127, 133-5, 196, 202, 246-7
-Keynesian state, 1n., 5, 56
-legitimacy, legitimation 2, 11, 146, 209
-liberal democratic state, 3, 74, 76, 77, 85, 207, 223
-liberal state, 5, 56, 59, 68
-medieval state, 202
-minimal state, 12-13, 34, 39, 71, 73, 196, 202, 239
-modern state, 5, 6, 8-10, 15, 27, 28, 32, 38, 75-6, 84, 85, 101, 106, 108, 161-3, 182, 196, 198, 202, 209, 211, 212, 214, 218, 225, 231, 246
-postmodern state, 6, 34-35, 196-223, 246
-regulation, 1, 2, 53, 55, 63, 69, 76, 80, 83, 90, 93, 100, 110, 225, 244, 246-7
-repression, 129, 135, 157, 216-17, 218
-retreat from, 17-24, 27-35
-size of, 2, 12, 28, 70, 71, 76, 245-6
-socialist state, 202, 221
-sovereign state, 9, 11, 17, 19, 161, 176, 184, 188-90
(*see also*: Sovereignty)
-state-building, 9-10, 161-3
-subjective responses to, 1-3, 4n.
-surveillance state, 3, 28, 216
(*see also*: Surveillance)
-traditional state, 9, 27, 32
(*see also*: Absolutism)
Weberian definition, 9n.
welfare state, 1, 5, 38, 40, 56, 58, 65-66, 68, 69, 102, 109-137, 155, 203
'withering away of', 245-6
Stretton, Hugh, 13
Structuralism, 1n., 72, 109, 164-5, 176-81, 186, 191-2, 193, 194, 229, *also*:
-realist structuralism, 168, 171, 172, 176

-structuration, 186-90
Structural functionalism, 19, 183
Superpowers, 174, 190, 191
Sustainable development, 74, 76, 90, 97ff., 104, *also*:
-unsustainable development, 220, 242
Surveillance, 1, 127, 133, 199, 217, 240, 247
(*see also*: State, surveillance)
Sweden, 62
System, the concept of, 19-20, 23, 53

Tariffs, 50, 55, 59, 68, 71, 243
Tasmanian Hydro-Electricity Corporation, 87
Taxation, 66, 79, 80, 90, 93, 100, 106, 114, 122, *also*:
-capital transaction tax, 244
-carbon tax, 80
-tax file number, 3
Technology, 8, 57, 177, 199, 200-2, 205, 216, 220, *also*:
-high-tech production, 198, 218
-Superhighway Project (SH), 244
-technocracy, 220
-technological mediation, 201-2, 207-9, 214, 215, 218, 222, 228, 244-5
-technological revolution, 206
Telecom, 244
Television, 3, 4, 124, 208
(*see also*: Media)
Territory, territoriality, 10, 11, 75, 211, 213, 225, 231-6, *also*:
-bioregions, 81-2
-regionalism, 212-13, 218, 220-1, 221, 248-9
(*see also*: De-territorialization; *and* State, boundaries)
Thatcher government, 80, 143
Thatcherism, 62
The Australian vocational certificate training system, 210
The gifthorse, 152
The sexual contract, 153
The virtual community, 245
Tilly, Charles, 25, 180
Time and temporality, 53, 76, 100, 186, 201, 230, 233-4, 247, 251
-Greenwich mean time, 233

INDEX

Trade, 69, 99, 104, 162, 178, 211, 242-3
Trade unions, 45, 51, 62, 63, 98, 118, 143, 160, 204
'Tragedy of the commons', 75, 78-9
Transnational corporations, 10, 34, 219, 242
Truman doctrine, 191

Unemployment, 51, 57, 63, 67, 110, 115-19, 124-30, 133, 134, 136, 145
-long-term, 71, 115, 125-7, 128, 129
'Unequal exchange', 177-8
Unfinished business, 147
Union movement, 46, 48, 51, 60, 62, 72
United Nations, 10, 18, 75, 145, 150, 193
-Human Rights Committee, 192-3
United States (USA) and North America, 18, 19, 21-23, 24, 25, 90, 91, 138, 153, 154, 155, 174, 178, 181, 182, 183, 184-5, 186, 224, 236, 237
Universities and academia, 27, 60, 61, 64, 146, 149, 159, 201, 245
Unknown Soldier, 239
Urbanization, 180
Uren, Tom, 62
Urry, John, 235

Walker, K., 93
Wallerstein, Immanuel, 176-81, 182
Waltz, Kenneth, 167, 168, 170, 183, 187
War, 180, 239
Warby, Michael, 246-7
Waters, Malcolm, 34-5, 246
Watkins, Frederick, 22n., 24
Watson, Don, 224, 226, 236, 237, 248
Watson, Sophie, 148, 150, 153, 159
Watts, Rob, ix, 6, 28, 30
Weber, Max, 9
Weberian concepts, 9n., 29, 103, 240
Welfare, 4, 28, 33, 37, 46, 56, 59, 62, 67, 69, 72, 82, 101, 109-137, 142, 152, 203, 216
(*see also*: State, welfare)
Welfare liberalism, 12, 57
Wendt, Alexander, 187-8
Wesley Vale pulp mill, 87-8
Wheelwright, Ted, 45
White, Rob, ix, 6, 28
White Australia, 50, 55, 234

White Paper on Employment (1994), 117, 126, 127
Whitlam, Gough, 46, 57-61 *passim*, 63, 148
Whitlam government, 4, 57-61, 68, 91, 140, 142, 160
Whitwell, G., 60
Willis, Ralph, 61, 62, 244
Wills, Sue, 148
Wilson, Elizabeth, 146
Women's Affairs Branch, 141, 142, 148
Women's Electoral Lobby (WEL), 140, 141
Women's liberation movement, 139-40, 142, *also*:
-suffrage movement, 149
Women, social science and public policy, 147
Women, social welfare and the state, 147, 149
Work, 53-4, 57, 117, 122, 136, 208, 210, 221, 227, *also*:
-and leisure, 219
-flexible skilling, 206, 210
-high-tech renovation, 202, 221
-of intellectuals, 208, 221
-Workcover Scheme, 116
World systems theory, 175-86

Yeatman, Anna, 138, 144, 148, 152
Youth, 67, 115, 123, 131-2
Yugoslavia, 11